CIVIL WAR II

X-MEN

CIVIL WAR II

X-MEN

WHEN A NEW INHUMAN NAMED ULYSSES MANIFESTS THE ABILITY TO PROFILE THE FUTURE, THE SUPERHUMAN COMMUNITY IS SPLIT AS TO WHETHER HIS POWER IS AN ASSET OR A DANGER.

THIS QUESTION IS ESPECIALLY RELEVANT TO THE X-MEN: TERRIGEN MISTS CIRCLE THE GLOBE, IGNITING THE INHUMAN RACE WHILE CRIPPLING MUTANTKIND—CUTTING DOWN THEIR NUMBERS AND SUPPRESSING NEW MUTANT MANIFESTATIONS. WHILE STORM AND HER TEAM OF X-MEN HAVE ALREADY JOINED IN THE USE OF ULYSSES' ABILITIES TO PREVENT MAJOR DISASTERS, MAGNETO SEES HIM AS A HARBINGER OF INHUMAN SUPREMACY AND THE FINAL NAIL IN MUTANTKIND'S COFFIN...

WRITER **CULLEN BUNN**	ARTIST **ANDREA BROCCARDO**
COLOR ARTIST **JESUS ABURTOV**	LETTERER **VC's JOE SABINO**
COVER ARTIST **DAVID YARDIN**	ASSISTANT EDITOR **CHRIS ROBINSON**
EDITOR **DANIEL KETCHUM**	X-MEN GROUP EDITOR **MARK PANICCIA**

X-MEN CREATED BY **STAN LEE** & **JACK KIRBY**

COLLECTION EDITOR **JENNIFER GRÜNWALD**	BOOK DESIGNER **JAY BOWEN**
ASSOCIATE MANAGING EDITOR **KATERI WOODY**	
ASSOCIATE EDITOR **SARAH BRUNSTAD**	EDITOR IN CHIEF **AXEL ALONSO**
EDITOR, SPECIAL PROJECTS **MARK D. BEAZLEY**	CHIEF CREATIVE OFFICER **JOE QUESADA**
VP PRODUCTION & SPECIAL PROJECTS **JEFF YOUNGQUIST**	PUBLISHER **DAN BUCKLEY**
SVP PRINT, SALES & MARKETING **DAVID GABRIEL**	EXECUTIVE PRODUCER **ALAN FINE**

CIVIL WAR II: X-MEN. Contains material originally published in magazine form as CIVIL WAR II: X-MEN #1-4 and AMAZING ADVENTURES #9. First printing 2016. ISBN# 978-1-302-90254-4. Published by MARVEL WORLDWIDE, INC., a subsidiary of MARVEL ENTERTAINMENT, LLC. OFFICE OF PUBLICATION: 135 West 50th Street, New York, NY 10020. Copyright © 2016 MARVEL No similarity between any of the names, characters, persons, and/or institutions in this magazine with those of any living or dead person or institution is intended, and any such similarity which may exist is purely coincidental. **Printed in Canada.** ALAN FINE, President, Marvel Entertainment; DAN BUCKLEY, President, TV, Publishing & Brand Management; JOE QUESADA, Chief Creative Officer; TOM BREVOORT, SVP of Publishing; DAVID BOGART, SVP of Business Affairs & Operations, Publishing & Partnership; C.B. CEBULSKI, VP of Brand Management & Development, Asia; DAVID GABRIEL, SVP of Sales & Marketing, Publishing; JEFF YOUNGQUIST, VP of Production & Special Projects; DAN CARR, Executive Director of Publishing Technology; ALEX MORALES, Director of Publishing Operations; SUSAN CRESPI, Production Manager; STAN LEE, Chairman Emeritus. For information regarding advertising in Marvel Comics or on Marvel.com, please contact Vit DeBellis, Integrated Sales Manager, at vdebellis@marvel.com. For Marvel subscription inquiries, please call 888-511-5480. **Manufactured between 9/23/2016 and 10/31/2016 by SOLISCO PRINTERS, SCOTT, QC, CANADA.**

10 9 8 7 6 5 4 3 2 1

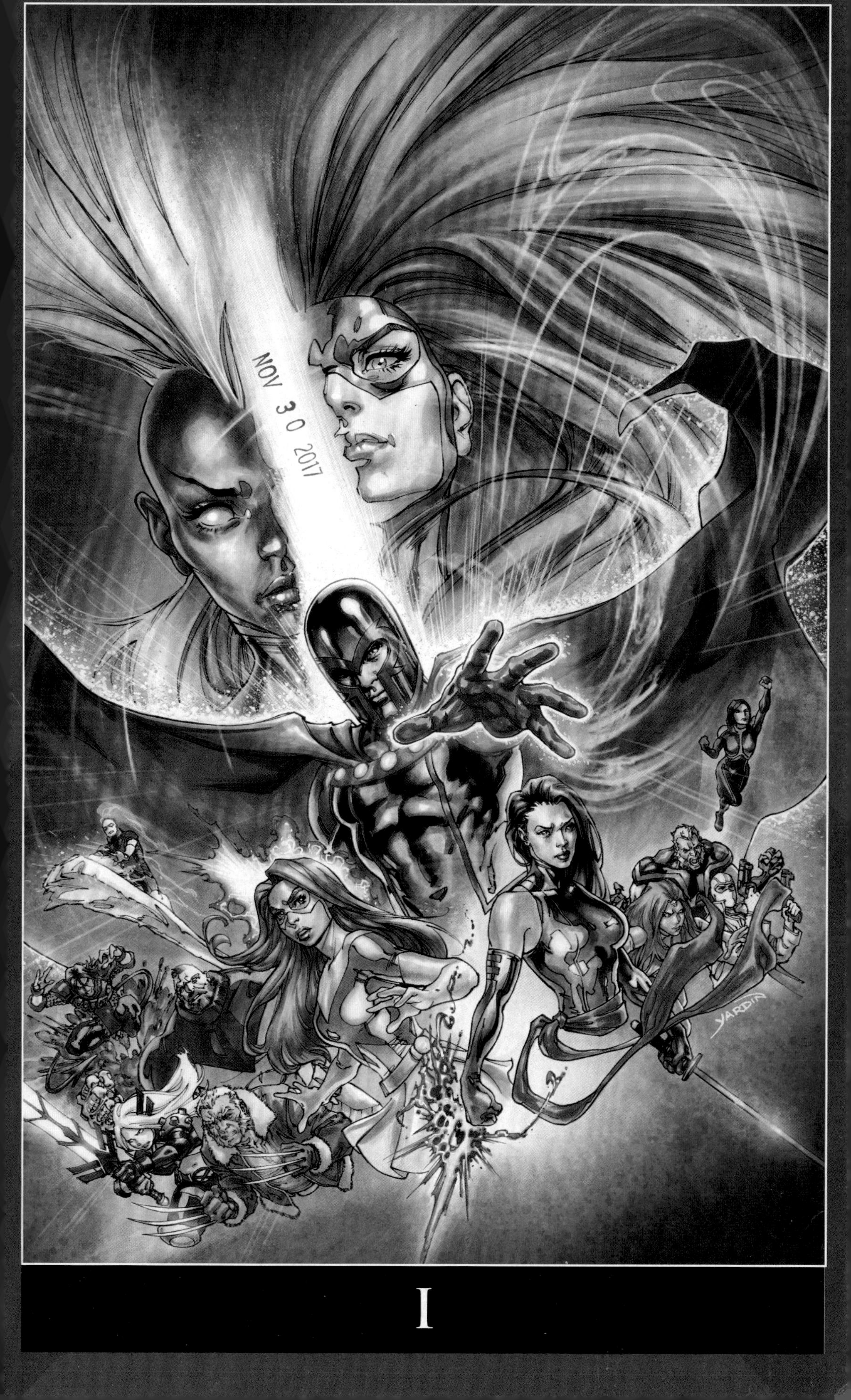
YARDIN

I

DUBAI.

A TOAST, MY FRIENDS...

...TO THE *TERRIGEN CLOUD* THAT, EVEN NOW, ROLLS TOWARD OUR CITY.

I AM TOLD THE CLOUD IS CONSIDERED HOLY BY THE *INHUMANS* OF ATTILAN.

IT GIVES THEM THEIR *STRENGTH*... THEIR *POWER*.

IT IS *LIFE!*

BUT TO *MUTANTS* LIKE US...THE CLOUD IS *DEATH!*

THE VAPORS WILL *KILL* US.

WELL... *SOME* OF US.

BECAUSE THESE CHAMBERS ARE *SEALED*.

WE WILL WATCH AS *DEATH* WASHES OVER US...

...AND W WILL KNOW H IT FEELS TO IMMORTA

SO ENJOY YOURSELVES, MY FELLOW CHILDREN OF THE ATOM...

...ENJOY WHAT MIGHT HAVE BEEN YOUR FINAL MOMENTS, BUT ARE INSTEAD--

WARNING.

HERMETIC SEALS HAVE BEEN DEACTIVATED.

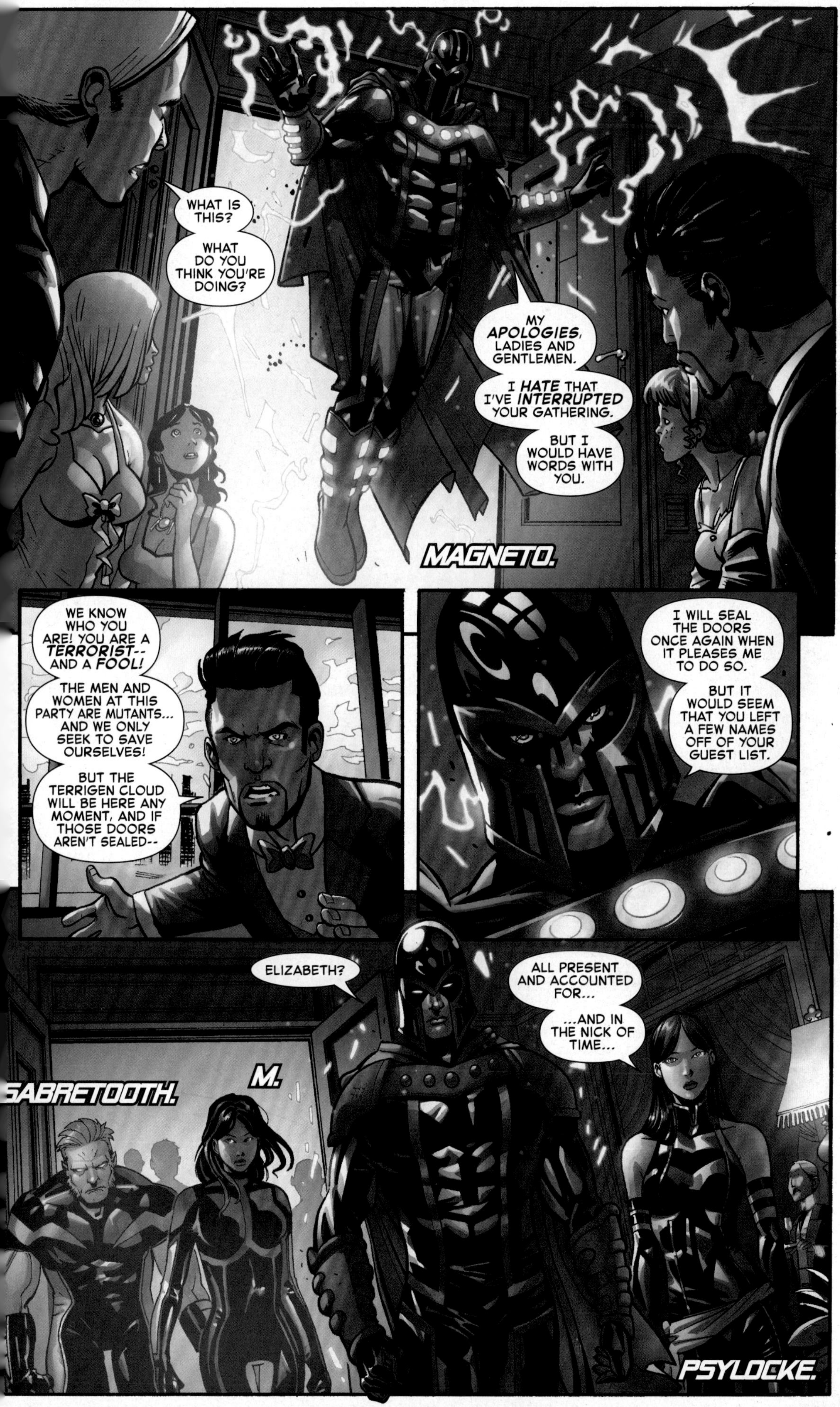
WHAT IS THIS?
WHAT DO YOU THINK YOU'RE DOING?
MY APOLOGIES, LADIES AND GENTLEMEN.
I HATE THAT I'VE INTERRUPTED YOUR GATHERING.
BUT I WOULD HAVE WORDS WITH YOU.
MAGNETO.
WE KNOW WHO YOU ARE! YOU ARE A TERRORIST-- AND A FOOL!
THE MEN AND WOMEN AT THIS PARTY ARE MUTANTS... AND WE ONLY SEEK TO SAVE OURSELVES!
BUT THE TERRIGEN CLOUD WILL BE HERE ANY MOMENT, AND IF THOSE DOORS AREN'T SEALED--
I WILL SEAL THE DOORS ONCE AGAIN WHEN IT PLEASES ME TO DO SO.
BUT IT WOULD SEEM THAT YOU LEFT A FEW NAMES OFF OF YOUR GUEST LIST.
ELIZABETH?
ALL PRESENT AND ACCOUNTED FOR...
...AND IN THE NICK OF TIME...
SABRETOOTH.
M.
PSYLOCKE.

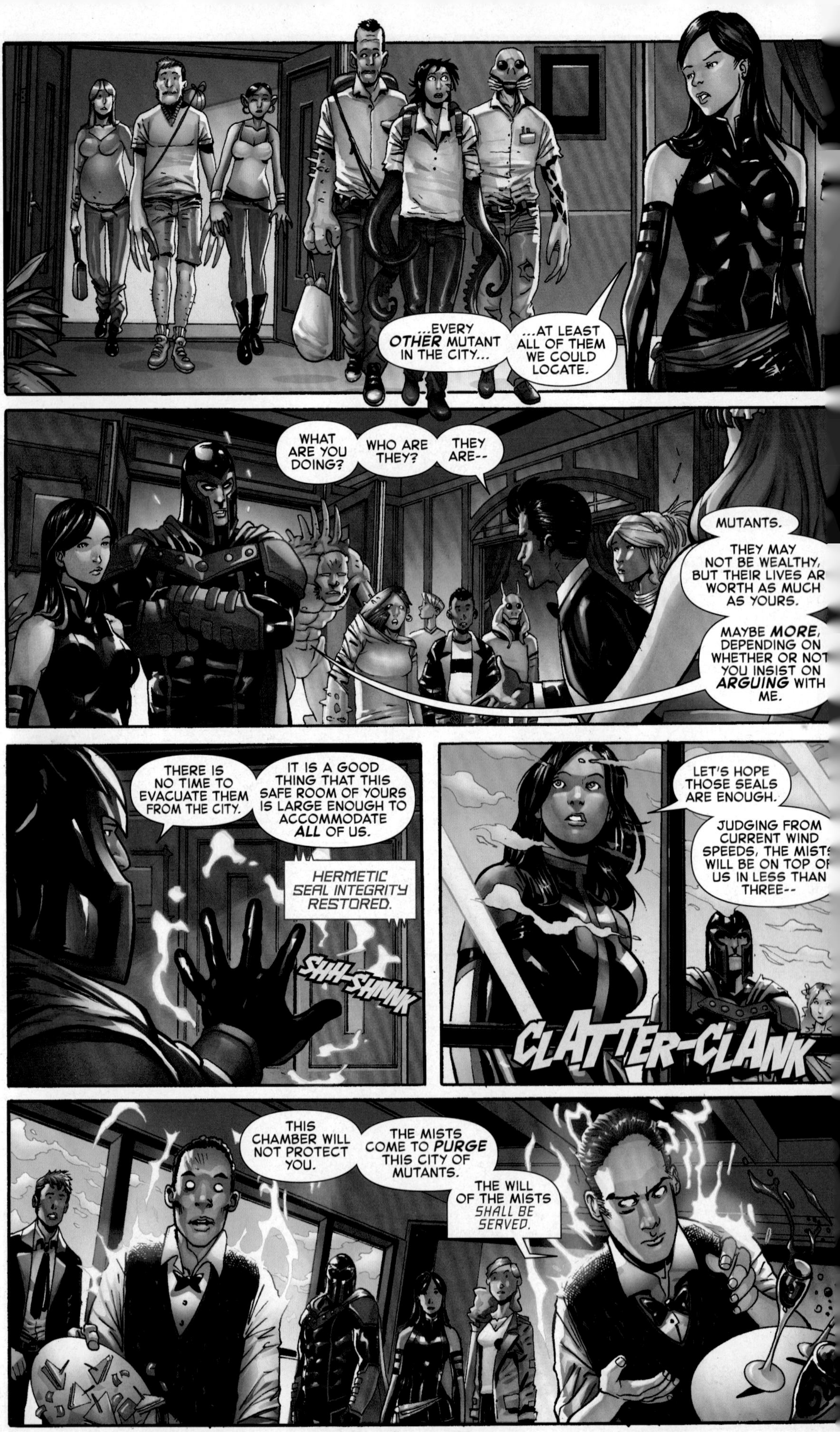
...EVERY OTHER MUTANT IN THE CITY...
...AT LEAST ALL OF THEM WE COULD LOCATE.
WHAT ARE YOU DOING?
WHO ARE THEY?
THEY ARE--
MUTANTS.
THEY MAY NOT BE WEALTHY, BUT THEIR LIVES AR WORTH AS MUCH AS YOURS.
MAYBE MORE, DEPENDING ON WHETHER OR NOT YOU INSIST ON ARGUING WITH ME.
THERE IS NO TIME TO EVACUATE THEM FROM THE CITY.
IT IS A GOOD THING THAT THIS SAFE ROOM OF YOURS IS LARGE ENOUGH TO ACCOMMODATE ALL OF US.
HERMETIC SEAL INTEGRITY RESTORED.
SHH-SHNNK
LET'S HOPE THOSE SEALS ARE ENOUGH.
JUDGING FROM CURRENT WIND SPEEDS, THE MISTS WILL BE ON TOP OF US IN LESS THAN THREE--
CLATTER-CLANK
THIS CHAMBER WILL NOT PROTECT YOU.
THE MISTS COME TO PURGE THIS CITY OF MUTANTS.
THE WILL OF THE MISTS SHALL BE SERVED.

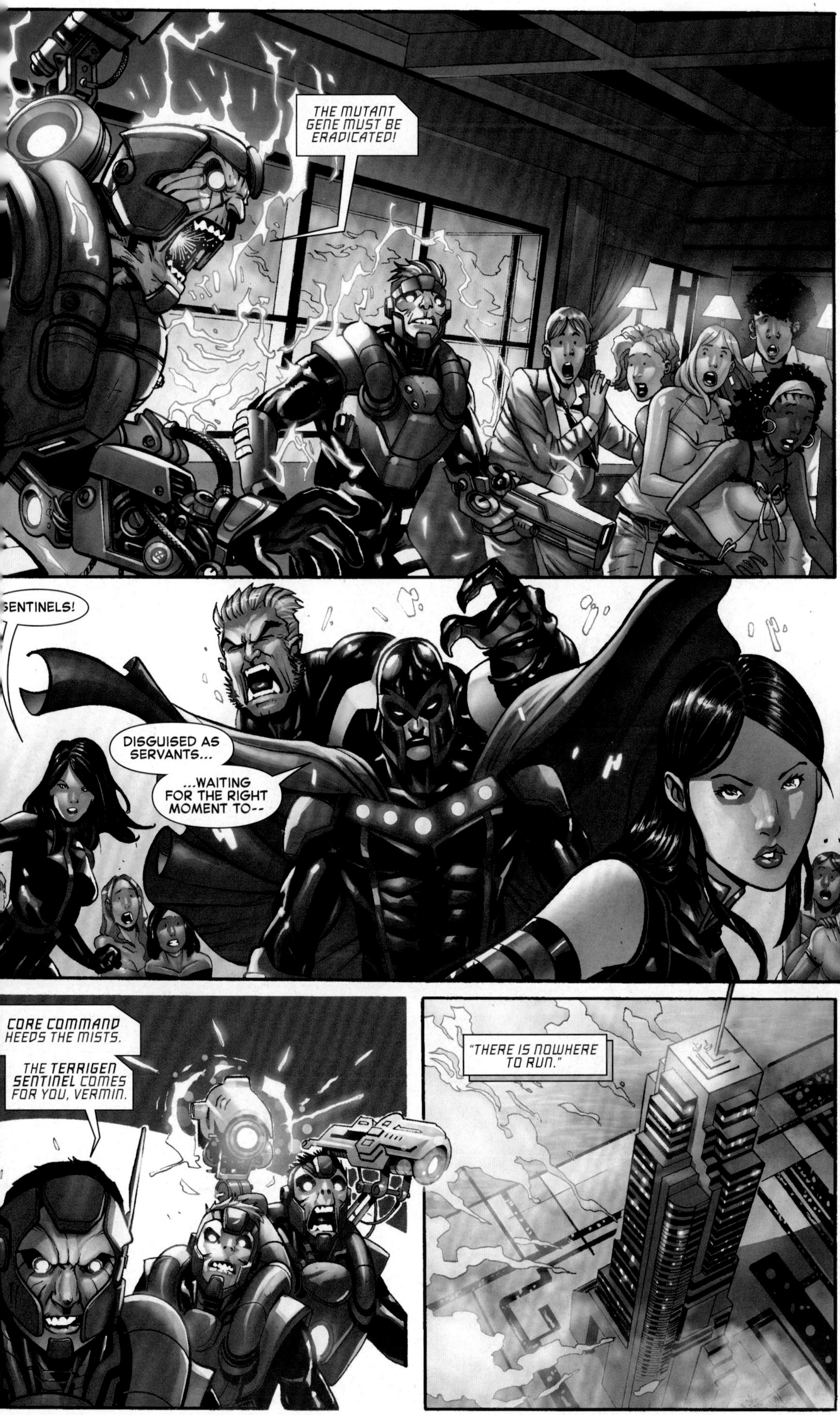
THE MUTANT GENE MUST BE ERADICATED!
SENTINELS!
DISGUISED AS SERVANTS...
...WAITING FOR THE RIGHT MOMENT TO--
CORE COMMAND HEEDS THE MISTS.
THE TERRIGEN SENTINEL COMES FOR YOU, VERMIN.
"THERE IS NOWHERE TO RUN."

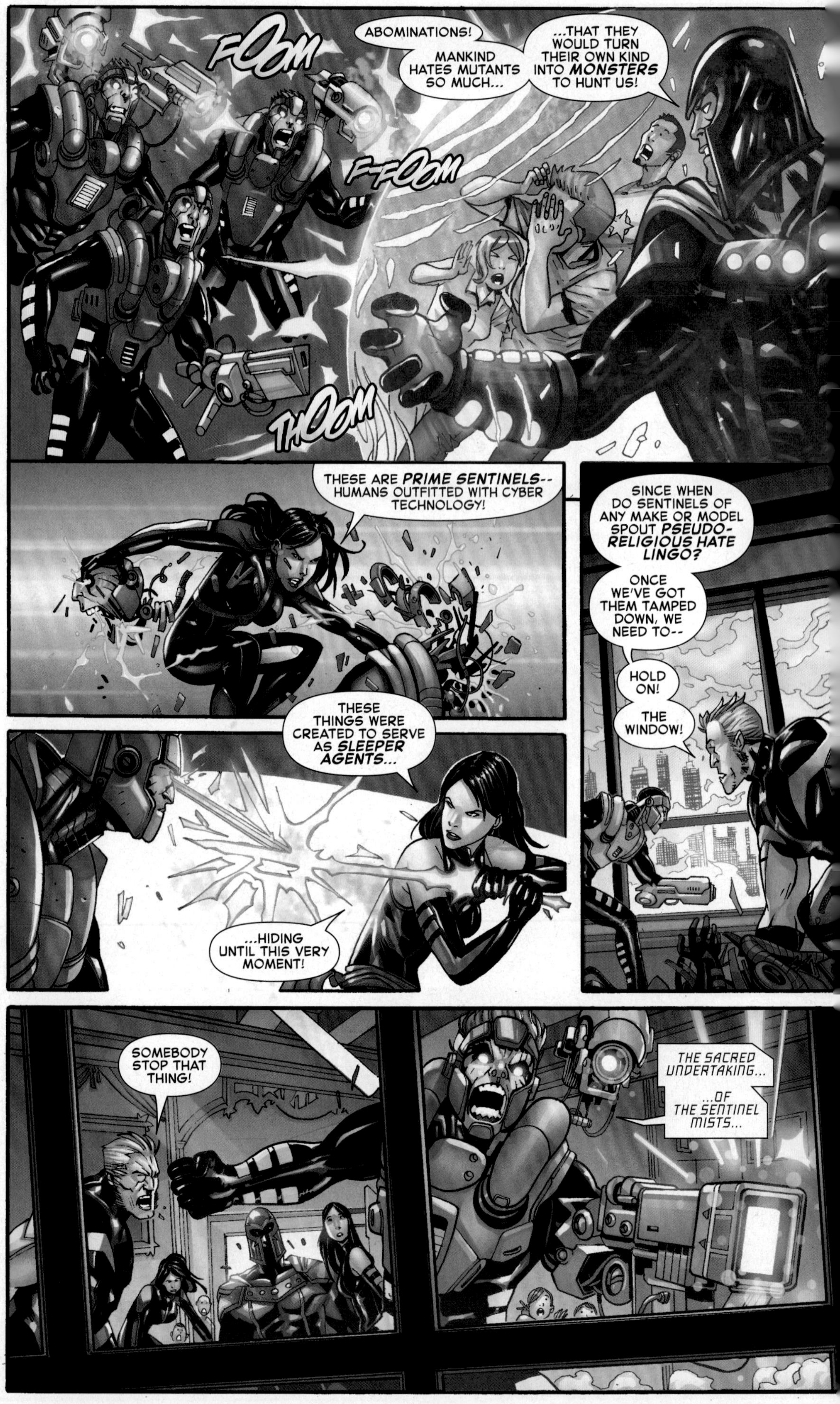
FOOM
ABOMINATIONS!
MANKIND HATES MUTANTS SO MUCH...
...THAT THEY WOULD TURN THEIR OWN KIND INTO MONSTERS TO HUNT US!
F-FOOM
THOOM
THESE ARE PRIME SENTINELS-- HUMANS OUTFITTED WITH CYBER TECHNOLOGY!
SINCE WHEN DO SENTINELS OF ANY MAKE OR MODEL SPOUT PSEUDO-RELIGIOUS HATE LINGO?
ONCE WE'VE GOT THEM TAMPED DOWN, WE NEED TO--
HOLD ON!
THE WINDOW!
THESE THINGS WERE CREATED TO SERVE AS SLEEPER AGENTS...
...HIDING UNTIL THIS VERY MOMENT!
SOMEBODY STOP THAT THING!
THE SACRED UNDERTAKING...
...OF THE SENTINEL MISTS...

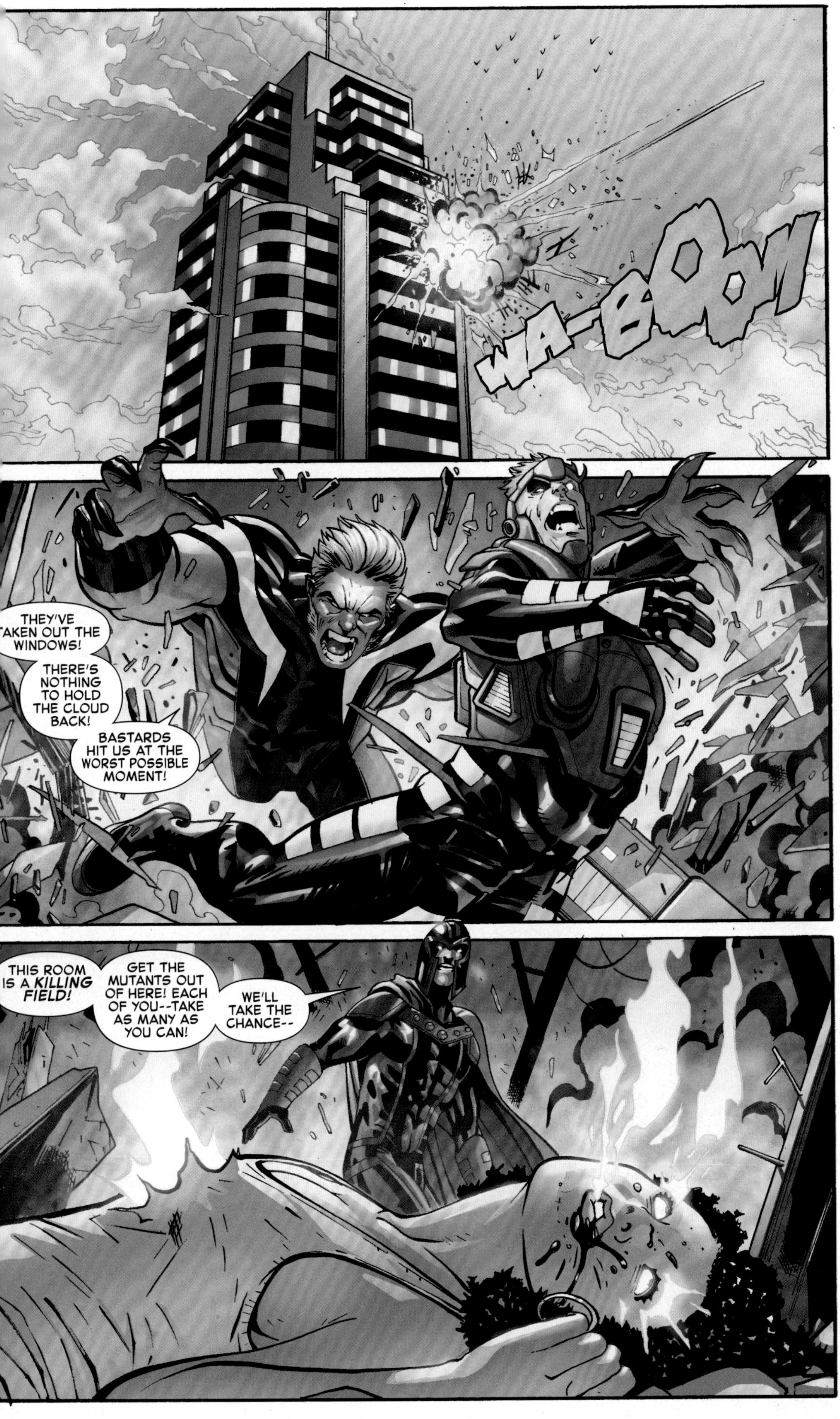
WA-BOOM
THEY'VE TAKEN OUT THE WINDOWS!
THERE'S NOTHING TO HOLD THE CLOUD BACK!
BASTARDS HIT US AT THE WORST POSSIBLE MOMENT!
THIS ROOM IS A *KILLING FIELD!*
GET THE MUTANTS OUT OF HERE! EACH OF YOU--TAKE AS MANY AS YOU CAN!
WE'LL TAKE THE CHANCE--

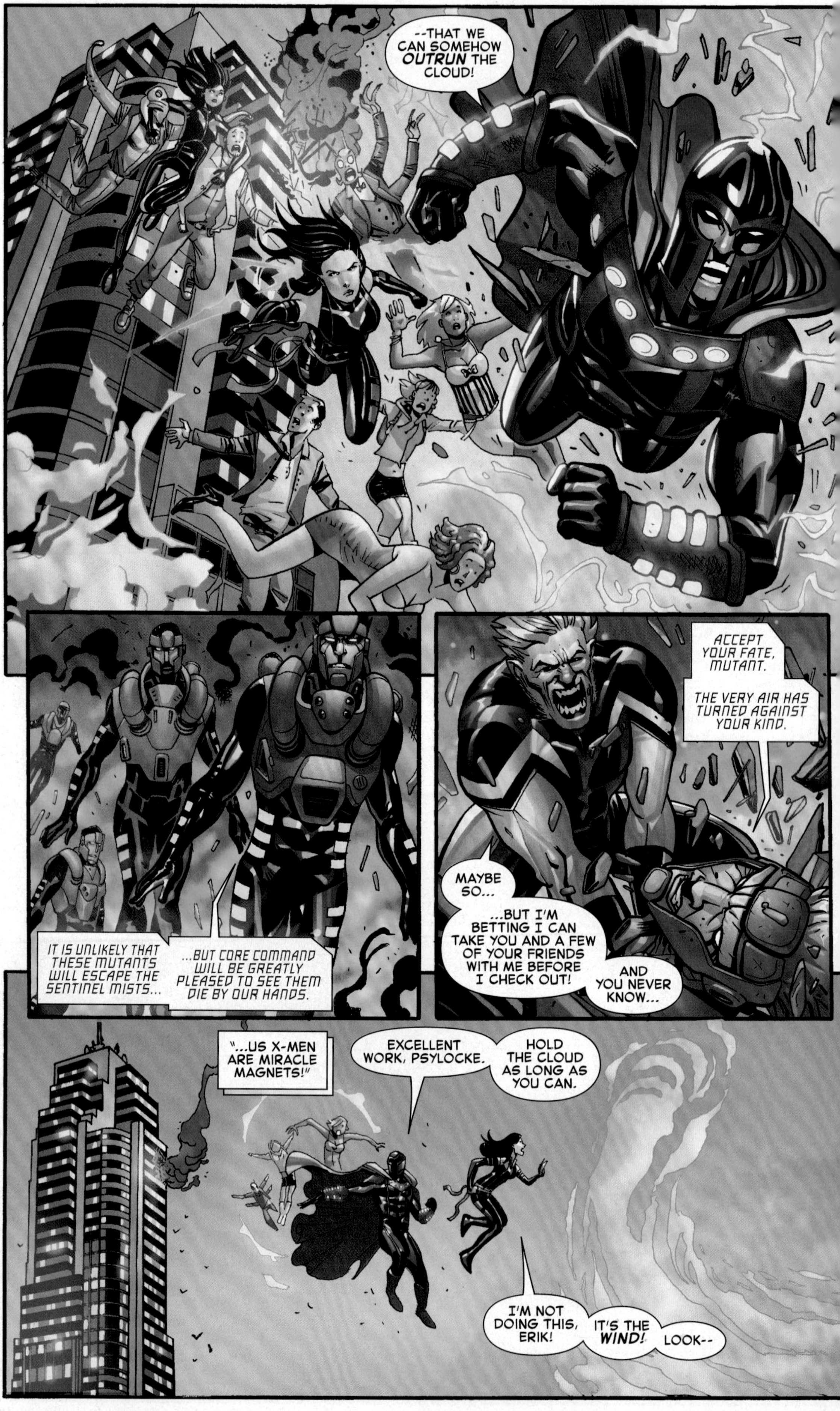
--THAT WE CAN SOMEHOW OUTRUN THE CLOUD!
IT IS UNLIKELY THAT THESE MUTANTS WILL ESCAPE THE SENTINEL MISTS...
...BUT CORE COMMAND WILL BE GREATLY PLEASED TO SEE THEM DIE BY OUR HANDS.
ACCEPT YOUR FATE, MUTANT.
THE VERY AIR HAS TURNED AGAINST YOUR KIND.
MAYBE SO...
...BUT I'M BETTING I CAN TAKE YOU AND A FEW OF YOUR FRIENDS WITH ME BEFORE I CHECK OUT!
AND YOU NEVER KNOW...
"...US X-MEN ARE MIRACLE MAGNETS!"
EXCELLENT WORK, PSYLOCKE.
HOLD THE CLOUD AS LONG AS YOU CAN.
I'M NOT DOING THIS, ERIK!
IT'S THE WIND!
LOOK--

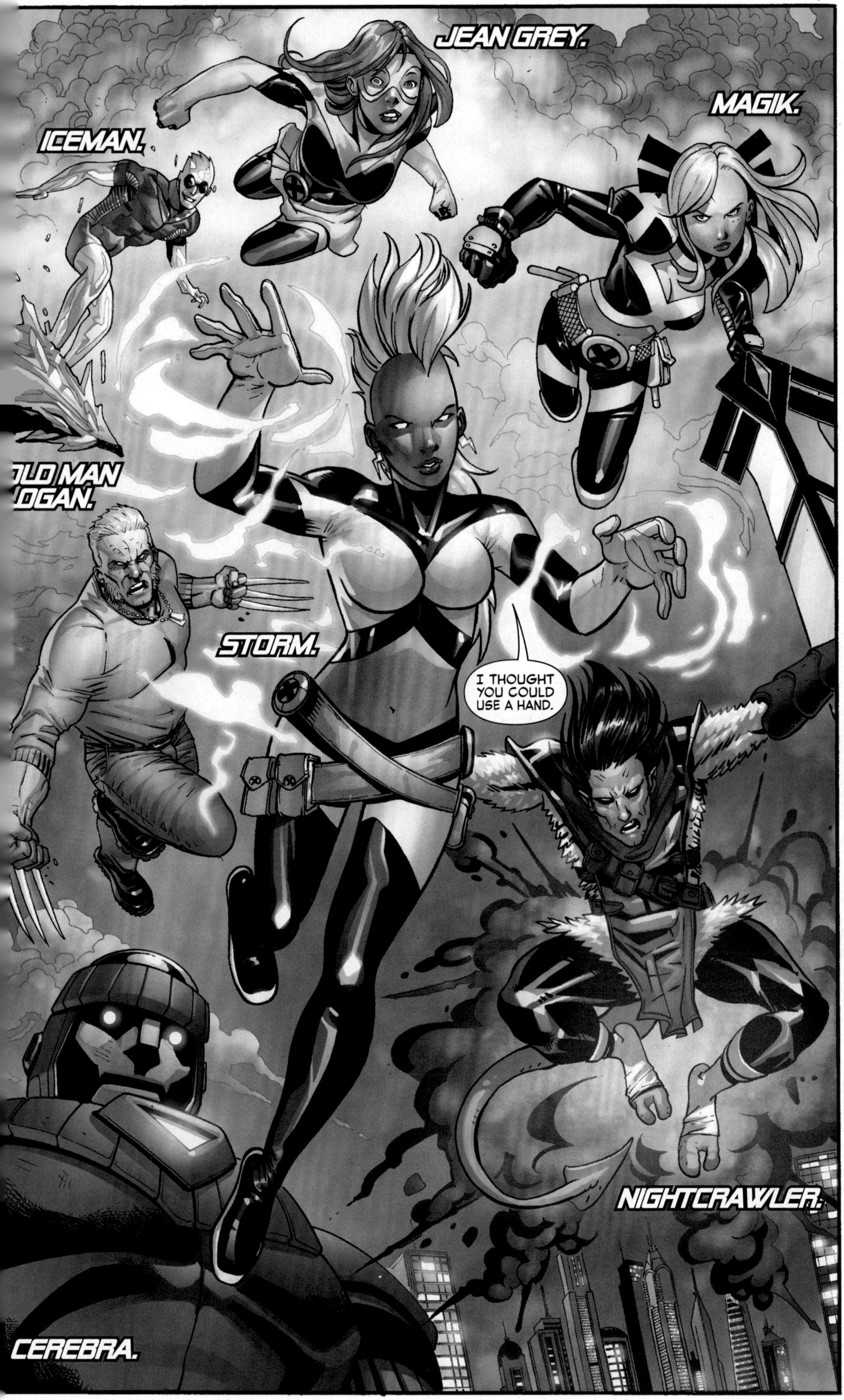
JEAN GREY.
MAGIK.
ICEMAN.
OLD MAN LOGAN.
STORM.
I THOUGHT YOU COULD USE A HAND.
NIGHTCRAWLER.
CEREBRA.

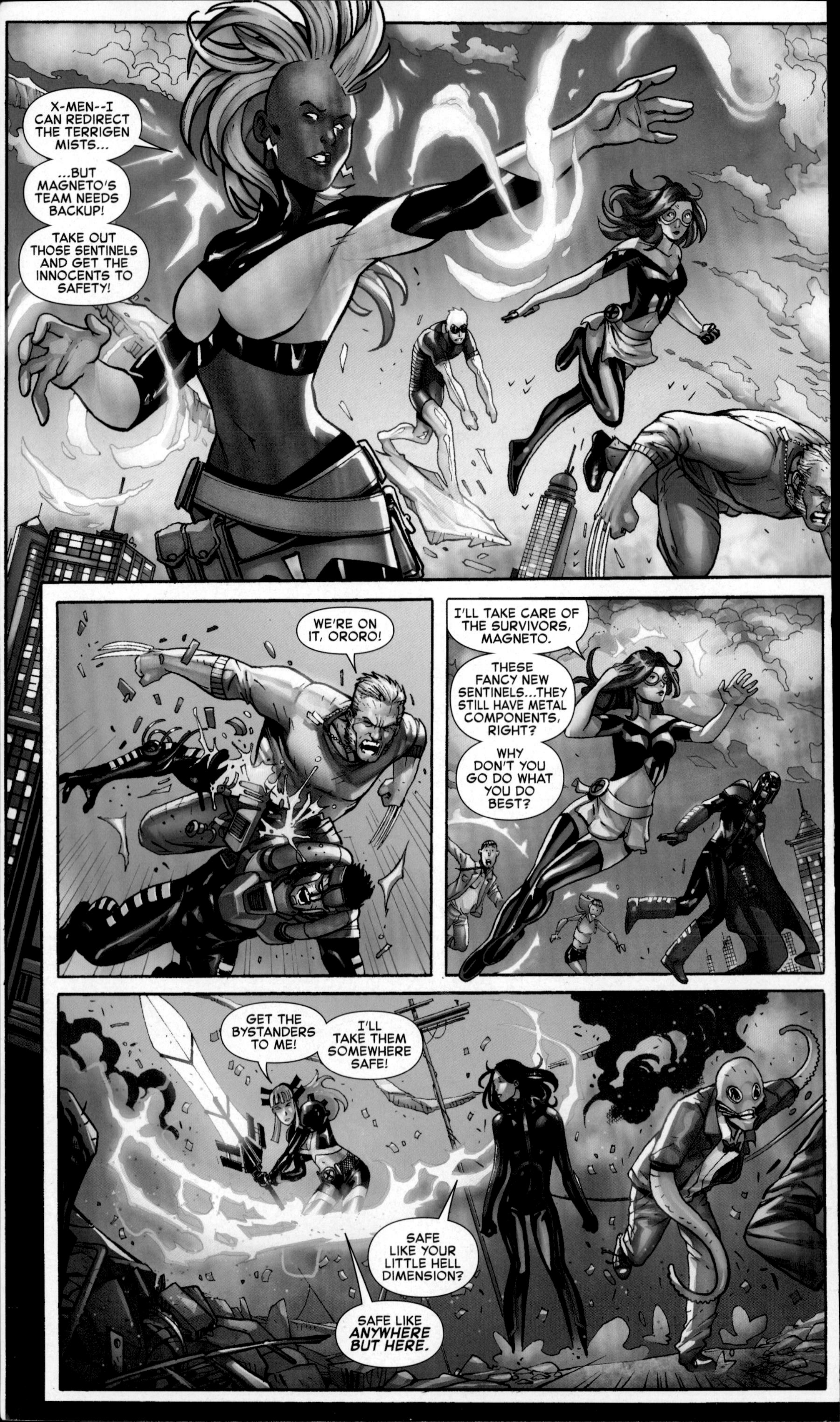
X-MEN--I CAN REDIRECT THE TERRIGEN MISTS...
...BUT MAGNETO'S TEAM NEEDS BACKUP!
TAKE OUT THOSE SENTINELS AND GET THE INNOCENTS TO SAFETY!
WE'RE ON IT, ORORO!
I'LL TAKE CARE OF THE SURVIVORS, MAGNETO.
THESE FANCY NEW SENTINELS...THEY STILL HAVE METAL COMPONENTS, RIGHT?
WHY DON'T YOU GO DO WHAT YOU DO BEST?
GET THE BYSTANDERS TO ME!
I'LL TAKE THEM SOMEWHERE SAFE!
SAFE LIKE YOUR LITTLE HELL DIMENSION?
SAFE LIKE *ANYWHERE BUT HERE.*

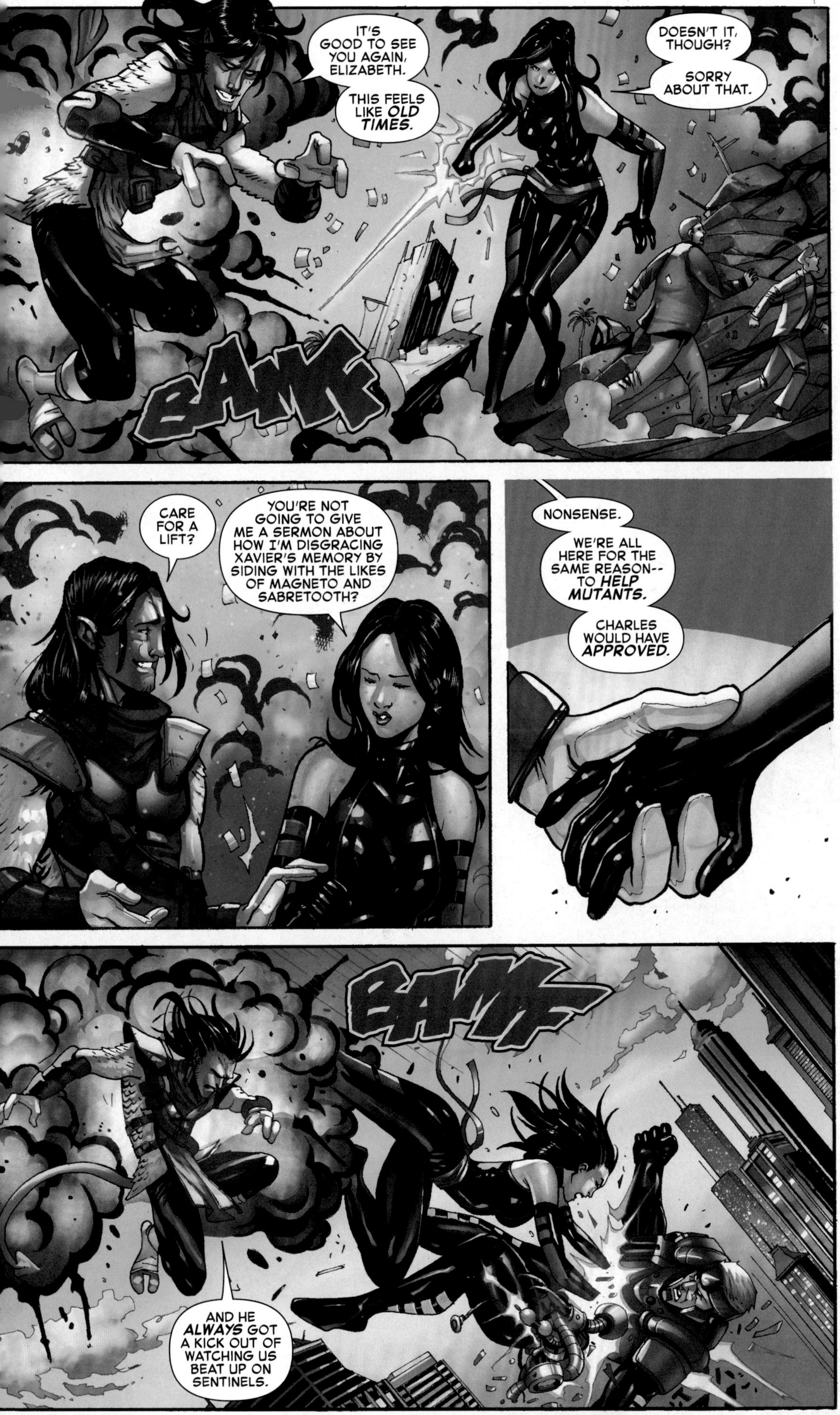

IT'S GOOD TO SEE YOU AGAIN, ELIZABETH.
THIS FEELS LIKE OLD TIMES.
DOESN'T IT, THOUGH?
SORRY ABOUT THAT.
BAMF
CARE FOR A LIFT?
YOU'RE NOT GOING TO GIVE ME A SERMON ABOUT HOW I'M DISGRACING XAVIER'S MEMORY BY SIDING WITH THE LIKES OF MAGNETO AND SABRETOOTH?
NONSENSE.
WE'RE ALL HERE FOR THE SAME REASON-- TO HELP MUTANTS.
CHARLES WOULD HAVE APPROVED.
BAMF
AND HE ALWAYS GOT A KICK OUT OF WATCHING US BEAT UP ON SENTINELS.

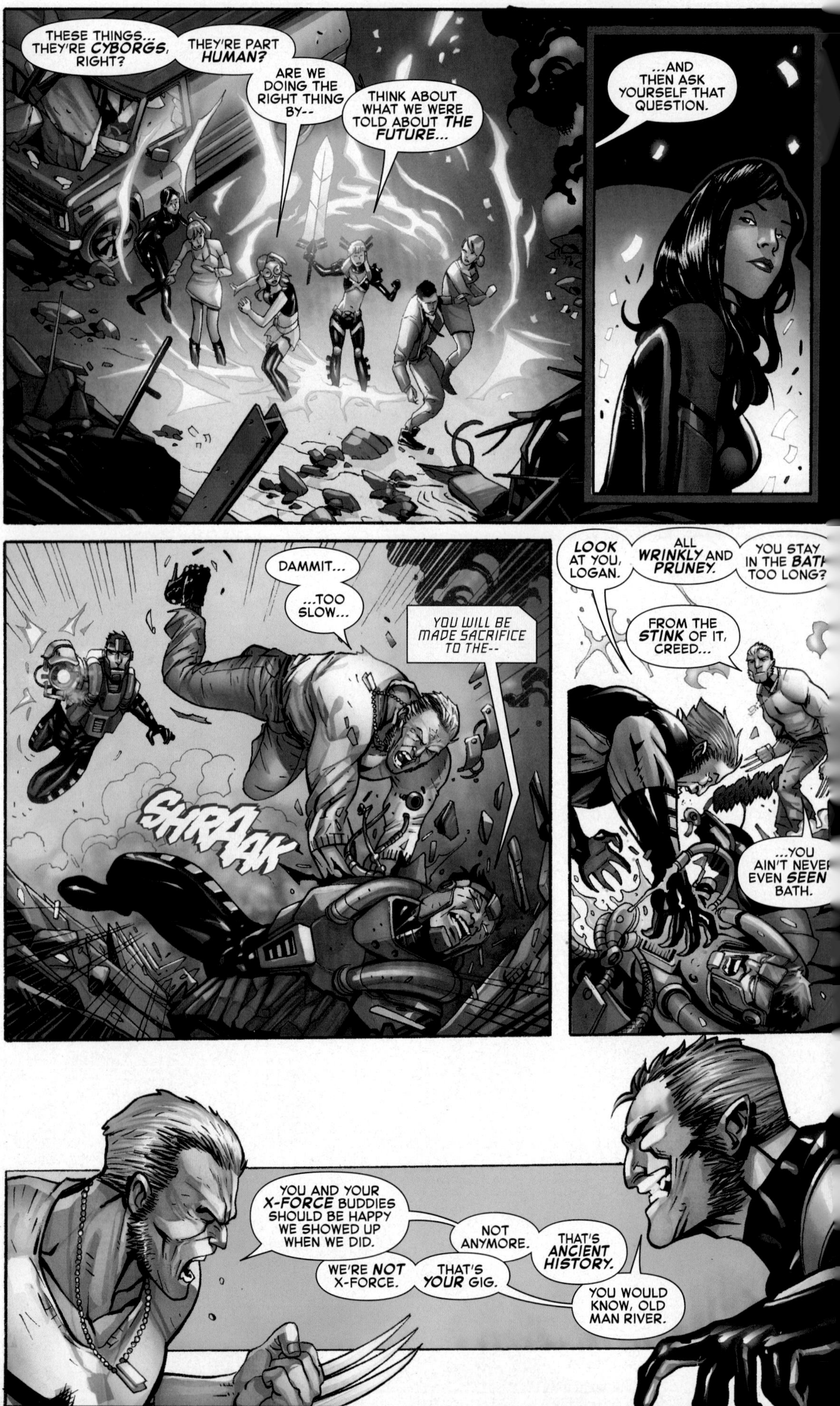
THESE THINGS... THEY'RE CYBORGS, RIGHT?
THEY'RE PART HUMAN?
ARE WE DOING THE RIGHT THING BY--
THINK ABOUT WHAT WE WERE TOLD ABOUT THE FUTURE...
...AND THEN ASK YOURSELF THAT QUESTION.
DAMMIT...
...TOO SLOW...
YOU WILL BE MADE SACRIFICE TO THE--
SHRAAK
LOOK AT YOU, LOGAN.
ALL WRINKLY AND PRUNEY.
YOU STAY IN THE BATH TOO LONG?
FROM THE STINK OF IT, CREED...
...YOU AIN'T NEVER EVEN SEEN BATH.
YOU AND YOUR X-FORCE BUDDIES SHOULD BE HAPPY WE SHOWED UP WHEN WE DID.
WE'RE NOT X-FORCE.
NOT ANYMORE.
THAT'S YOUR GIG.
THAT'S ANCIENT HISTORY.
YOU WOULD KNOW, OLD MAN RIVER.

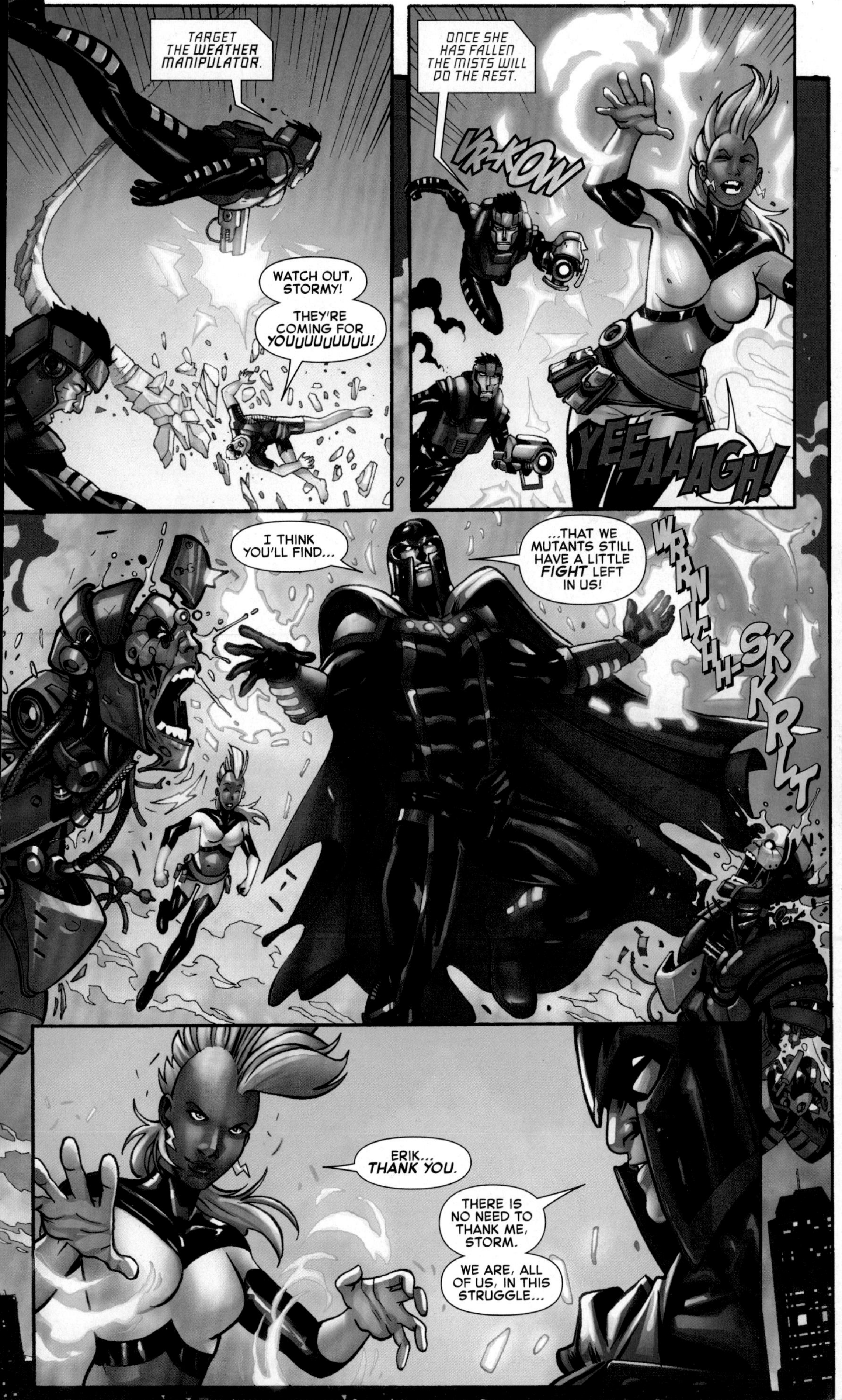
TARGET THE WEATHER MANIPULATOR.
WATCH OUT, STORMY!
THEY'RE COMING FOR YOUUUUUUUUU!
ONCE SHE HAS FALLEN THE MISTS WILL DO THE REST.
VR-KOW
YEEAAAAGH!
I THINK YOU'LL FIND...
...THAT WE MUTANTS STILL HAVE A LITTLE FIGHT LEFT IN US!
WRRNCHH-SKKRLT
ERIK... THANK YOU.
THERE IS NO NEED TO THANK ME, STORM.
WE ARE, ALL OF US, IN THIS STRUGGLE...

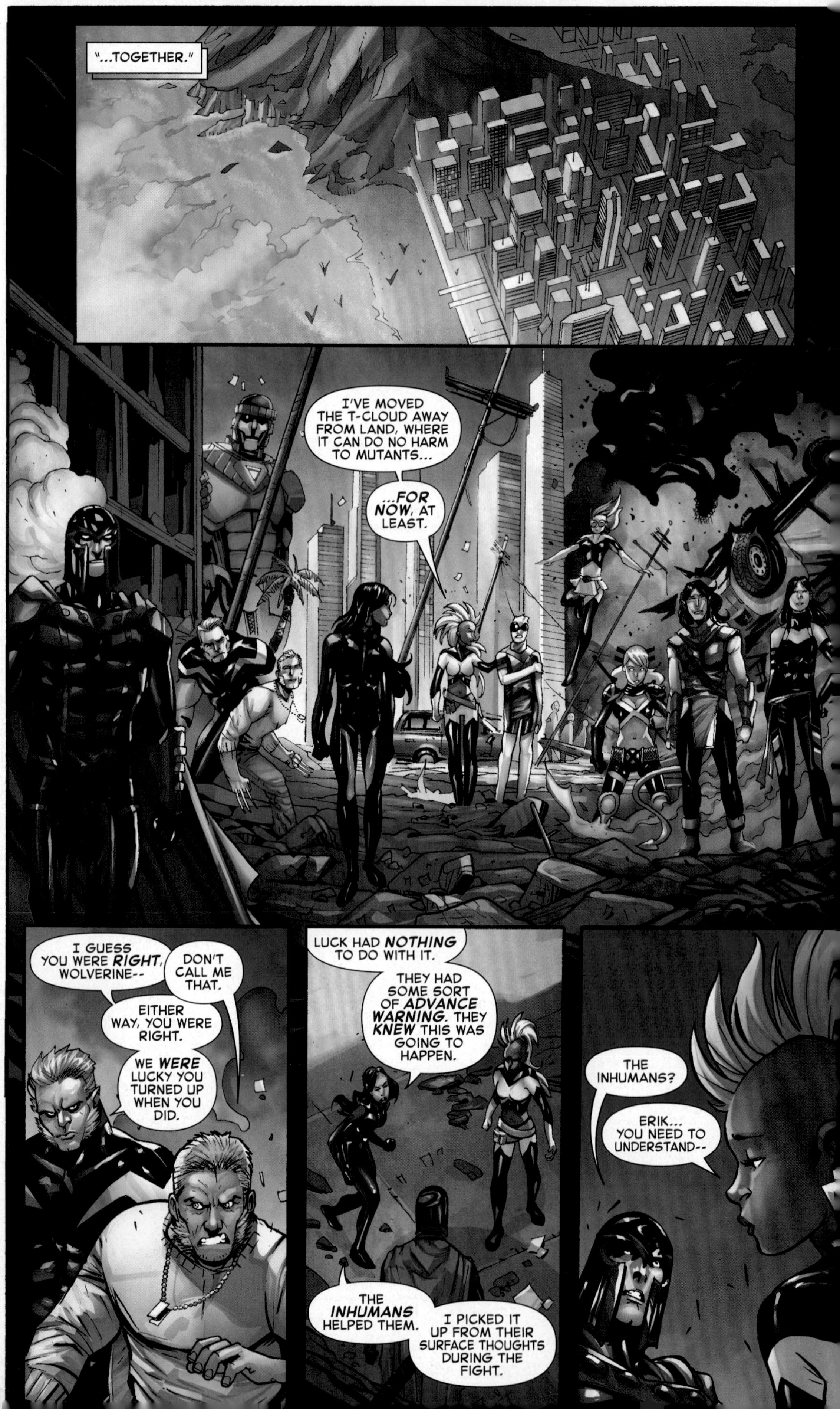
"...TOGETHER."
I'VE MOVED THE T-CLOUD AWAY FROM LAND, WHERE IT CAN DO NO HARM TO MUTANTS...
...FOR NOW, AT LEAST.
I GUESS YOU WERE RIGHT, WOLVERINE--
DON'T CALL ME THAT.
EITHER WAY, YOU WERE RIGHT.
WE WERE LUCKY YOU TURNED UP WHEN YOU DID.
LUCK HAD NOTHING TO DO WITH IT.
THEY HAD SOME SORT OF ADVANCE WARNING. THEY KNEW THIS WAS GOING TO HAPPEN.
THE INHUMANS HELPED THEM.
I PICKED IT UP FROM THEIR SURFACE THOUGHTS DURING THE FIGHT.
THE INHUMANS?
ERIK... YOU NEED TO UNDERSTAND--

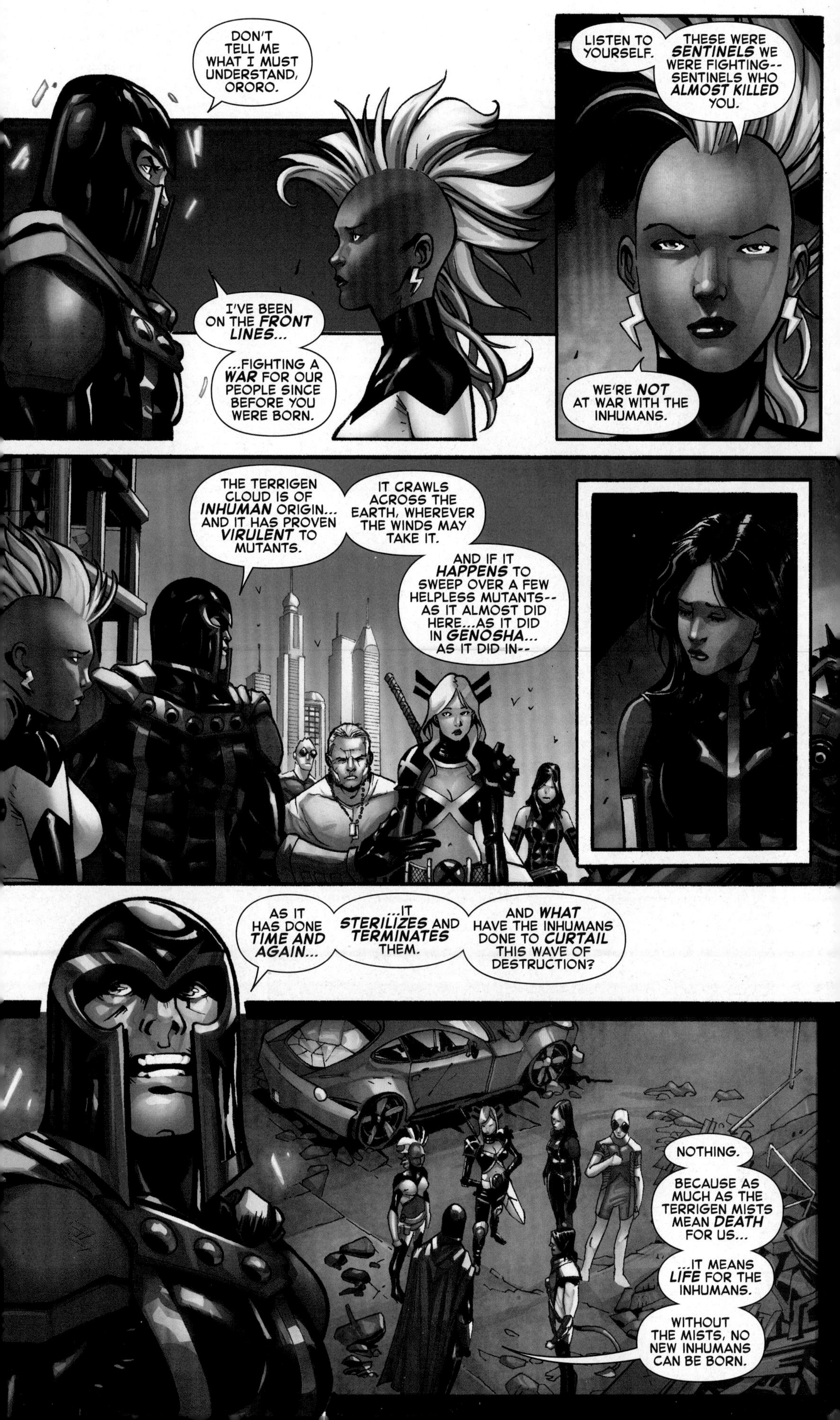
DON'T TELL ME WHAT I MUST UNDERSTAND, ORORO.
I'VE BEEN ON THE FRONT LINES...
...FIGHTING A WAR FOR OUR PEOPLE SINCE BEFORE YOU WERE BORN.
LISTEN TO YOURSELF.
THESE WERE SENTINELS WE WERE FIGHTING-- SENTINELS WHO ALMOST KILLED YOU.
WE'RE NOT AT WAR WITH THE INHUMANS.
THE TERRIGEN CLOUD IS OF INHUMAN ORIGIN... AND IT HAS PROVEN VIRULENT TO MUTANTS.
IT CRAWLS ACROSS THE EARTH, WHEREVER THE WINDS MAY TAKE IT.
AND IF IT HAPPENS TO SWEEP OVER A FEW HELPLESS MUTANTS-- AS IT ALMOST DID HERE...AS IT DID IN GENOSHA... AS IT DID IN--
AS IT HAS DONE TIME AND AGAIN...
...IT STERILIZES AND TERMINATES THEM.
AND WHAT HAVE THE INHUMANS DONE TO CURTAIL THIS WAVE OF DESTRUCTION?
NOTHING.
BECAUSE AS MUCH AS THE TERRIGEN MISTS MEAN DEATH FOR US...
...IT MEANS LIFE FOR THE INHUMANS.
WITHOUT THE MISTS, NO NEW INHUMANS CAN BE BORN.

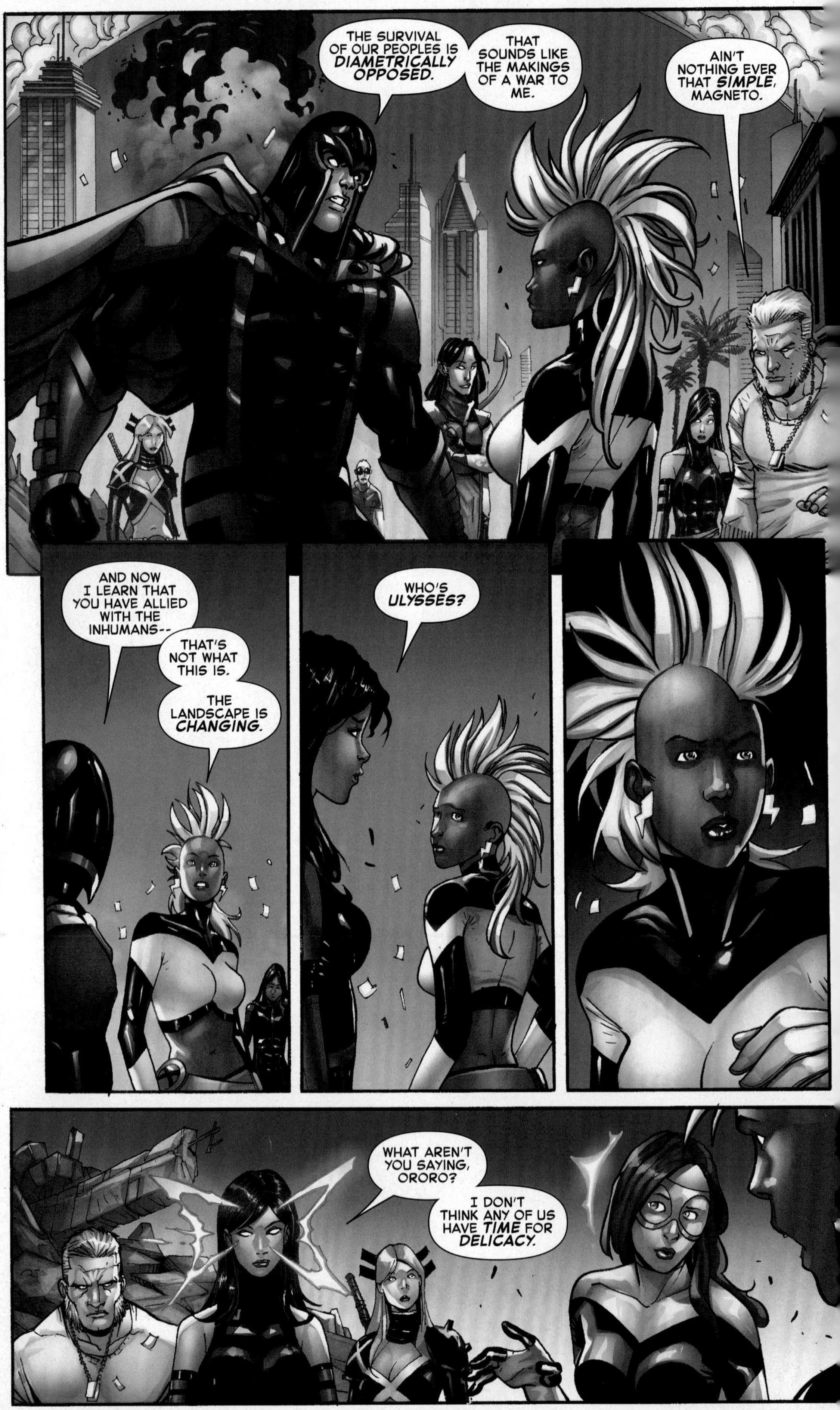
THE SURVIVAL OF OUR PEOPLES IS DIAMETRICALLY OPPOSED.
THAT SOUNDS LIKE THE MAKINGS OF A WAR TO ME.
AIN'T NOTHING EVER THAT SIMPLE, MAGNETO.
AND NOW I LEARN THAT YOU HAVE ALLIED WITH THE INHUMANS--
THAT'S NOT WHAT THIS IS.
THE LANDSCAPE IS CHANGING.
WHO'S ULYSSES?
WHAT AREN'T YOU SAYING, ORORO?
I DON'T THINK ANY OF US HAVE TIME FOR DELICACY.

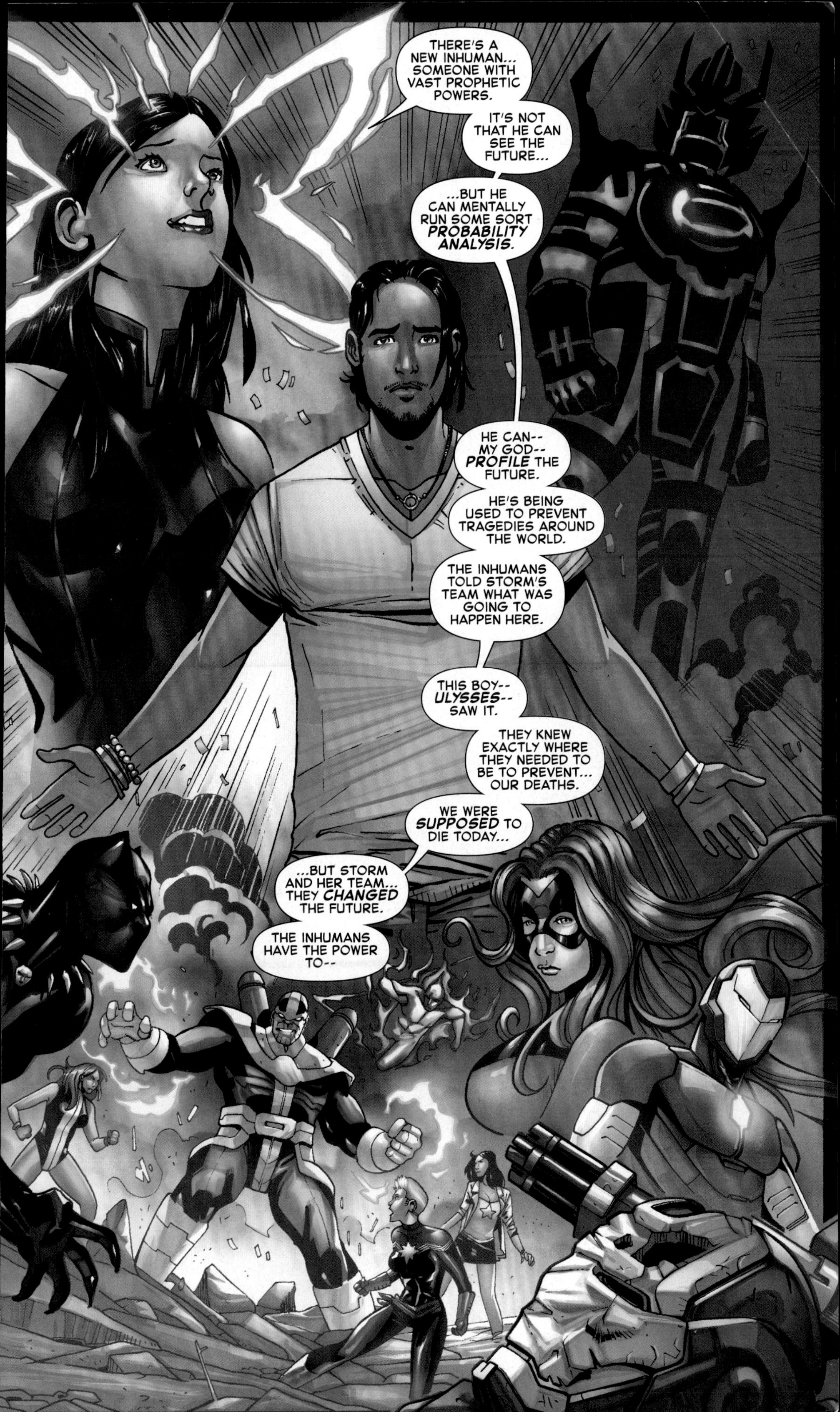
THERE'S A NEW INHUMAN... SOMEONE WITH VAST PROPHETIC POWERS.
IT'S NOT THAT HE CAN SEE THE FUTURE...
...BUT HE CAN MENTALLY RUN SOME SORT PROBABILITY ANALYSIS.
HE CAN-- MY GOD-- PROFILE THE FUTURE.
HE'S BEING USED TO PREVENT TRAGEDIES AROUND THE WORLD.
THE INHUMANS TOLD STORM'S TEAM WHAT WAS GOING TO HAPPEN HERE.
THIS BOY-- ULYSSES-- SAW IT.
THEY KNEW EXACTLY WHERE THEY NEEDED TO BE TO PREVENT... OUR DEATHS.
WE WERE SUPPOSED TO DIE TODAY...
...BUT STORM AND HER TEAM... THEY CHANGED THE FUTURE.
THE INHUMANS HAVE THE POWER TO--

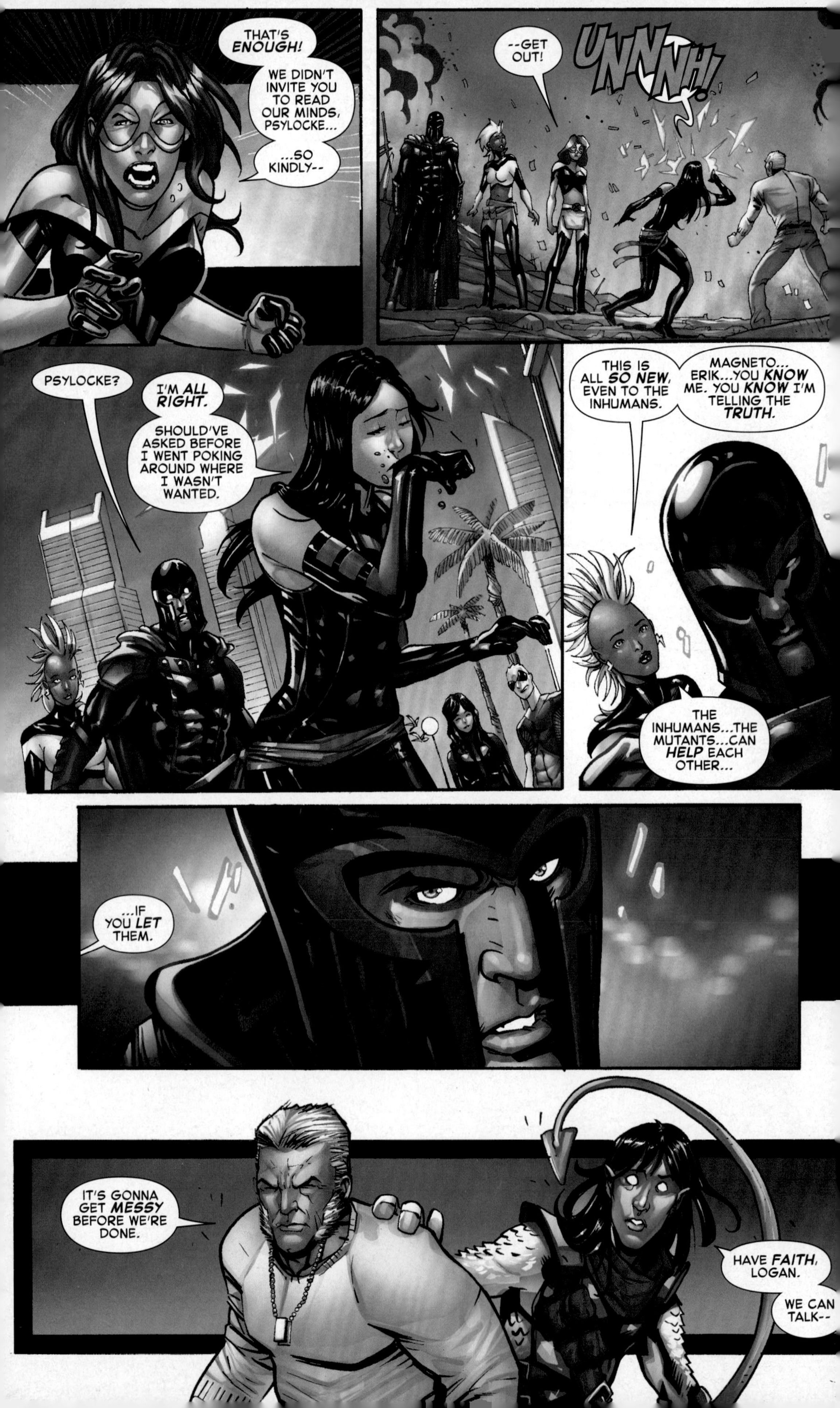
THAT'S ENOUGH!
WE DIDN'T INVITE YOU TO READ OUR MINDS, PSYLOCKE...
...SO KINDLY--
--GET OUT!
UNNNH!
PSYLOCKE?
I'M ALL RIGHT.
SHOULD'VE ASKED BEFORE I WENT POKING AROUND WHERE I WASN'T WANTED.
THIS IS ALL SO NEW, EVEN TO THE INHUMANS.
MAGNETO... ERIK...YOU KNOW ME. YOU KNOW I'M TELLING THE TRUTH.
THE INHUMANS...THE MUTANTS...CAN HELP EACH OTHER...
...IF YOU LET THEM.
IT'S GONNA GET MESSY BEFORE WE'RE DONE.
HAVE FAITH, LOGAN.
WE CAN TALK--

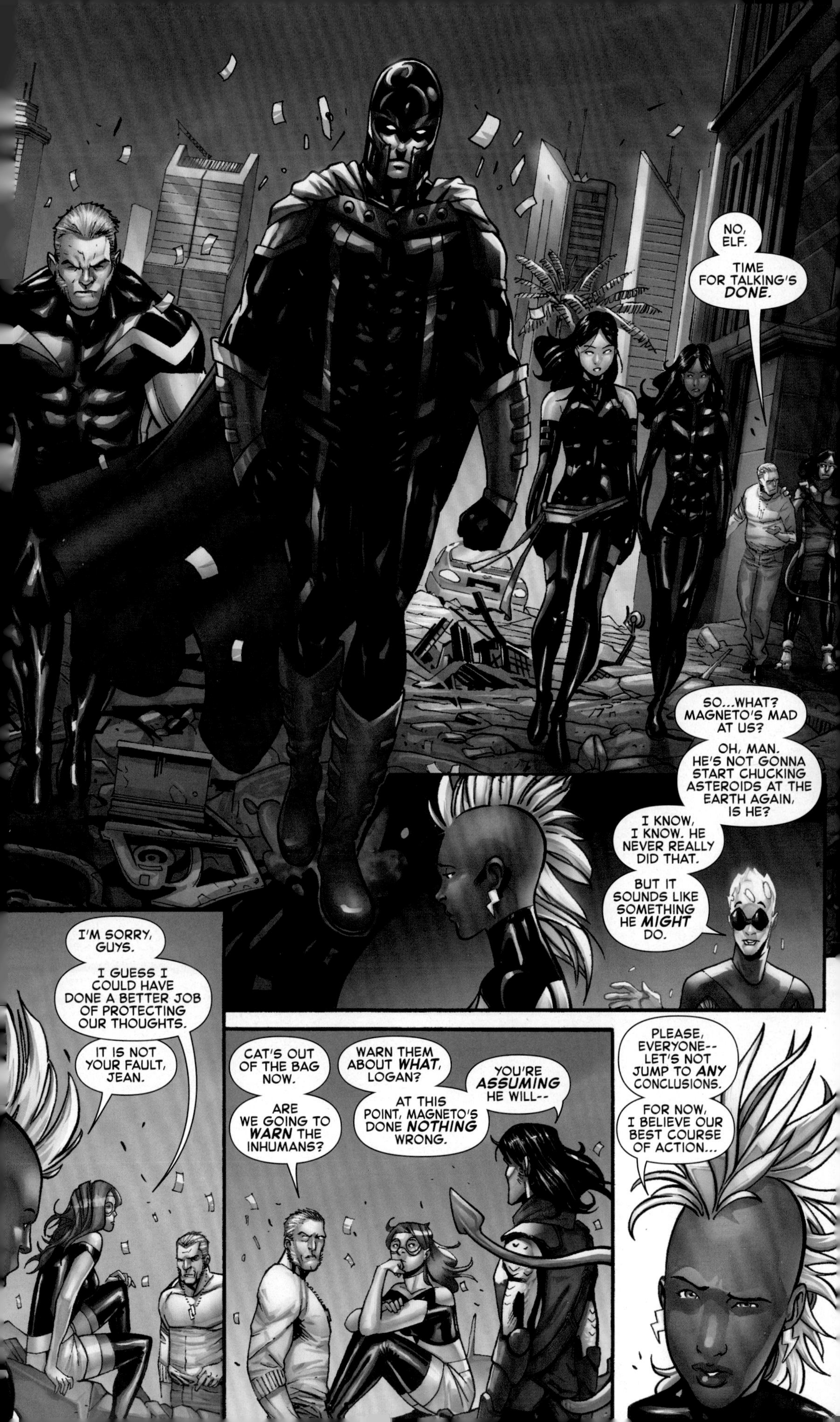

NO, ELF.
TIME FOR TALKING'S DONE.
SO...WHAT? MAGNETO'S MAD AT US?
OH, MAN. HE'S NOT GONNA START CHUCKING ASTEROIDS AT THE EARTH AGAIN, IS HE?
I KNOW, I KNOW. HE NEVER REALLY DID THAT.
BUT IT SOUNDS LIKE SOMETHING HE MIGHT DO.
I'M SORRY, GUYS.
I GUESS I COULD HAVE DONE A BETTER JOB OF PROTECTING OUR THOUGHTS.
IT IS NOT YOUR FAULT, JEAN.
CAT'S OUT OF THE BAG NOW.
ARE WE GOING TO WARN THE INHUMANS?
WARN THEM ABOUT WHAT, LOGAN?
AT THIS POINT, MAGNETO'S DONE NOTHING WRONG.
YOU'RE ASSUMING HE WILL--
PLEASE, EVERYONE-- LET'S NOT JUMP TO ANY CONCLUSIONS.
FOR NOW, I BELIEVE OUR BEST COURSE OF ACTION...

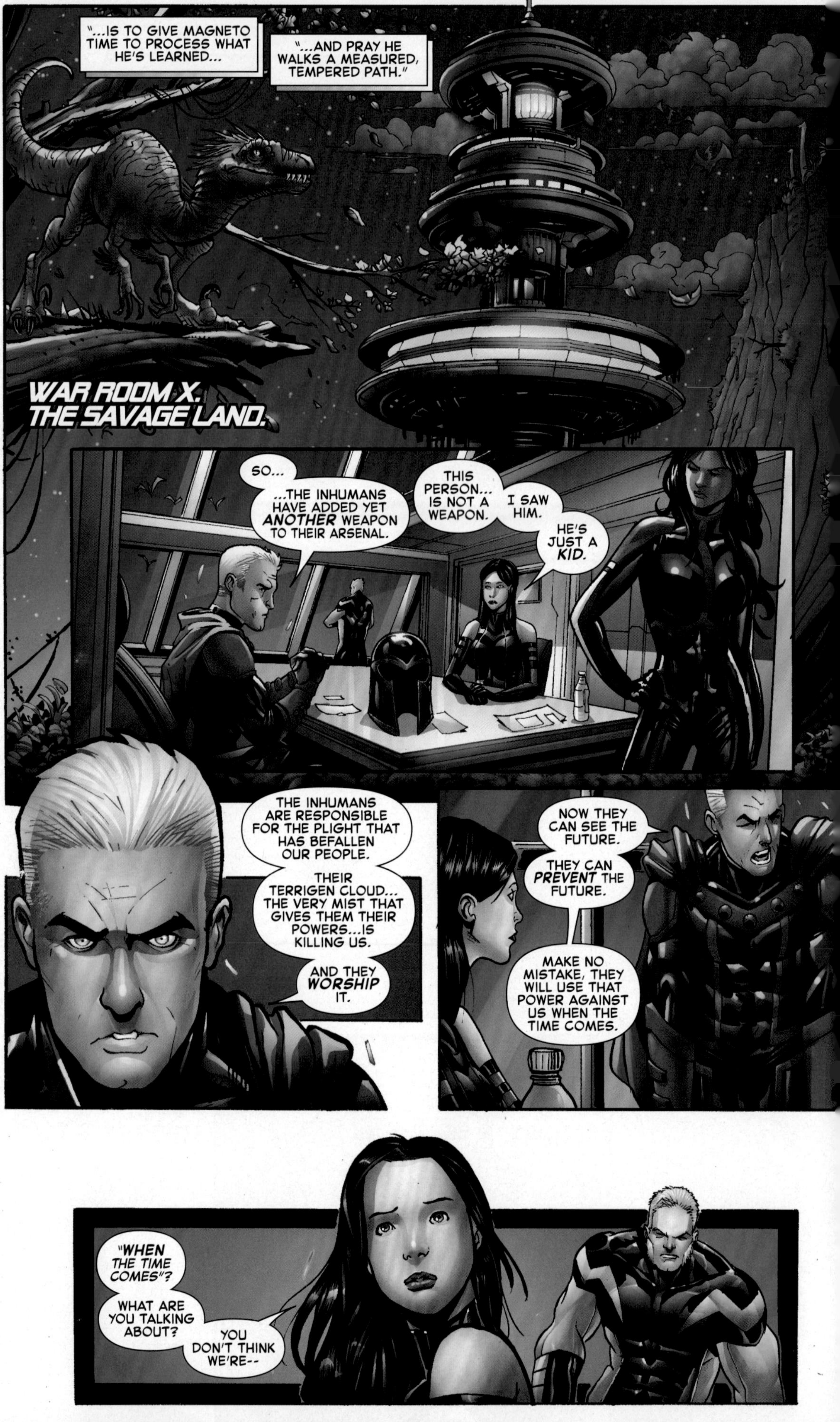
"...IS TO GIVE MAGNETO TIME TO PROCESS WHAT HE'S LEARNED...
"...AND PRAY HE WALKS A MEASURED, TEMPERED PATH."
WAR ROOM X. THE SAVAGE LAND.
SO...
...THE INHUMANS HAVE ADDED YET ANOTHER WEAPON TO THEIR ARSENAL.
THIS PERSON... IS NOT A WEAPON.
I SAW HIM.
HE'S JUST A KID.
THE INHUMANS ARE RESPONSIBLE FOR THE PLIGHT THAT HAS BEFALLEN OUR PEOPLE.
THEIR TERRIGEN CLOUD... THE VERY MIST THAT GIVES THEM THEIR POWERS...IS KILLING US.
AND THEY WORSHIP IT.
NOW THEY CAN SEE THE FUTURE.
THEY CAN PREVENT THE FUTURE.
MAKE NO MISTAKE, THEY WILL USE THAT POWER AGAINST US WHEN THE TIME COMES.
"WHEN THE TIME COMES"?
WHAT ARE YOU TALKING ABOUT?
YOU DON'T THINK WE'RE--

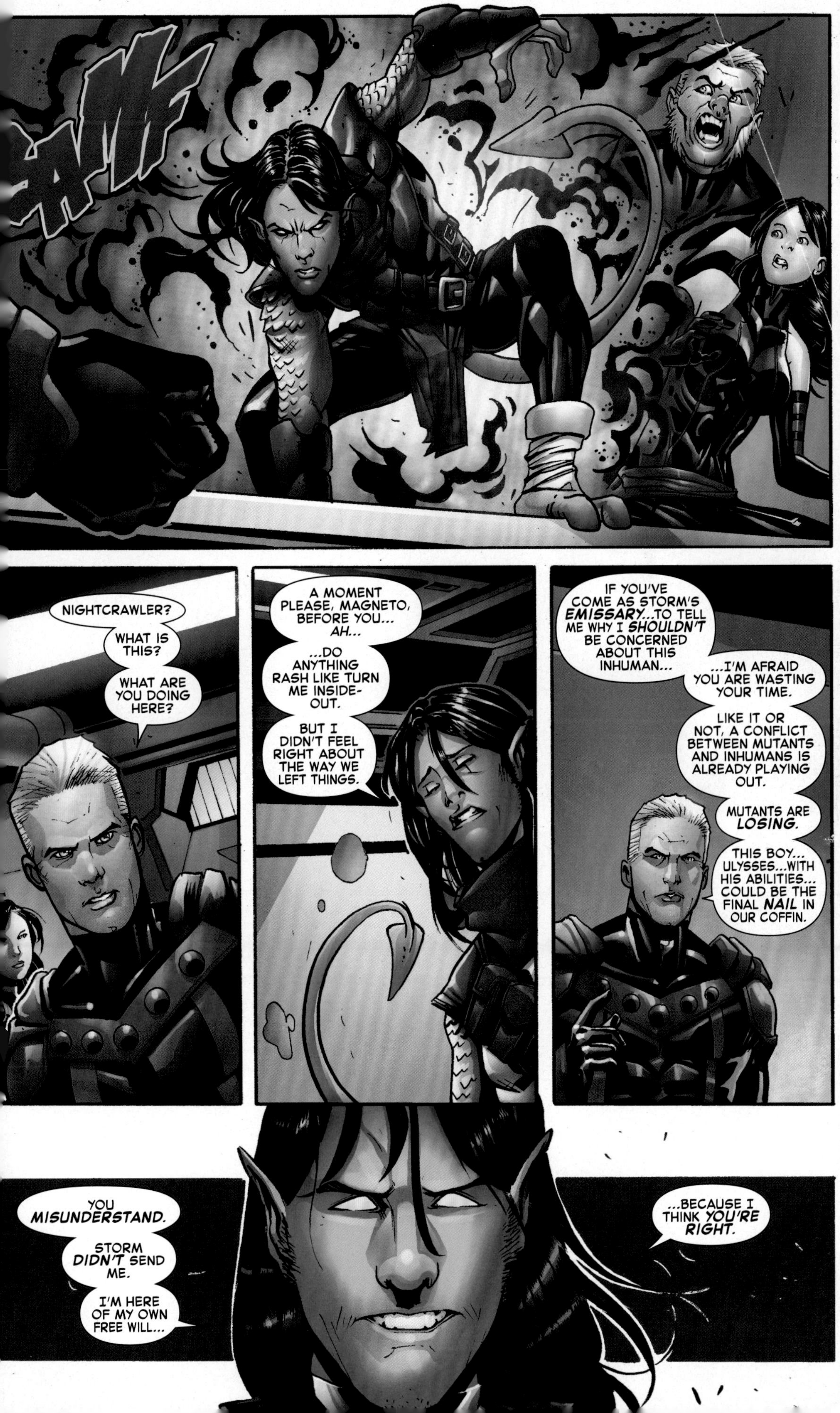

BAMF
NIGHTCRAWLER?
WHAT IS THIS?
WHAT ARE YOU DOING HERE?
A MOMENT PLEASE, MAGNETO, BEFORE YOU... AH...
...DO ANYTHING RASH LIKE TURN ME INSIDE-OUT.
BUT I DIDN'T FEEL RIGHT ABOUT THE WAY WE LEFT THINGS.
IF YOU'VE COME AS STORM'S EMISSARY...TO TELL ME WHY I SHOULDN'T BE CONCERNED ABOUT THIS INHUMAN...
...I'M AFRAID YOU ARE WASTING YOUR TIME.
LIKE IT OR NOT, A CONFLICT BETWEEN MUTANTS AND INHUMANS IS ALREADY PLAYING OUT.
MUTANTS ARE LOSING.
THIS BOY... ULYSSES...WITH HIS ABILITIES... COULD BE THE FINAL NAIL IN OUR COFFIN.
YOU MISUNDERSTAND.
STORM DIDN'T SEND ME.
I'M HERE OF MY OWN FREE WILL...
...BECAUSE I THINK YOU'RE RIGHT.

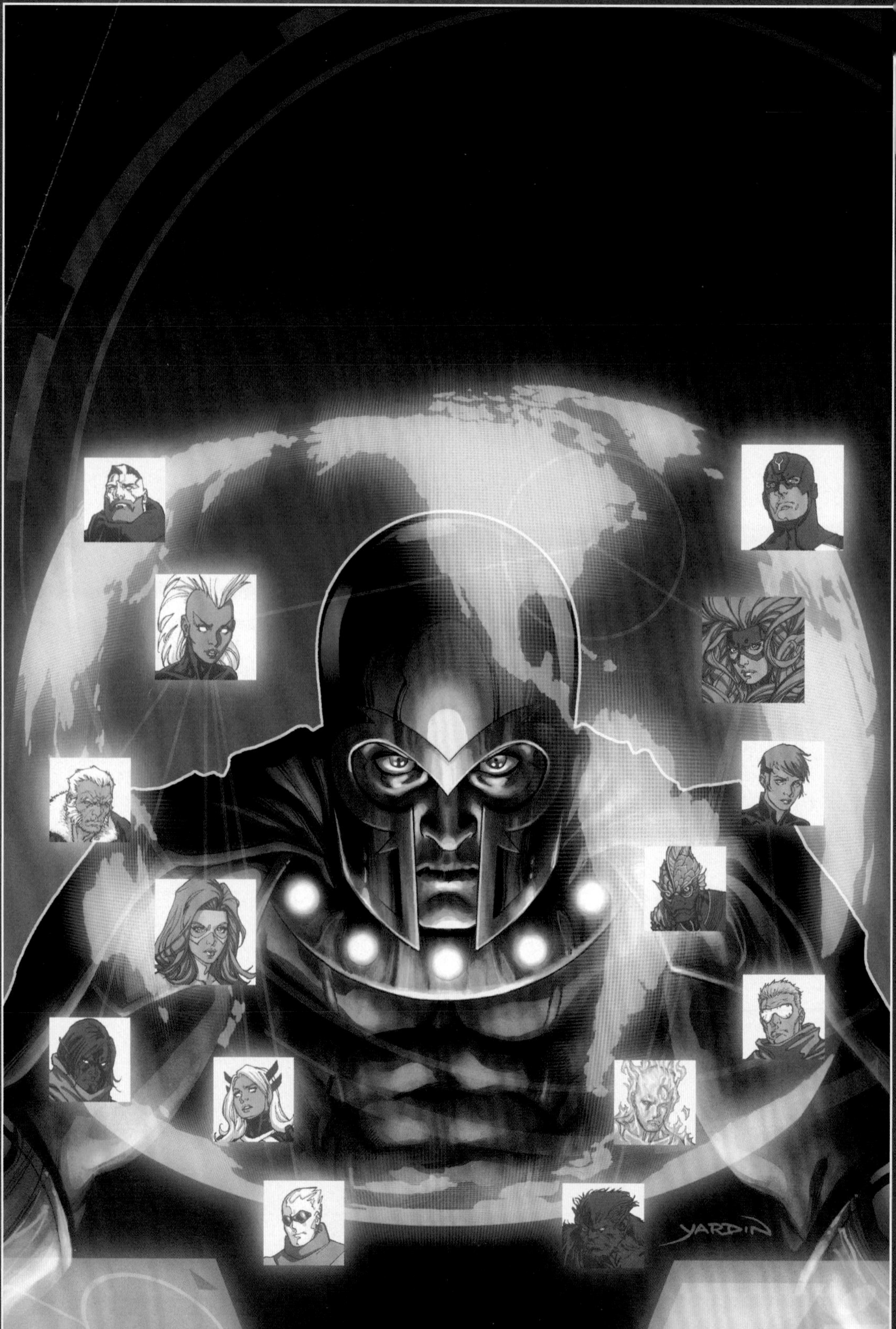
YARDIN

II

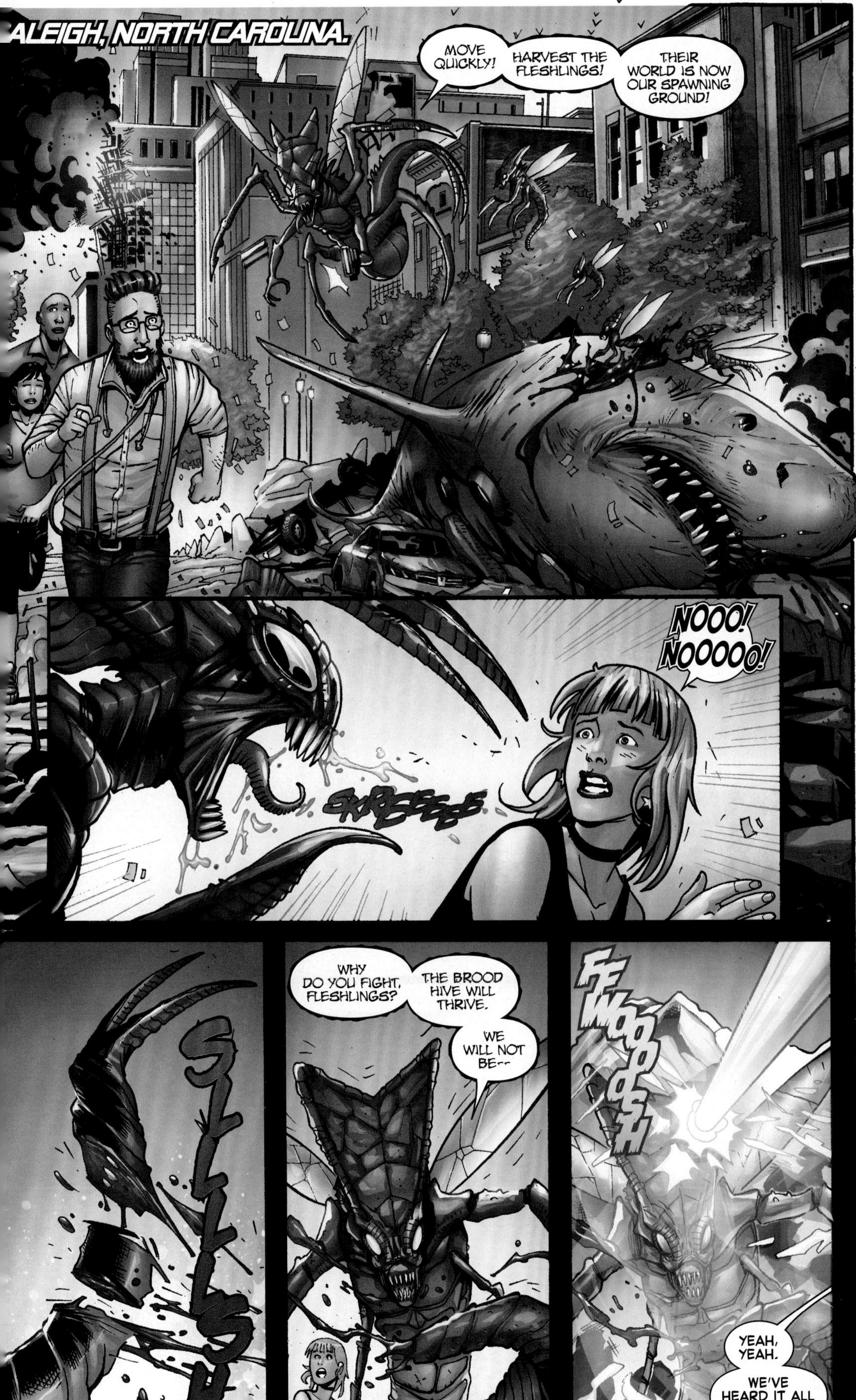
ALEIGH, NORTH CAROLINA.
MOVE QUICKLY!
HARVEST THE FLESHLINGS!
THEIR WORLD IS NOW OUR SPAWNING GROUND!
NOOO! NOOOOO!
SKREEEEE
SHLLLSH
WHY DO YOU FIGHT, FLESHLINGS?
THE BROOD HIVE WILL THRIVE.
WE WILL NOT BE--
FFWOOOOOSH
YEAH, YEAH.
WE'VE HEARD IT ALL BEFORE.

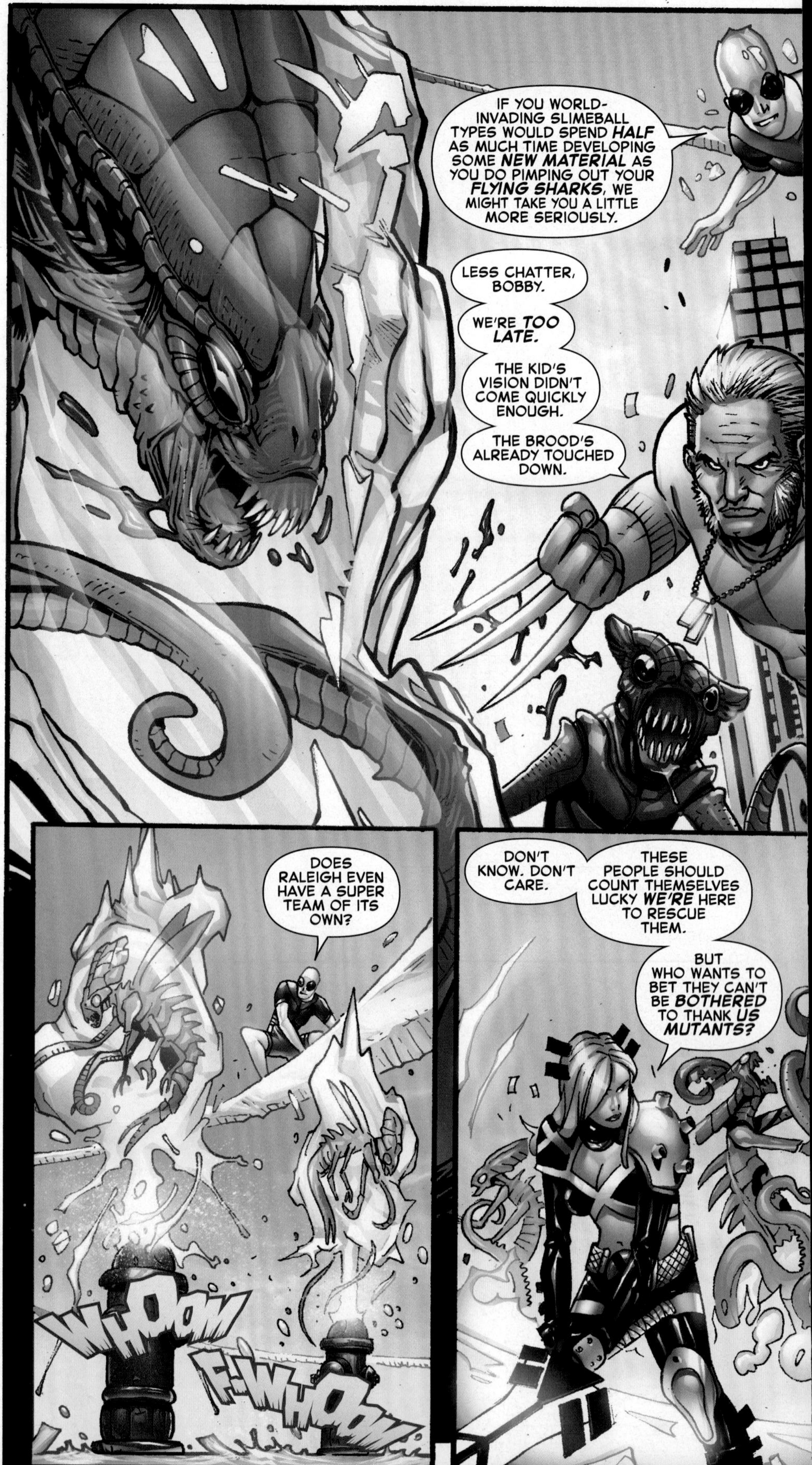
IF YOU WORLD-INVADING SLIMEBALL TYPES WOULD SPEND HALF AS MUCH TIME DEVELOPING SOME NEW MATERIAL AS YOU DO PIMPING OUT YOUR FLYING SHARKS, WE MIGHT TAKE YOU A LITTLE MORE SERIOUSLY.
LESS CHATTER, BOBBY.
WE'RE TOO LATE.
THE KID'S VISION DIDN'T COME QUICKLY ENOUGH.
THE BROOD'S ALREADY TOUCHED DOWN.
DOES RALEIGH EVEN HAVE A SUPER TEAM OF ITS OWN?
WHOOM
F-WHOOM
DON'T KNOW. DON'T CARE.
THESE PEOPLE SHOULD COUNT THEMSELVES LUCKY WE'RE HERE TO RESCUE THEM.
BUT WHO WANTS TO BET THEY CAN'T BE BOTHERED TO THANK US MUTANTS?

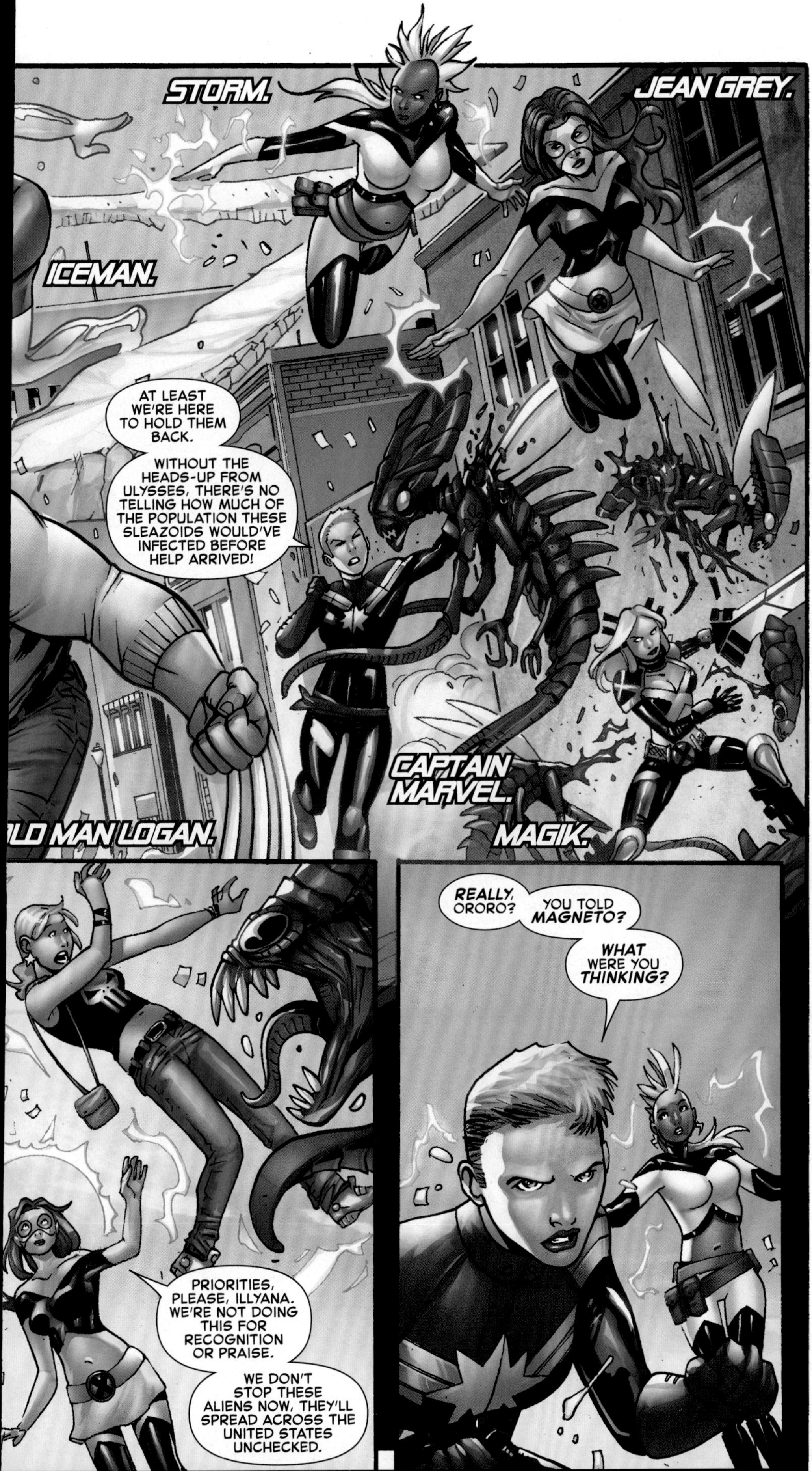
STORM.
JEAN GREY.
ICEMAN.
AT LEAST WE'RE HERE TO HOLD THEM BACK.
WITHOUT THE HEADS-UP FROM ULYSSES, THERE'S NO TELLING HOW MUCH OF THE POPULATION THESE SLEAZOIDS WOULD'VE INFECTED BEFORE HELP ARRIVED!
CAPTAIN MARVEL.
MAGIK.
LD MAN LOGAN.
PRIORITIES, PLEASE, ILLYANA. WE'RE NOT DOING THIS FOR RECOGNITION OR PRAISE.
WE DON'T STOP THESE ALIENS NOW, THEY'LL SPREAD ACROSS THE UNITED STATES UNCHECKED.
REALLY, ORORO?
YOU TOLD MAGNETO?
WHAT WERE YOU THINKING?

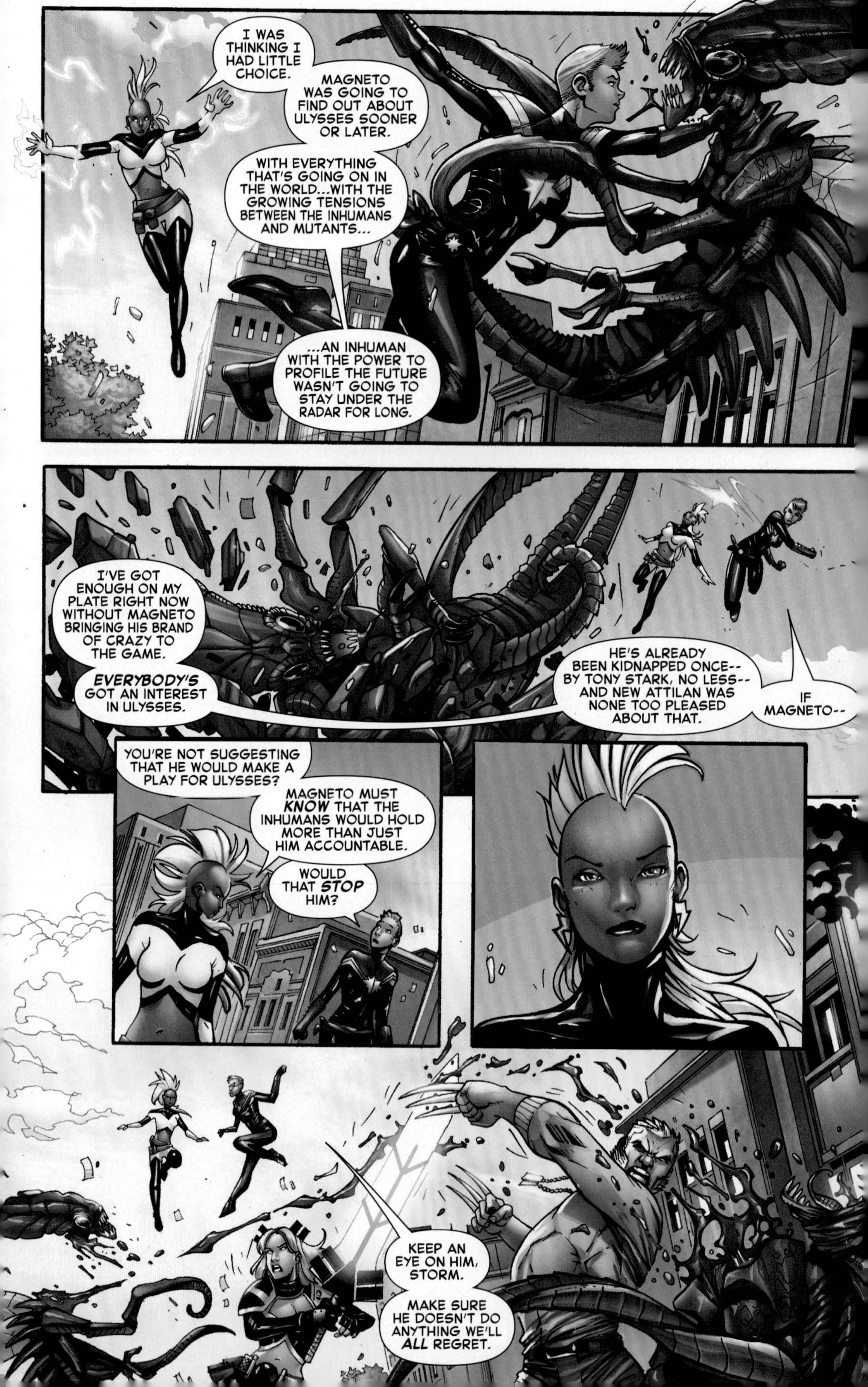
I WAS THINKING I HAD LITTLE CHOICE.
MAGNETO WAS GOING TO FIND OUT ABOUT ULYSSES SOONER OR LATER.
WITH EVERYTHING THAT'S GOING ON IN THE WORLD...WITH THE GROWING TENSIONS BETWEEN THE INHUMANS AND MUTANTS...
...AN INHUMAN WITH THE POWER TO PROFILE THE FUTURE WASN'T GOING TO STAY UNDER THE RADAR FOR LONG.
I'VE GOT ENOUGH ON MY PLATE RIGHT NOW WITHOUT MAGNETO BRINGING HIS BRAND OF CRAZY TO THE GAME.
EVERYBODY'S GOT AN INTEREST IN ULYSSES.
HE'S ALREADY BEEN KIDNAPPED ONCE-- BY TONY STARK, NO LESS-- AND NEW ATTILAN WAS NONE TOO PLEASED ABOUT THAT.
IF MAGNETO--
YOU'RE NOT SUGGESTING THAT HE WOULD MAKE A PLAY FOR ULYSSES?
MAGNETO MUST KNOW THAT THE INHUMANS WOULD HOLD MORE THAN JUST HIM ACCOUNTABLE.
WOULD THAT STOP HIM?
KEEP AN EYE ON HIM, STORM.
MAKE SURE HE DOESN'T DO ANYTHING WE'LL ALL REGRET.

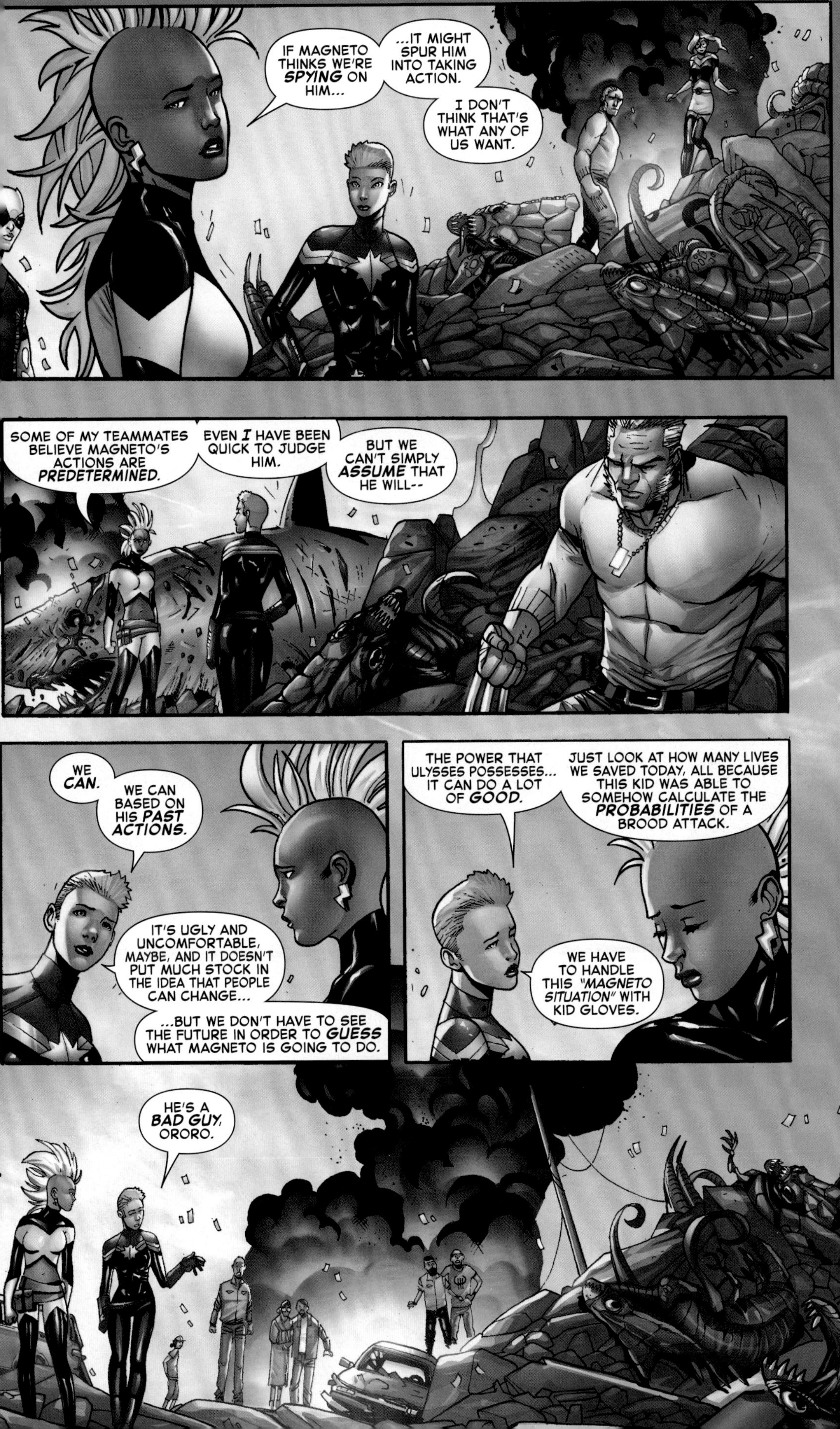
IF MAGNETO THINKS WE'RE SPYING ON HIM...
...IT MIGHT SPUR HIM INTO TAKING ACTION.
I DON'T THINK THAT'S WHAT ANY OF US WANT.
SOME OF MY TEAMMATES BELIEVE MAGNETO'S ACTIONS ARE PREDETERMINED.
EVEN I HAVE BEEN QUICK TO JUDGE HIM.
BUT WE CAN'T SIMPLY ASSUME THAT HE WILL--
WE CAN.
WE CAN BASED ON HIS PAST ACTIONS.
IT'S UGLY AND UNCOMFORTABLE, MAYBE, AND IT DOESN'T PUT MUCH STOCK IN THE IDEA THAT PEOPLE CAN CHANGE...
...BUT WE DON'T HAVE TO SEE THE FUTURE IN ORDER TO GUESS WHAT MAGNETO IS GOING TO DO.
THE POWER THAT ULYSSES POSSESSES... IT CAN DO A LOT OF GOOD.
JUST LOOK AT HOW MANY LIVES WE SAVED TODAY, ALL BECAUSE THIS KID WAS ABLE TO SOMEHOW CALCULATE THE PROBABILITIES OF A BROOD ATTACK.
WE HAVE TO HANDLE THIS "MAGNETO SITUATION" WITH KID GLOVES.
HE'S A BAD GUY, ORORO.

"TREAT HIM LIKE ONE."

WAR ROOM X. THE SAVAGE LAND.

HE'S TELLING THE TRUTH. NIGHTCRAWLER HERE ON HIS O- NOT AT STORM REQUEST.

PSYLOCKE.

THANKS FOR ALLOWING ME TO SCAN YOUR THOUGHTS, KURT.

I KNOW IT'S NOT A COMFORTABLE SITUATION.

IT'S ALL RIGHT, ELIZABETH.

IT SADDENS ME, THOUGH...

...THAT *TRUST* BETWEEN MUTANTS IS IN SUCH *SHORT SUPPLY* THESE DAYS.

NIGHTCRAWLER.

MY RESERVOIRS OF TRUST RAN DRY ABOUT THE TIME MY FELLOW MUTANTS STARTED SIDING WITH OUR ENEMIES ABOVE THEIR OWN KIND.

IN SHORT, A LONG, LONG, LONG TIME AGO.

MAGNETO

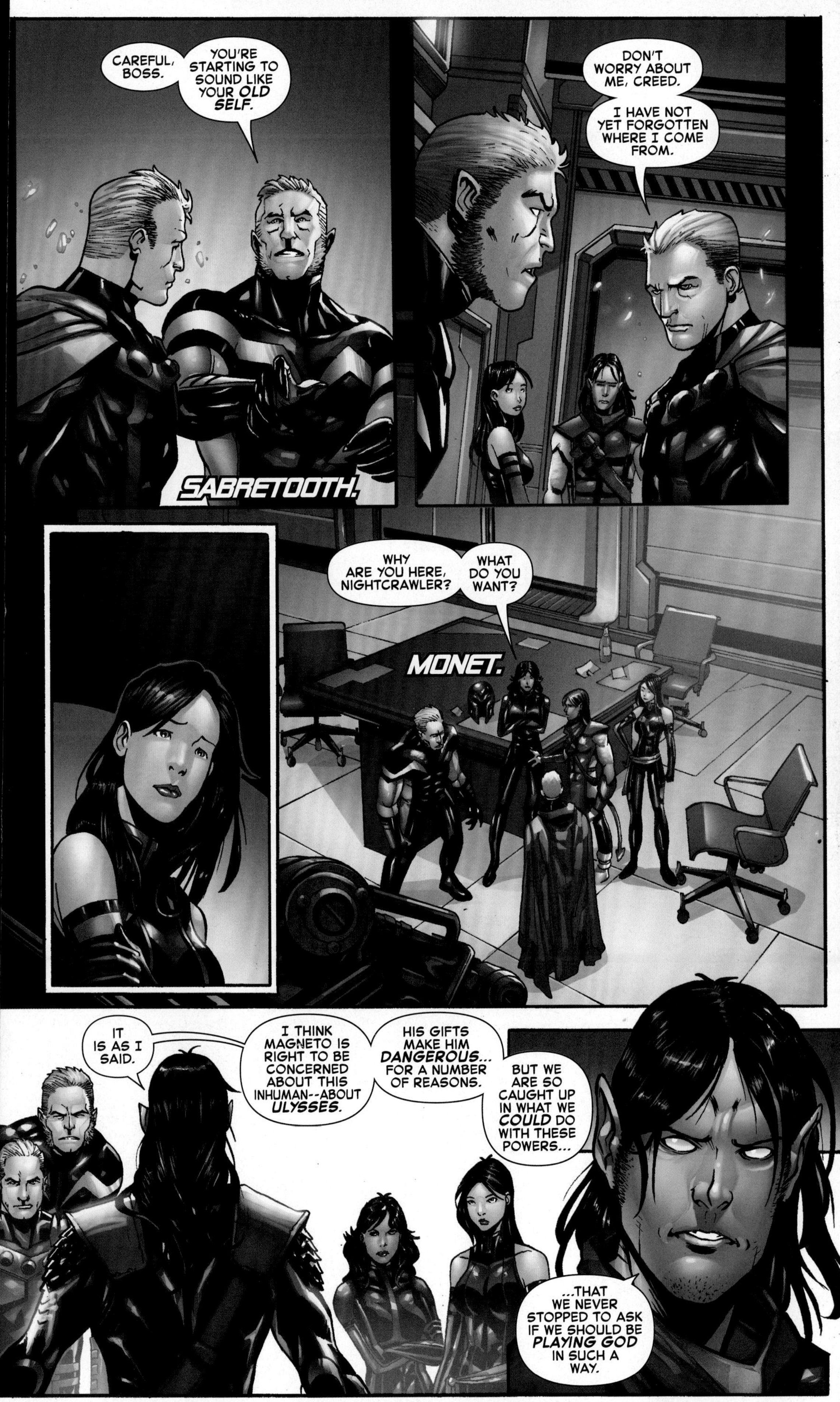
CAREFUL, BOSS.
YOU'RE STARTING TO SOUND LIKE YOUR OLD SELF.
SABRETOOTH.
DON'T WORRY ABOUT ME, CREED.
I HAVE NOT YET FORGOTTEN WHERE I COME FROM.
WHY ARE YOU HERE, NIGHTCRAWLER?
WHAT DO YOU WANT?
MONET.
IT IS AS I SAID.
I THINK MAGNETO IS RIGHT TO BE CONCERNED ABOUT THIS INHUMAN--ABOUT ULYSSES.
HIS GIFTS MAKE HIM DANGEROUS... FOR A NUMBER OF REASONS.
BUT WE ARE SO CAUGHT UP IN WHAT WE COULD DO WITH THESE POWERS...
...THAT WE NEVER STOPPED TO ASK IF WE SHOULD BE PLAYING GOD IN SUCH A WAY.

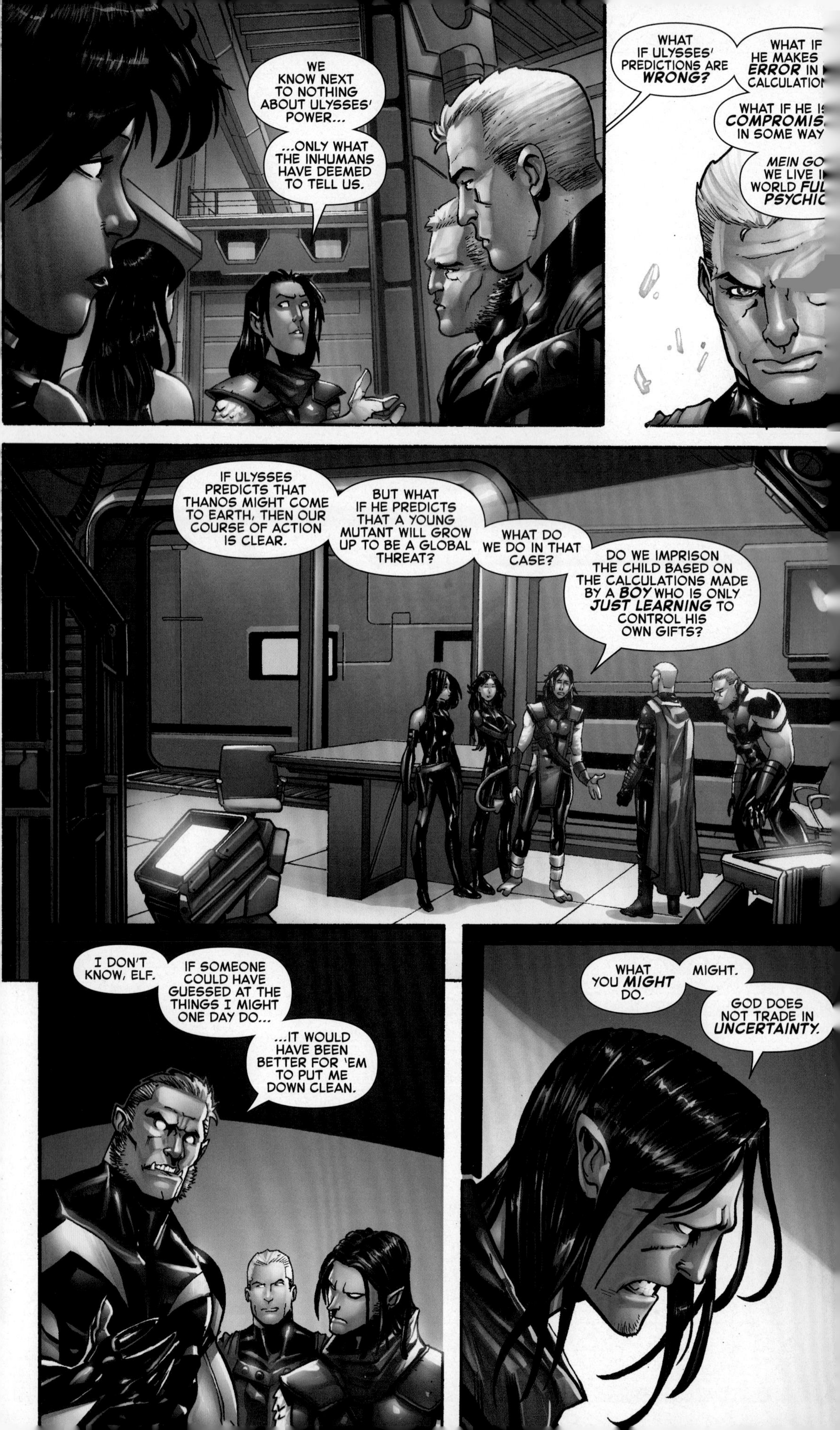

WE KNOW NEXT TO NOTHING ABOUT ULYSSES' POWER...
...ONLY WHAT THE INHUMANS HAVE DEEMED TO TELL US.
WHAT IF ULYSSES' PREDICTIONS ARE *WRONG?*
WHAT IF HE MAKES *ERROR* IN CALCULATION
WHAT IF HE IS *COMPROMIS* IN SOME WAY
MEIN GO WE LIVE I WORLD *FUL* *PSYCHIC*
IF ULYSSES PREDICTS THAT THANOS MIGHT COME TO EARTH, THEN OUR COURSE OF ACTION IS CLEAR.
BUT WHAT IF HE PREDICTS THAT A YOUNG MUTANT WILL GROW UP TO BE A GLOBAL THREAT?
WHAT DO WE DO IN THAT CASE?
DO WE IMPRISON THE CHILD BASED ON THE CALCULATIONS MADE BY A *BOY* WHO IS ONLY *JUST LEARNING* TO CONTROL HIS OWN GIFTS?
I DON'T KNOW, ELF.
IF SOMEONE COULD HAVE GUESSED AT THE THINGS I MIGHT ONE DAY DO...
...IT WOULD HAVE BEEN BETTER FOR 'EM TO PUT ME DOWN CLEAN.
WHAT YOU *MIGHT* DO.
MIGHT.
GOD DOES NOT TRADE IN *UNCERTAINTY.*

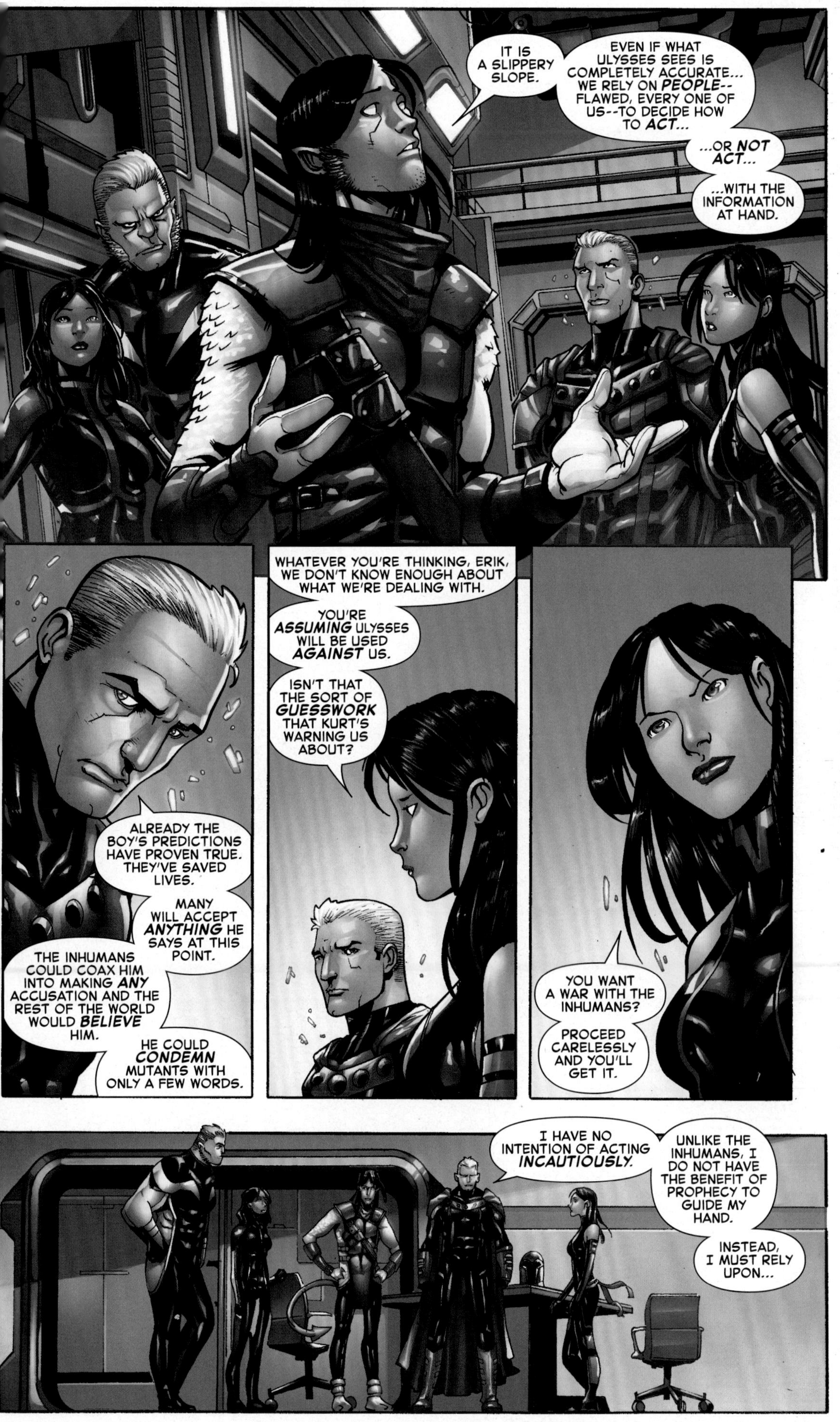
IT IS A SLIPPERY SLOPE.
EVEN IF WHAT ULYSSES SEES IS COMPLETELY ACCURATE... WE RELY ON PEOPLE-- FLAWED, EVERY ONE OF US--TO DECIDE HOW TO ACT...
...OR NOT ACT...
...WITH THE INFORMATION AT HAND.
ALREADY THE BOY'S PREDICTIONS HAVE PROVEN TRUE. THEY'VE SAVED LIVES.
MANY WILL ACCEPT ANYTHING HE SAYS AT THIS POINT.
THE INHUMANS COULD COAX HIM INTO MAKING ANY ACCUSATION AND THE REST OF THE WORLD WOULD BELIEVE HIM.
HE COULD CONDEMN MUTANTS WITH ONLY A FEW WORDS.
WHATEVER YOU'RE THINKING, ERIK, WE DON'T KNOW ENOUGH ABOUT WHAT WE'RE DEALING WITH.
YOU'RE ASSUMING ULYSSES WILL BE USED AGAINST US.
ISN'T THAT THE SORT OF GUESSWORK THAT KURT'S WARNING US ABOUT?
YOU WANT A WAR WITH THE INHUMANS?
PROCEED CARELESSLY AND YOU'LL GET IT.
I HAVE NO INTENTION OF ACTING INCAUTIOUSLY.
UNLIKE THE INHUMANS, I DO NOT HAVE THE BENEFIT OF PROPHECY TO GUIDE MY HAND.
INSTEAD, I MUST RELY UPON...

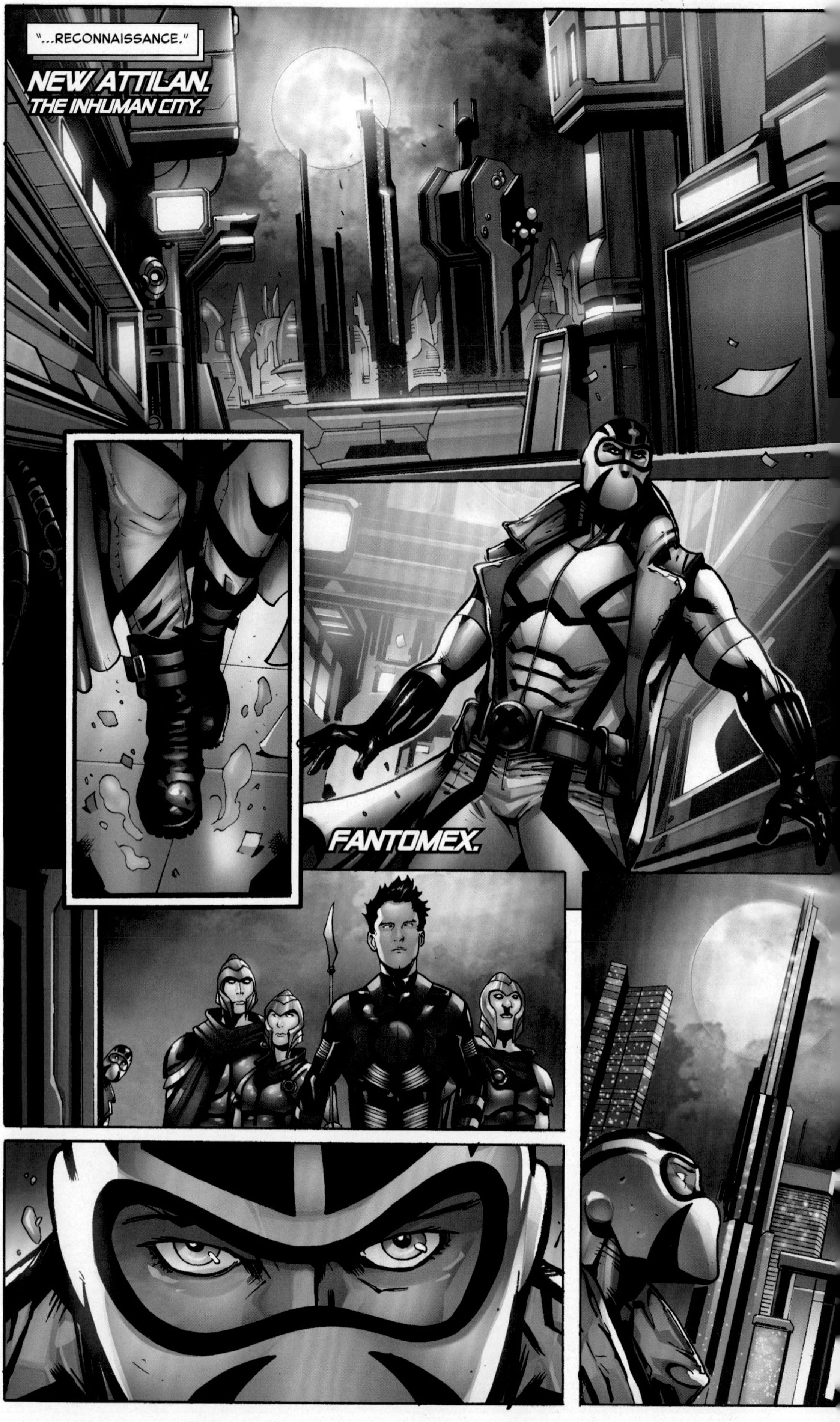
"...RECONNAISSANCE."
NEW ATTILAN.
THE INHUMAN CITY.
FANTOMEX.

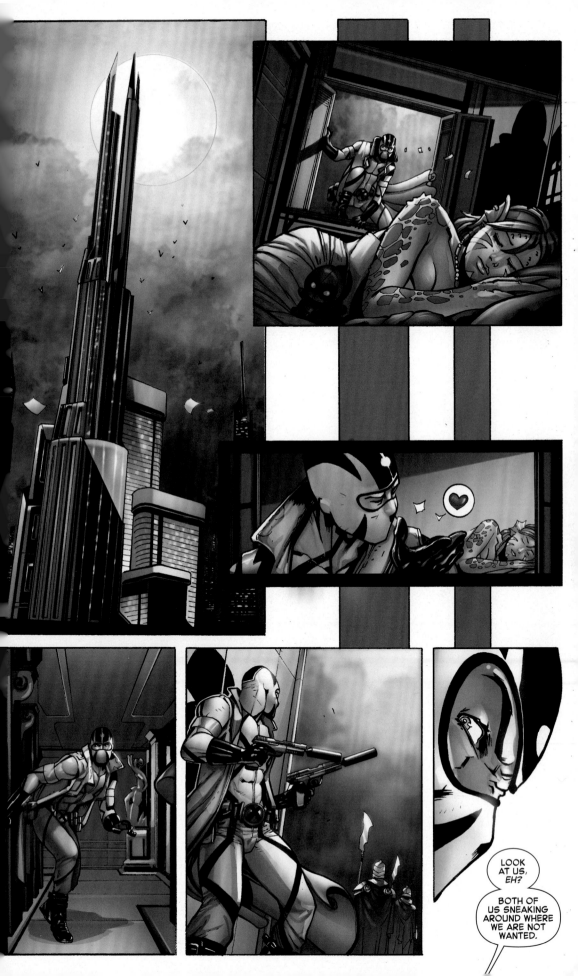

LOOK AT US, EH?

BOTH OF US SNEAKING AROUND WHERE WE ARE NOT WANTED.

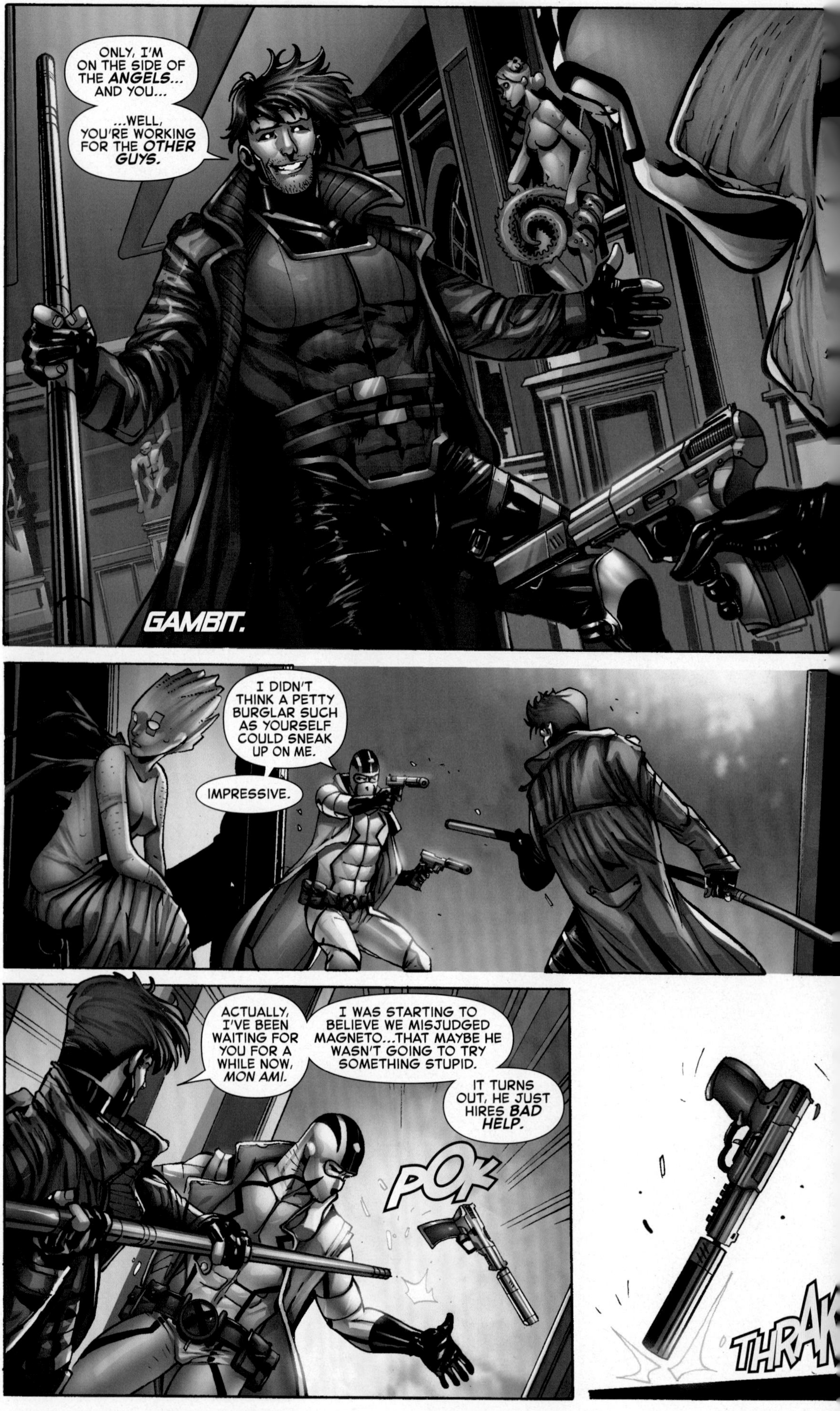
ONLY, I'M ON THE SIDE OF THE *ANGELS*... AND YOU...
...WELL, YOU'RE WORKING FOR THE *OTHER GUYS.*
GAMBIT.
I DIDN'T THINK A PETTY BURGLAR SUCH AS YOURSELF COULD SNEAK UP ON ME.
IMPRESSIVE.
ACTUALLY, I'VE BEEN WAITING FOR YOU FOR A WHILE NOW, *MON AMI.*
I WAS STARTING TO BELIEVE WE MISJUDGED MAGNETO...THAT MAYBE HE WASN'T GOING TO TRY SOMETHING STUPID.
IT TURNS OUT, HE JUST HIRES *BAD HELP.*
POK
THRAK

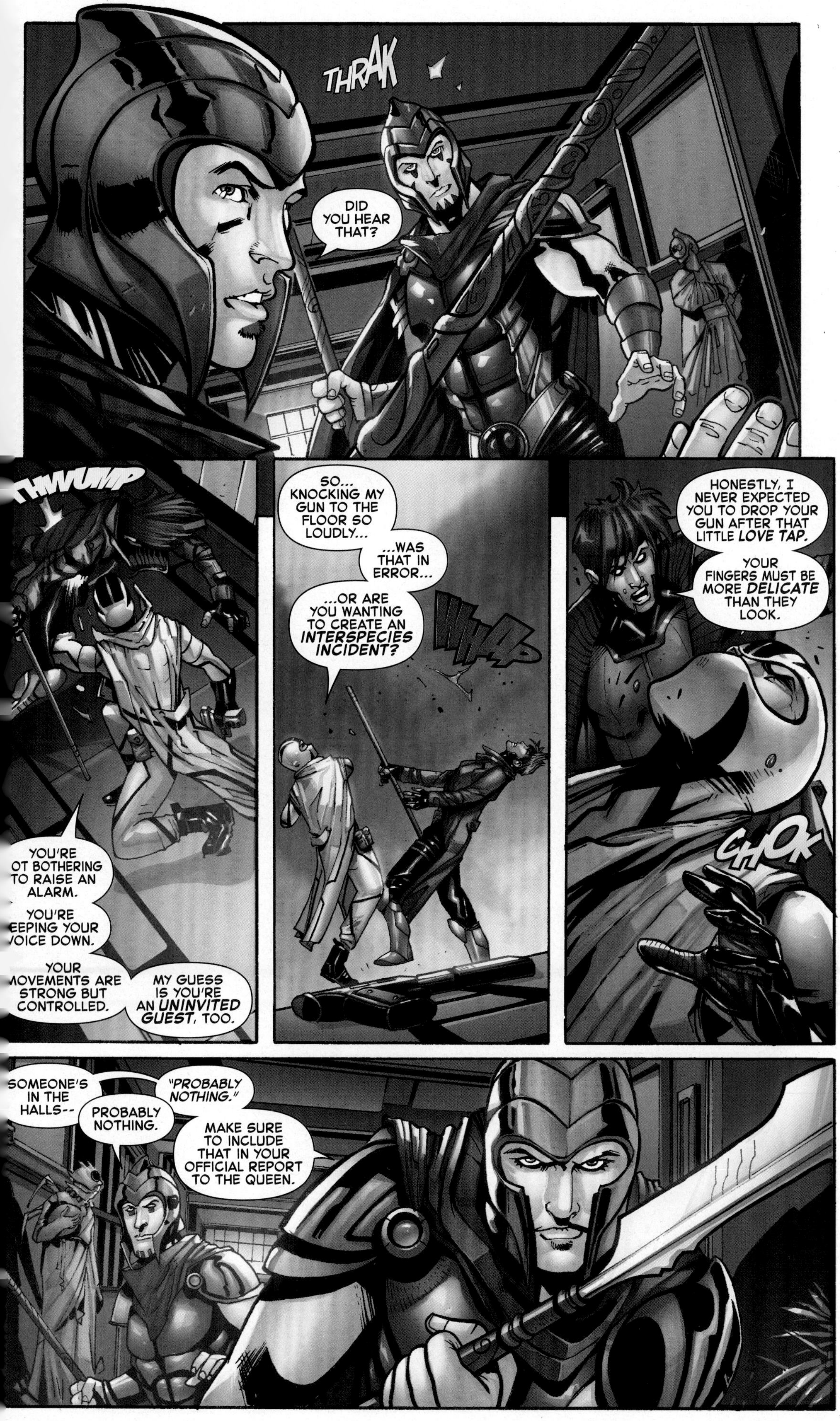
THRAK
DID YOU HEAR THAT?
THWUMP
YOU'RE OT BOTHERING TO RAISE AN ALARM.
YOU'RE EEPING YOUR VOICE DOWN.
YOUR MOVEMENTS ARE STRONG BUT CONTROLLED.
MY GUESS IS YOU'RE AN *UNINVITED GUEST*, TOO.
SO... KNOCKING MY GUN TO THE FLOOR SO LOUDLY...
...WAS THAT IN ERROR...
...OR ARE YOU WANTING TO CREATE AN *INTERSPECIES INCIDENT?*
WHAP
HONESTLY, I NEVER EXPECTED YOU TO DROP YOUR GUN AFTER THAT LITTLE *LOVE TAP.*
YOUR FINGERS MUST BE MORE *DELICATE* THAN THEY LOOK.
CHOK
SOMEONE'S IN THE HALLS--
PROBABLY NOTHING.
"PROBABLY NOTHING."
MAKE SURE TO INCLUDE THAT IN YOUR OFFICIAL REPORT TO THE QUEEN.

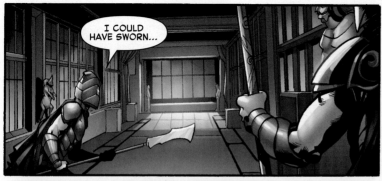

I COULD HAVE SWORN...

SEE? I TOLD YOU.

MAYBE SO. I GUESS I'M JUST ON EDGE...

...JUMPING AT SHADOWS.

...SOMEONE WAS HERE...

NOW, *THAT* GIMMICK COMES IN HANDY.

MISDIRECTION.

A LITTLE *MENTAL NUDGE* TO HELP THEM SEE EVERYTHING *EXCEPT* THE TWO OF US.

BUT WE'RE STILL FIGHTING, ARE WE NOT?

OUI.

JUST CHECKING.

KRAK

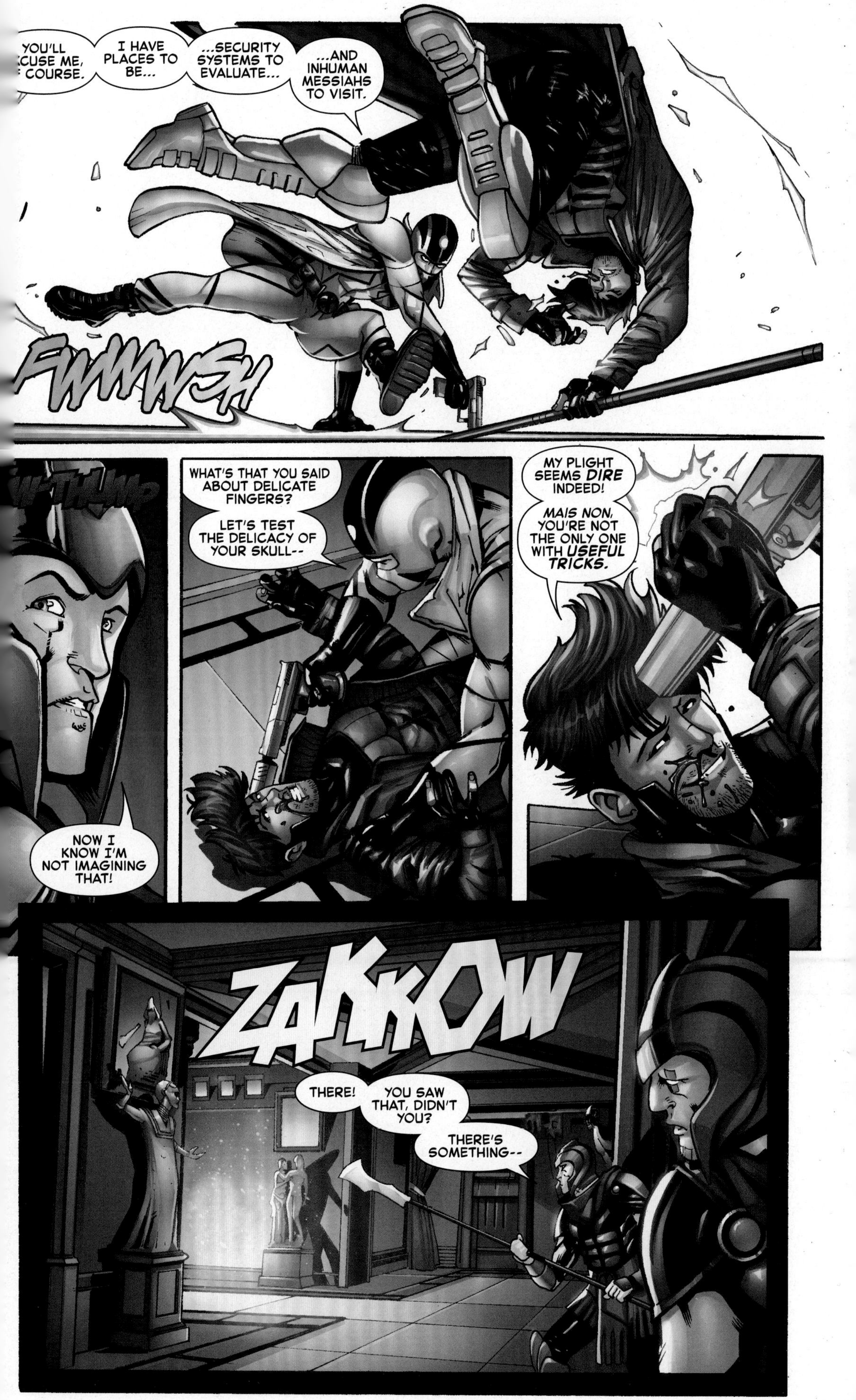
YOU'LL XCUSE ME, F COURSE.
I HAVE PLACES TO BE...
...SECURITY SYSTEMS TO EVALUATE...
...AND INHUMAN MESSIAHS TO VISIT.
FWWWSH
WHAT'S THAT YOU SAID ABOUT DELICATE FINGERS?
LET'S TEST THE DELICACY OF YOUR SKULL--
MY PLIGHT SEEMS DIRE INDEED!
MAIS NON, YOU'RE NOT THE ONLY ONE WITH USEFUL TRICKS.
NOW I KNOW I'M NOT IMAGINING THAT!
ZAKKOW
THERE!
YOU SAW THAT, DIDN'T YOU?
THERE'S SOMETHING--

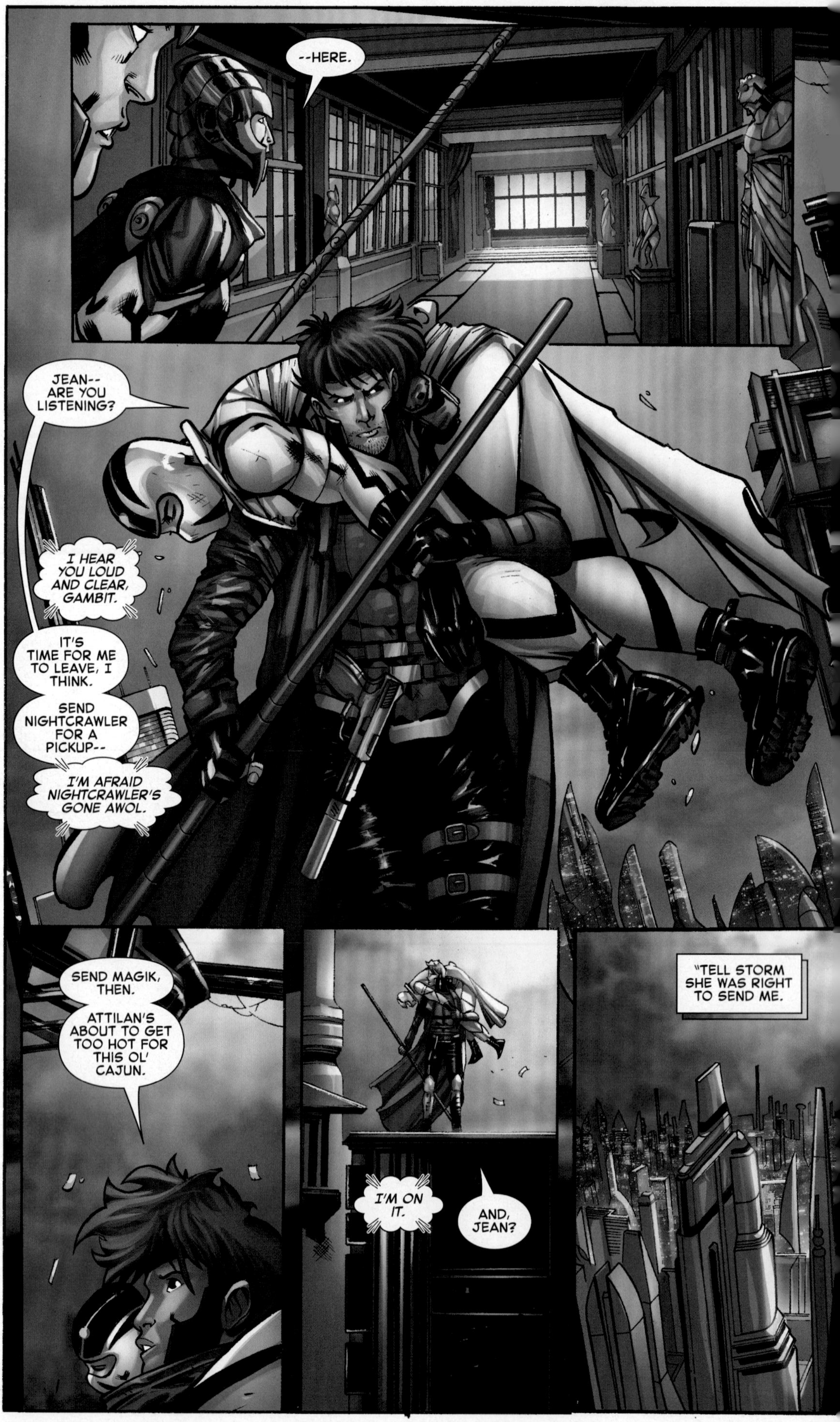
--HERE.
JEAN-- ARE YOU LISTENING?
I HEAR YOU LOUD AND CLEAR, GAMBIT.
IT'S TIME FOR ME TO LEAVE, I THINK.
SEND NIGHTCRAWLER FOR A PICKUP--
I'M AFRAID NIGHTCRAWLER'S GONE AWOL.
SEND MAGIK, THEN.
ATTILAN'S ABOUT TO GET TOO HOT FOR THIS OL' CAJUN.
I'M ON IT.
AND, JEAN?
"TELL STORM SHE WAS RIGHT TO SEND ME.

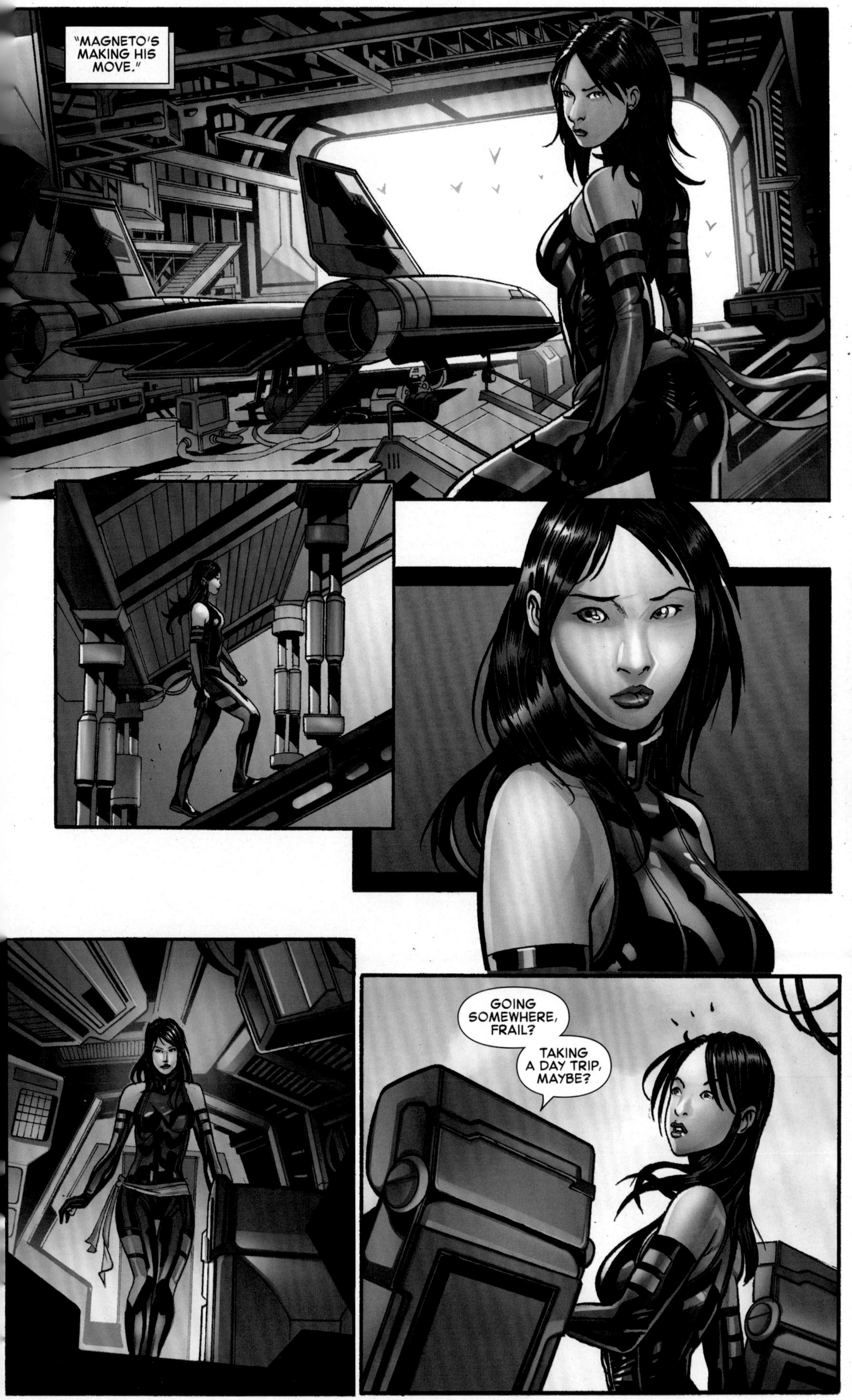
"MAGNETO'S MAKING HIS MOVE."
GOING SOMEWHERE, FRAIL?
TAKING A DAY TRIP, MAYBE?

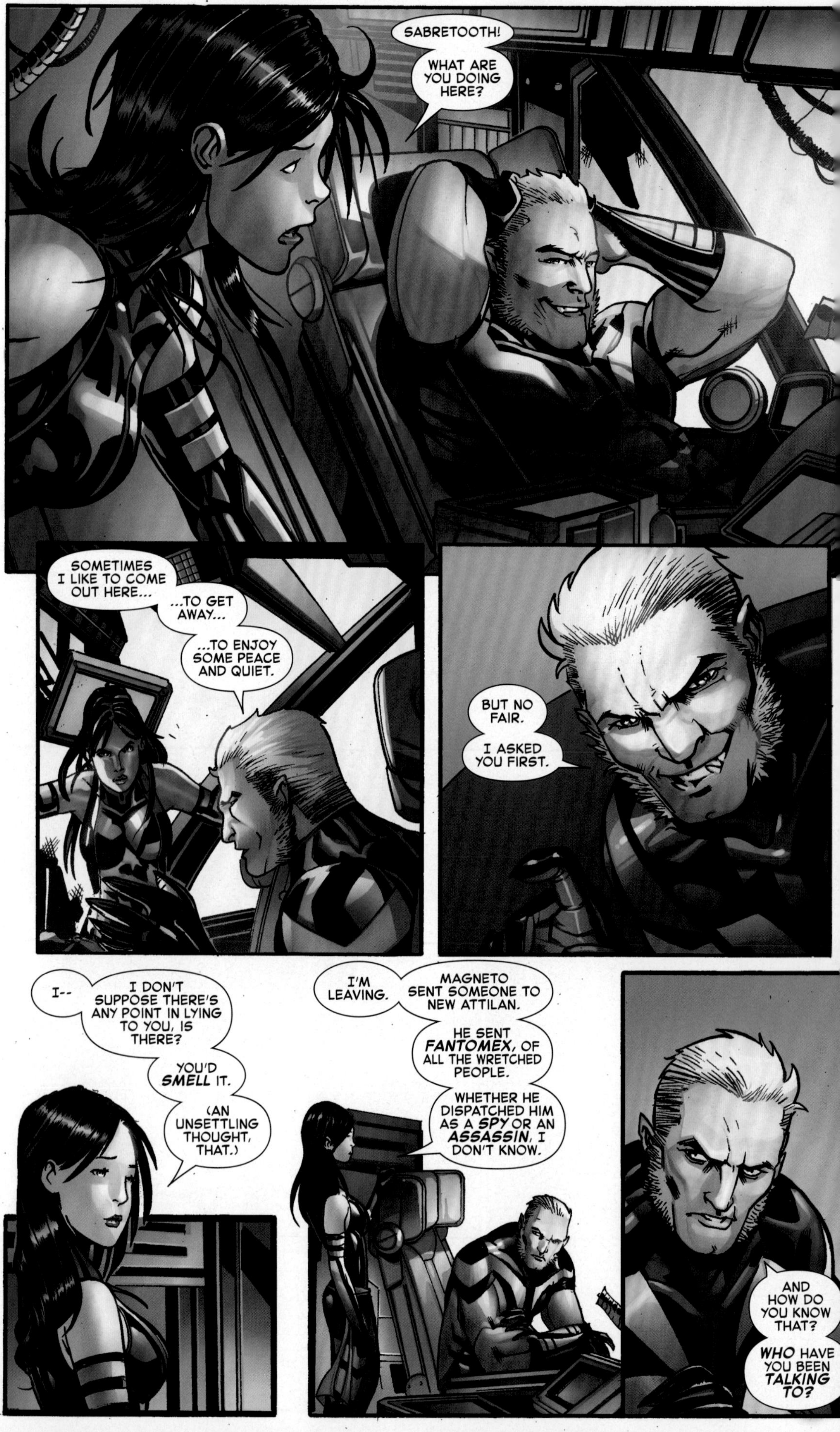
SABRETOOTH!
WHAT ARE YOU DOING HERE?
SOMETIMES I LIKE TO COME OUT HERE...
...TO GET AWAY...
...TO ENJOY SOME PEACE AND QUIET.
BUT NO FAIR.
I ASKED YOU FIRST.
I--
I DON'T SUPPOSE THERE'S ANY POINT IN LYING TO YOU, IS THERE?
YOU'D SMELL IT.
(AN UNSETTLING THOUGHT, THAT.)
I'M LEAVING.
MAGNETO SENT SOMEONE TO NEW ATTILAN.
HE SENT FANTOMEX, OF ALL THE WRETCHED PEOPLE.
WHETHER HE DISPATCHED HIM AS A SPY OR AN ASSASSIN, I DON'T KNOW.
AND HOW DO YOU KNOW THAT?
WHO HAVE YOU BEEN TALKING TO?

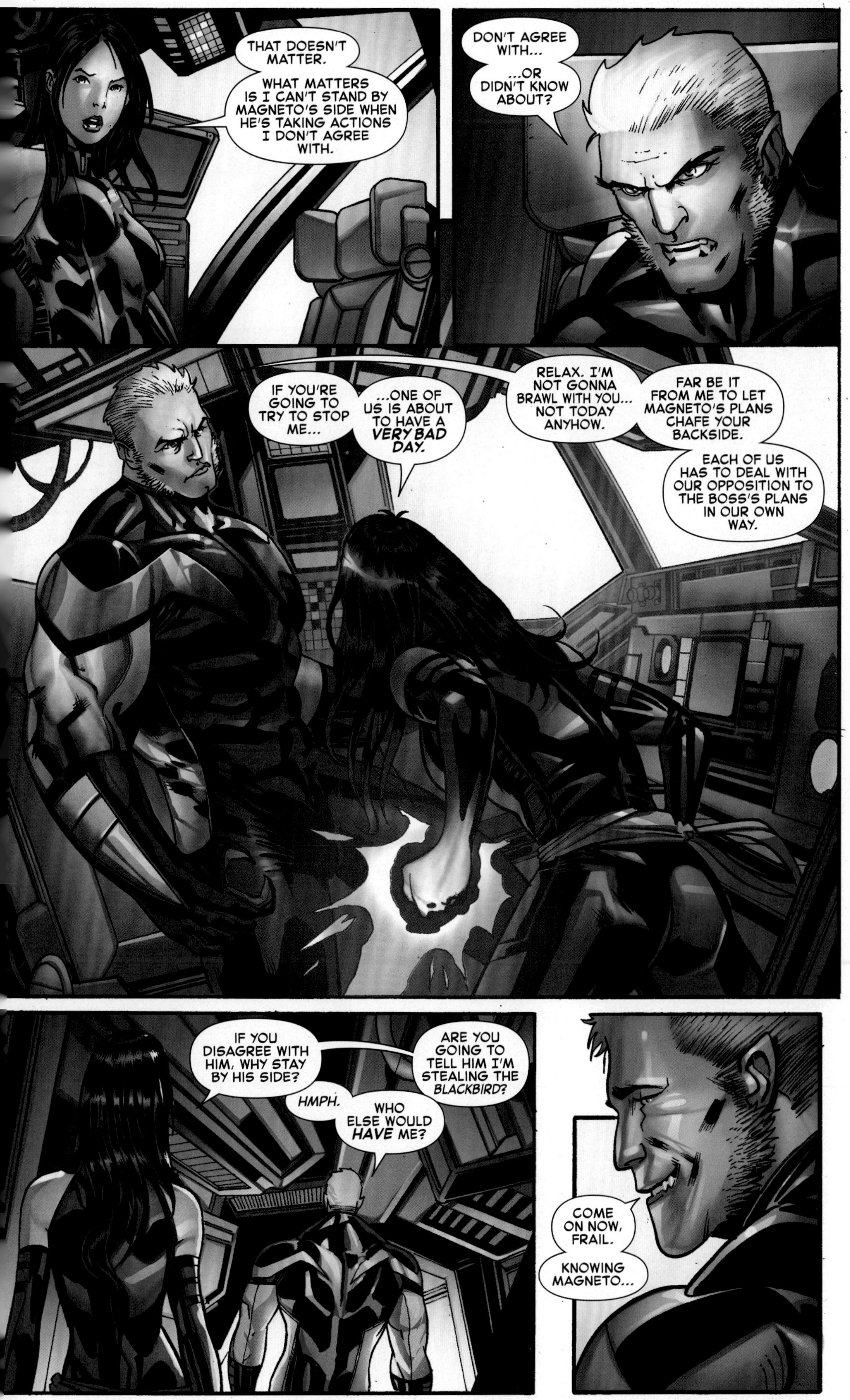
THAT DOESN'T MATTER.
WHAT MATTERS IS I CAN'T STAND BY MAGNETO'S SIDE WHEN HE'S TAKING ACTIONS I DON'T AGREE WITH.
DON'T AGREE WITH...
...OR DIDN'T KNOW ABOUT?
IF YOU'RE GOING TO TRY TO STOP ME...
...ONE OF US IS ABOUT TO HAVE A VERY BAD DAY.
RELAX. I'M NOT GONNA BRAWL WITH YOU... NOT TODAY ANYHOW.
FAR BE IT FROM ME TO LET MAGNETO'S PLANS CHAFE YOUR BACKSIDE.
EACH OF US HAS TO DEAL WITH OUR OPPOSITION TO THE BOSS'S PLANS IN OUR OWN WAY.
IF YOU DISAGREE WITH HIM, WHY STAY BY HIS SIDE?
ARE YOU GOING TO TELL HIM I'M STEALING THE BLACKBIRD?
HMPH.
WHO ELSE WOULD HAVE ME?
COME ON NOW, FRAIL.
KNOWING MAGNETO...

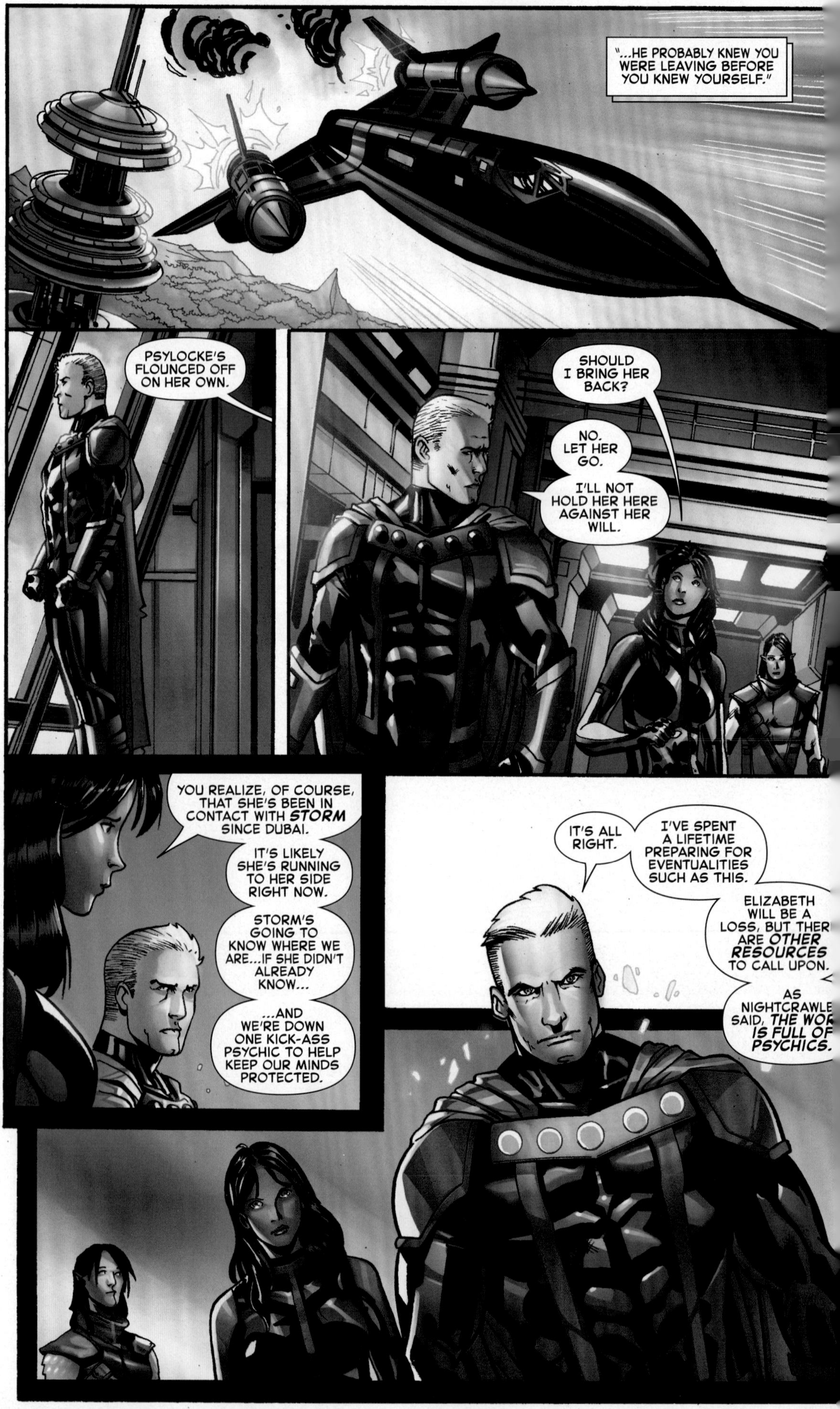
"...HE PROBABLY KNEW YOU WERE LEAVING BEFORE YOU KNEW YOURSELF."
PSYLOCKE'S FLOUNCED OFF ON HER OWN.
SHOULD I BRING HER BACK?
NO. LET HER GO.
I'LL NOT HOLD HER HERE AGAINST HER WILL.
YOU REALIZE, OF COURSE, THAT SHE'S BEEN IN CONTACT WITH STORM SINCE DUBAI.
IT'S LIKELY SHE'S RUNNING TO HER SIDE RIGHT NOW.
STORM'S GOING TO KNOW WHERE WE ARE...IF SHE DIDN'T ALREADY KNOW...
...AND WE'RE DOWN ONE KICK-ASS PSYCHIC TO HELP KEEP OUR MINDS PROTECTED.
IT'S ALL RIGHT.
I'VE SPENT A LIFETIME PREPARING FOR EVENTUALITIES SUCH AS THIS.
ELIZABETH WILL BE A LOSS, BUT THER ARE OTHER RESOURCES TO CALL UPON.
AS NIGHTCRAWLE SAID, THE WOR IS FULL OF PSYCHICS.

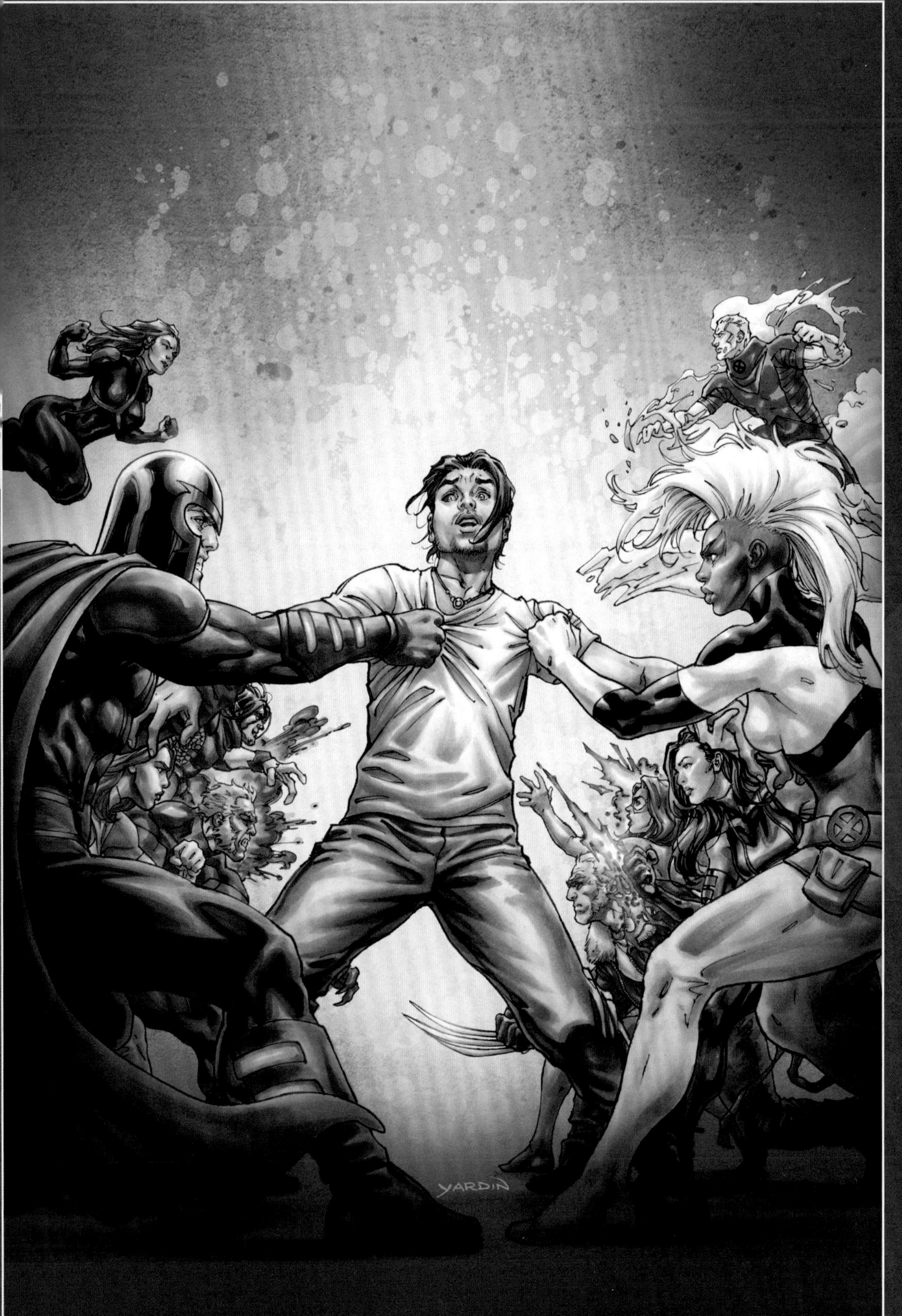
YARDIN

III

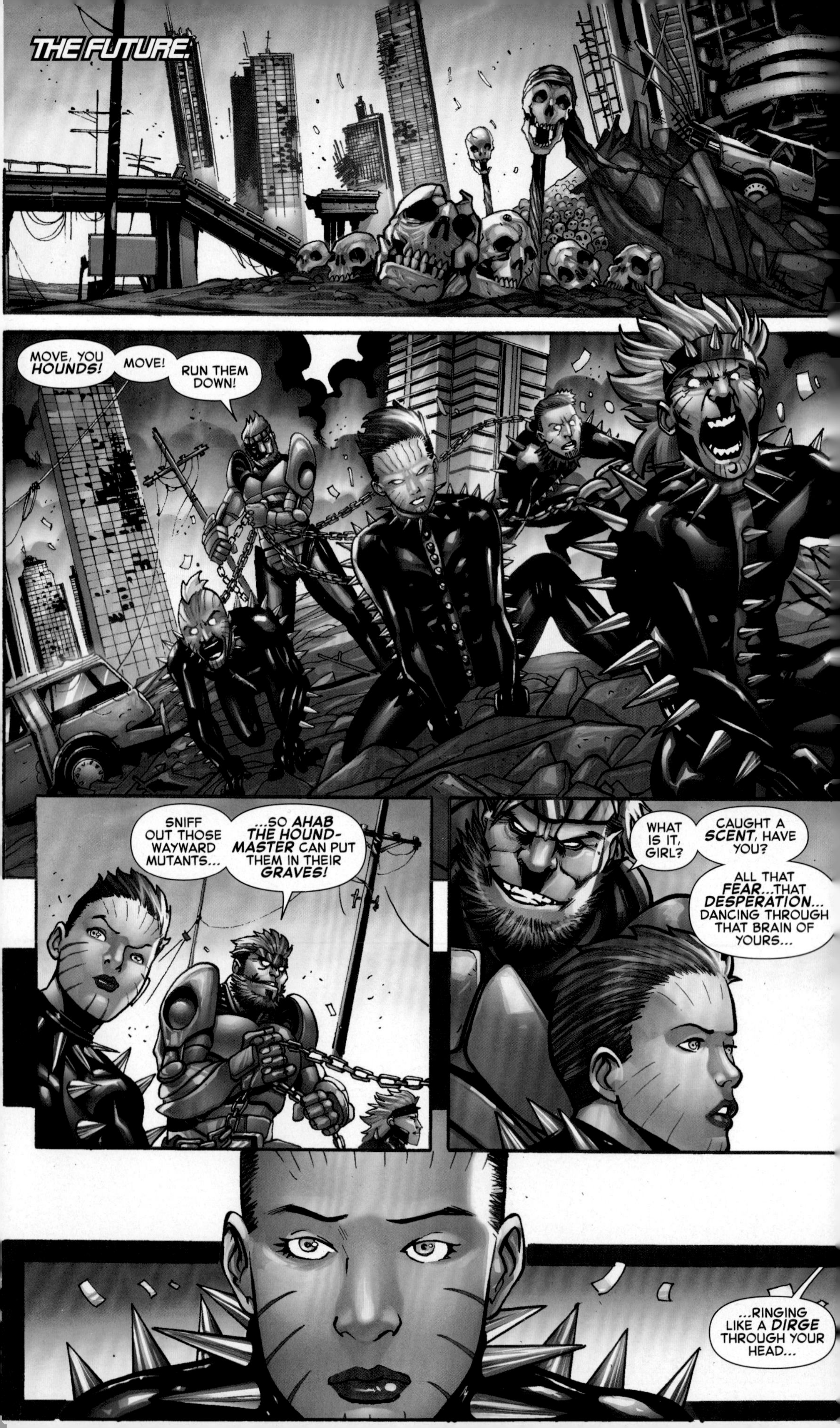

THE FUTURE.
MOVE, YOU HOUNDS!
MOVE!
RUN THEM DOWN!
SNIFF OUT THOSE WAYWARD MUTANTS...
...SO AHAB THE HOUND-MASTER CAN PUT THEM IN THEIR GRAVES!
WHAT IS IT, GIRL?
CAUGHT A SCENT, HAVE YOU?
ALL THAT FEAR...THAT DESPERATION... DANCING THROUGH THAT BRAIN OF YOURS...
...RINGING LIKE A DIRGE THROUGH YOUR HEAD...

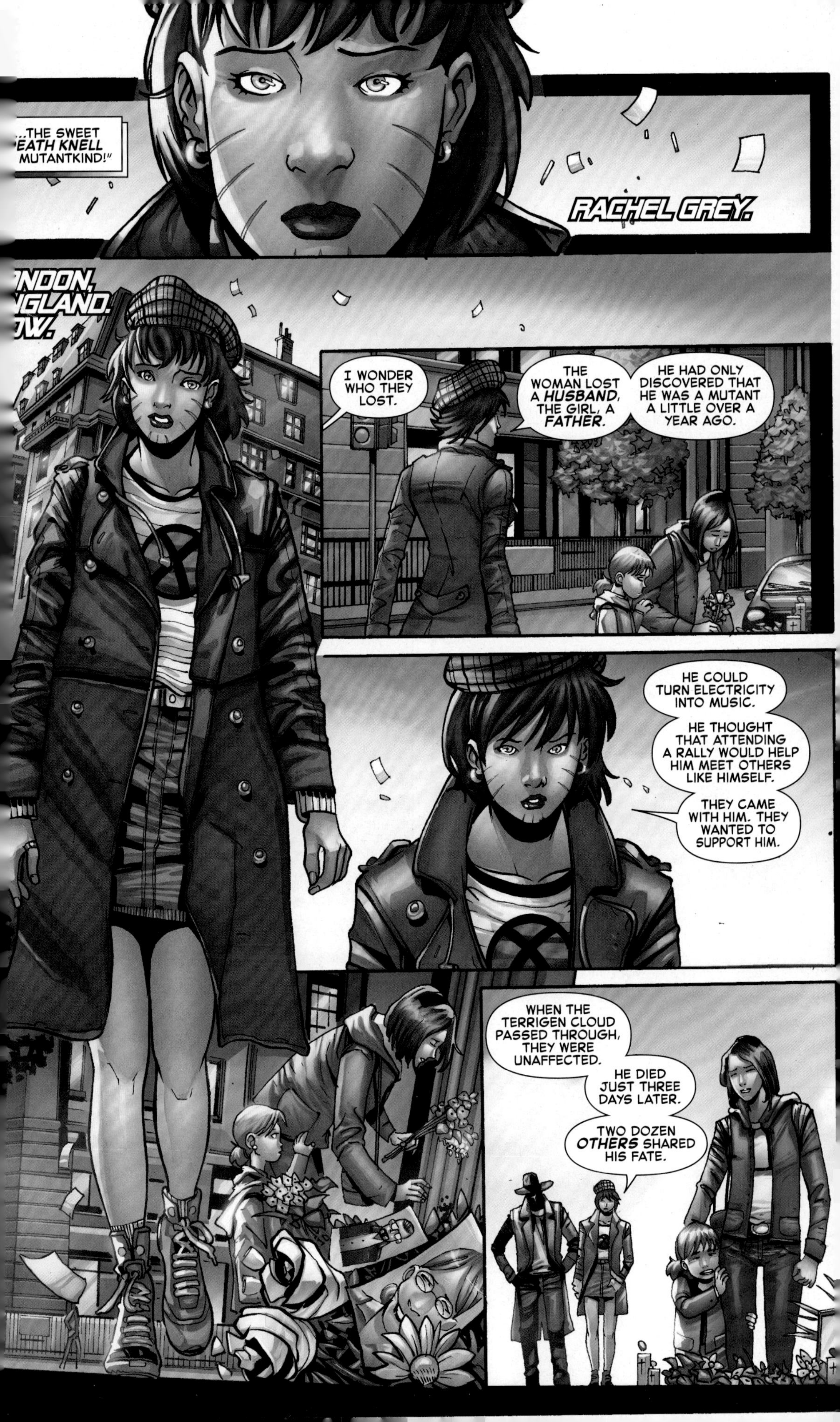
...THE SWEET
EATH KNELL
MUTANTKIND!"
RACHEL GREY.
NDON,
NGLAND.
OW.
I WONDER WHO THEY LOST.
THE WOMAN LOST A HUSBAND, THE GIRL, A FATHER.
HE HAD ONLY DISCOVERED THAT HE WAS A MUTANT A LITTLE OVER A YEAR AGO.
HE COULD TURN ELECTRICITY INTO MUSIC.
HE THOUGHT THAT ATTENDING A RALLY WOULD HELP HIM MEET OTHERS LIKE HIMSELF.
THEY CAME WITH HIM. THEY WANTED TO SUPPORT HIM.
WHEN THE TERRIGEN CLOUD PASSED THROUGH, THEY WERE UNAFFECTED.
HE DIED JUST THREE DAYS LATER.
TWO DOZEN OTHERS SHARED HIS FATE.

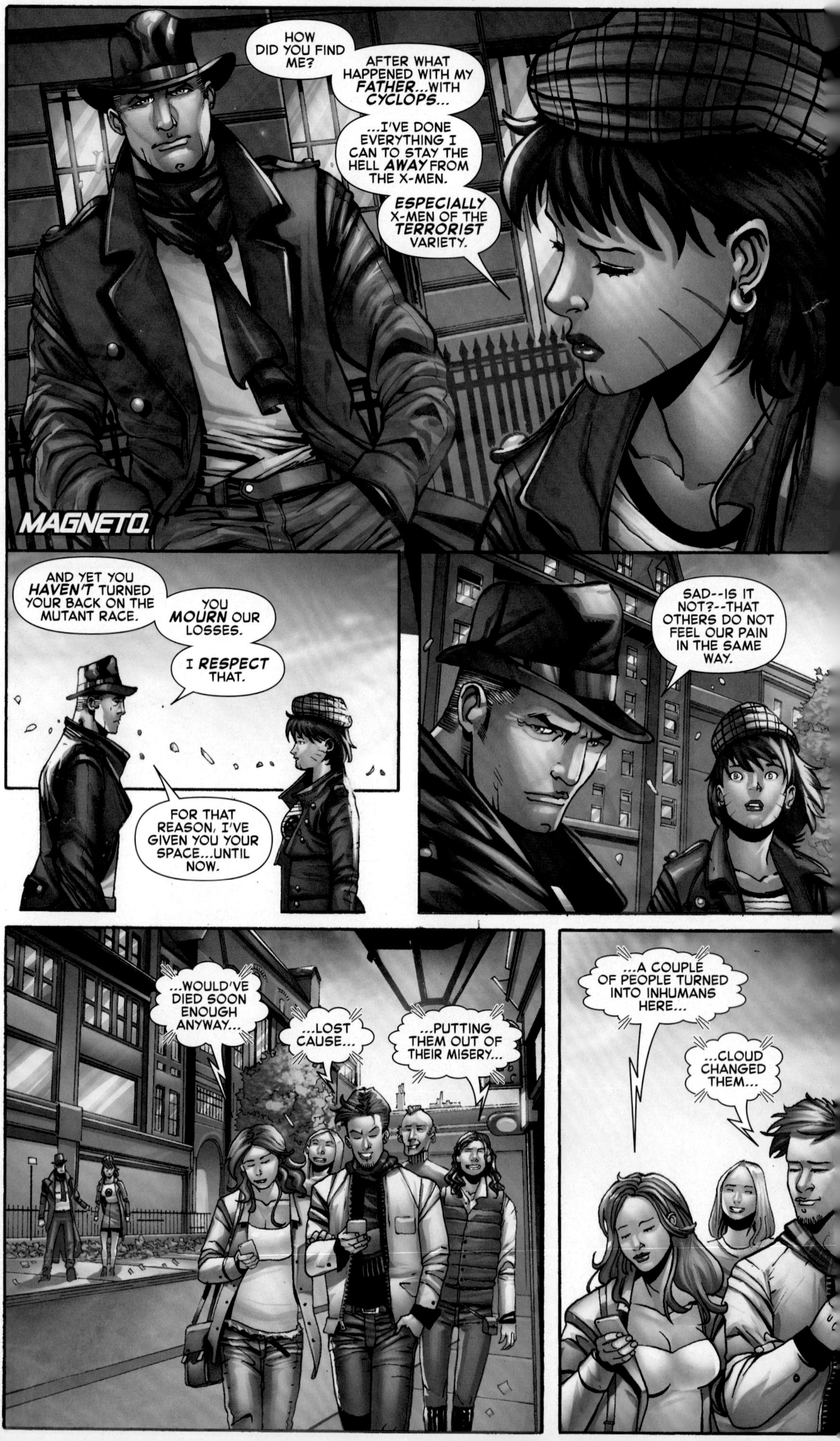
HOW DID YOU FIND ME?
AFTER WHAT HAPPENED WITH MY FATHER...WITH CYCLOPS...
...I'VE DONE EVERYTHING I CAN TO STAY THE HELL AWAY FROM THE X-MEN.
ESPECIALLY X-MEN OF THE TERRORIST VARIETY.
MAGNETO.
AND YET YOU HAVEN'T TURNED YOUR BACK ON THE MUTANT RACE.
YOU MOURN OUR LOSSES.
I RESPECT THAT.
FOR THAT REASON, I'VE GIVEN YOU YOUR SPACE...UNTIL NOW.
SAD--IS IT NOT?--THAT OTHERS DO NOT FEEL OUR PAIN IN THE SAME WAY.
...WOULD'VE DIED SOON ENOUGH ANYWAY...
...LOST CAUSE...
...PUTTING THEM OUT OF THEIR MISERY...
...A COUPLE OF PEOPLE TURNED INTO INHUMANS HERE...
...CLOUD CHANGED THEM...

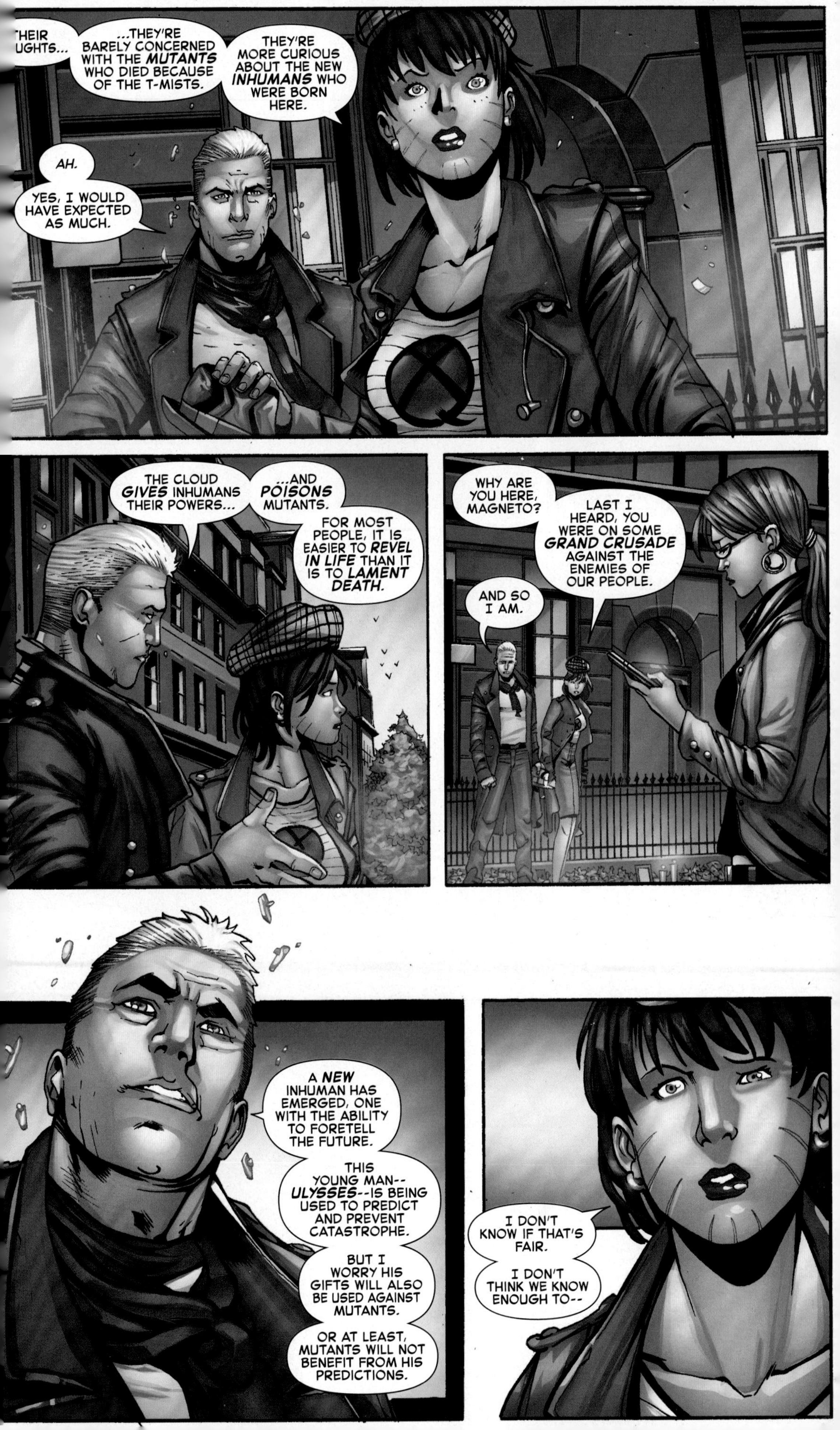
THEIR
...UGHTS...
...THEY'RE BARELY CONCERNED WITH THE MUTANTS WHO DIED BECAUSE OF THE T-MISTS.
THEY'RE MORE CURIOUS ABOUT THE NEW INHUMANS WHO WERE BORN HERE.
AH.
YES, I WOULD HAVE EXPECTED AS MUCH.
THE CLOUD GIVES INHUMANS THEIR POWERS...
...AND POISONS MUTANTS.
FOR MOST PEOPLE, IT IS EASIER TO REVEL IN LIFE THAN IT IS TO LAMENT DEATH.
WHY ARE YOU HERE, MAGNETO?
LAST I HEARD, YOU WERE ON SOME GRAND CRUSADE AGAINST THE ENEMIES OF OUR PEOPLE.
AND SO I AM.
A NEW INHUMAN HAS EMERGED, ONE WITH THE ABILITY TO FORETELL THE FUTURE.
THIS YOUNG MAN--ULYSSES--IS BEING USED TO PREDICT AND PREVENT CATASTROPHE.
BUT I WORRY HIS GIFTS WILL ALSO BE USED AGAINST MUTANTS.
OR AT LEAST, MUTANTS WILL NOT BENEFIT FROM HIS PREDICTIONS.
I DON'T KNOW IF THAT'S FAIR.
I DON'T THINK WE KNOW ENOUGH TO--

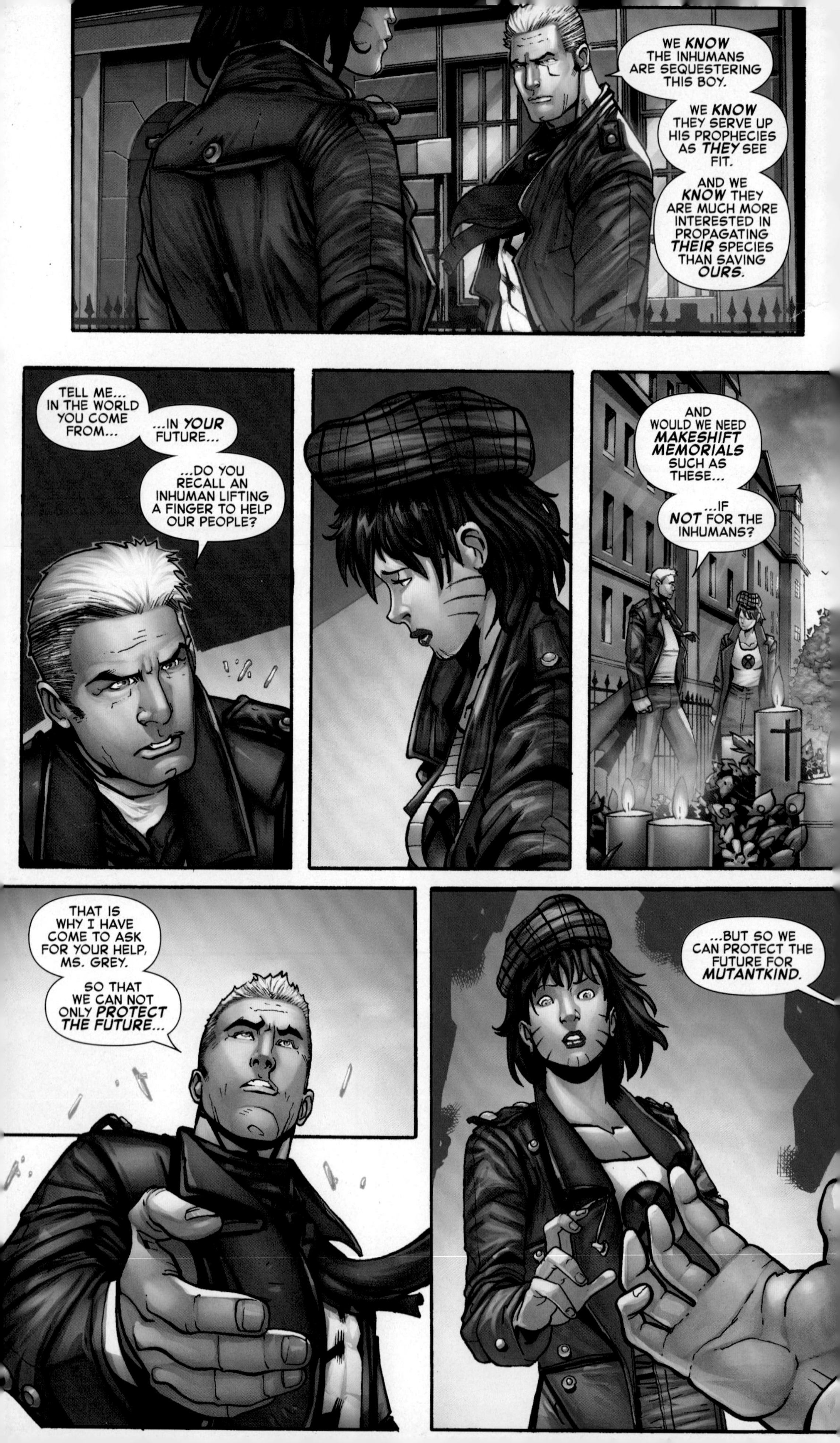
WE KNOW THE INHUMANS ARE SEQUESTERING THIS BOY.
WE KNOW THEY SERVE UP HIS PROPHECIES AS THEY SEE FIT.
AND WE KNOW THEY ARE MUCH MORE INTERESTED IN PROPAGATING THEIR SPECIES THAN SAVING OURS.
TELL ME... IN THE WORLD YOU COME FROM...
...IN YOUR FUTURE...
...DO YOU RECALL AN INHUMAN LIFTING A FINGER TO HELP OUR PEOPLE?
AND WOULD WE NEED MAKESHIFT MEMORIALS SUCH AS THESE...
...IF NOT FOR THE INHUMANS?
THAT IS WHY I HAVE COME TO ASK FOR YOUR HELP, MS. GREY.
SO THAT WE CAN NOT ONLY PROTECT THE FUTURE...
...BUT SO WE CAN PROTECT THE FUTURE FOR MUTANTKIND.

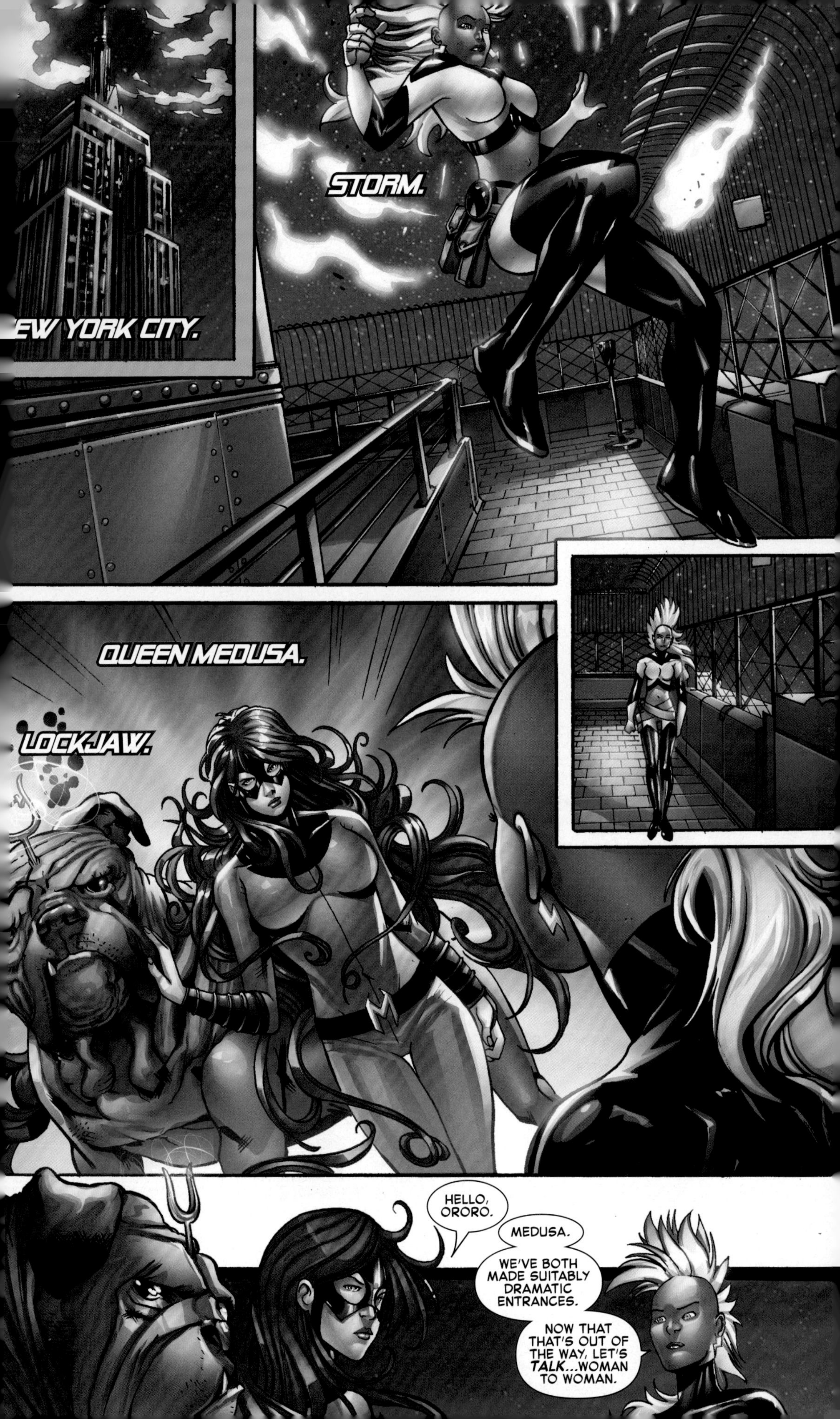

EW YORK CITY.
STORM.
QUEEN MEDUSA.
LOCKJAW.
HELLO, ORORO.
MEDUSA.
WE'VE BOTH MADE SUITABLY DRAMATIC ENTRANCES.
NOW THAT THAT'S OUT OF THE WAY, LET'S TALK...WOMAN TO WOMAN.

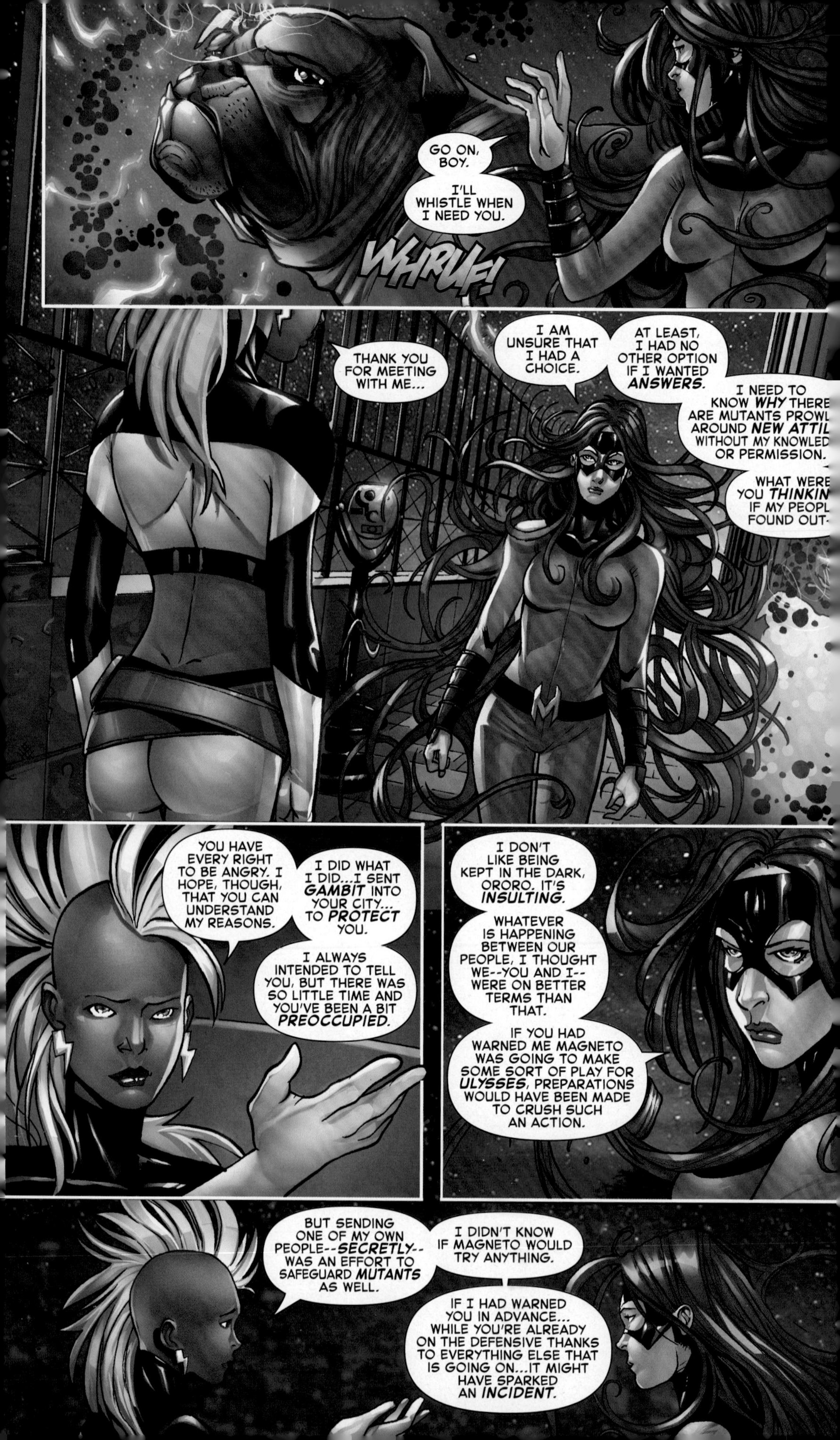
GO ON, BOY.
I'LL WHISTLE WHEN I NEED YOU.
WHRUF!
THANK YOU FOR MEETING WITH ME...
I AM UNSURE THAT I HAD A CHOICE.
AT LEAST, I HAD NO OTHER OPTION IF I WANTED ANSWERS.
I NEED TO KNOW WHY THERE ARE MUTANTS PROWL AROUND NEW ATTIL WITHOUT MY KNOWLED OR PERMISSION.
WHAT WERE YOU THINKIN IF MY PEOPL FOUND OUT-
YOU HAVE EVERY RIGHT TO BE ANGRY. I HOPE, THOUGH, THAT YOU CAN UNDERSTAND MY REASONS.
I DID WHAT I DID...I SENT GAMBIT INTO YOUR CITY... TO PROTECT YOU.
I ALWAYS INTENDED TO TELL YOU, BUT THERE WAS SO LITTLE TIME AND YOU'VE BEEN A BIT PREOCCUPIED.
I DON'T LIKE BEING KEPT IN THE DARK, ORORO. IT'S INSULTING.
WHATEVER IS HAPPENING BETWEEN OUR PEOPLE, I THOUGHT WE--YOU AND I--WERE ON BETTER TERMS THAN THAT.
IF YOU HAD WARNED ME MAGNETO WAS GOING TO MAKE SOME SORT OF PLAY FOR ULYSSES, PREPARATIONS WOULD HAVE BEEN MADE TO CRUSH SUCH AN ACTION.
BUT SENDING ONE OF MY OWN PEOPLE--SECRETLY--WAS AN EFFORT TO SAFEGUARD MUTANTS AS WELL.
I DIDN'T KNOW IF MAGNETO WOULD TRY ANYTHING.
IF I HAD WARNED YOU IN ADVANCE... WHILE YOU'RE ALREADY ON THE DEFENSIVE THANKS TO EVERYTHING ELSE THAT IS GOING ON...IT MIGHT HAVE SPARKED AN INCIDENT.

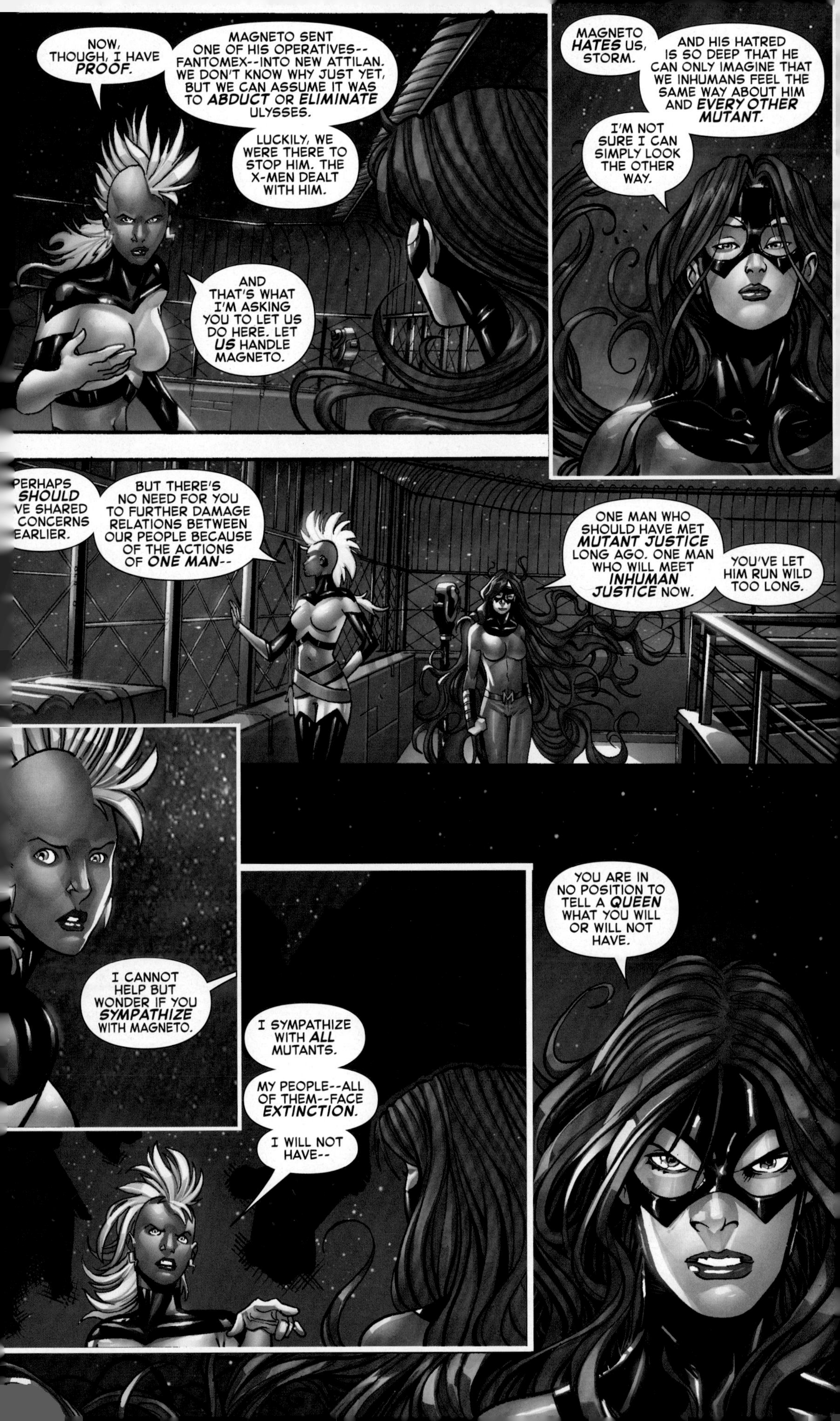
NOW, THOUGH, I HAVE PROOF.
MAGNETO SENT ONE OF HIS OPERATIVES--FANTOMEX--INTO NEW ATTILAN. WE DON'T KNOW WHY JUST YET, BUT WE CAN ASSUME IT WAS TO ABDUCT OR ELIMINATE ULYSSES.
LUCKILY, WE WERE THERE TO STOP HIM. THE X-MEN DEALT WITH HIM.
AND THAT'S WHAT I'M ASKING YOU TO LET US DO HERE. LET US HANDLE MAGNETO.
MAGNETO HATES US, STORM.
AND HIS HATRED IS SO DEEP THAT HE CAN ONLY IMAGINE THAT WE INHUMANS FEEL THE SAME WAY ABOUT HIM AND EVERY OTHER MUTANT.
I'M NOT SURE I CAN SIMPLY LOOK THE OTHER WAY.
PERHAPS SHOULD VE SHARED CONCERNS EARLIER.
BUT THERE'S NO NEED FOR YOU TO FURTHER DAMAGE RELATIONS BETWEEN OUR PEOPLE BECAUSE OF THE ACTIONS OF ONE MAN--
ONE MAN WHO SHOULD HAVE MET MUTANT JUSTICE LONG AGO. ONE MAN WHO WILL MEET INHUMAN JUSTICE NOW.
YOU'VE LET HIM RUN WILD TOO LONG.
I CANNOT HELP BUT WONDER IF YOU SYMPATHIZE WITH MAGNETO.
I SYMPATHIZE WITH ALL MUTANTS.
MY PEOPLE--ALL OF THEM--FACE EXTINCTION.
I WILL NOT HAVE--
YOU ARE IN NO POSITION TO TELL A QUEEN WHAT YOU WILL OR WILL NOT HAVE.

I *RESPECT* YOU, MEDUSA, AND YOUR POSITION, BUT DO NOT FORGET THAT I, TOO, HAVE BEEN A QUEEN.

WE *BOTH* KNOW THE BURDEN OF RULE.

KRA-KOW

SURELY THAT WAS NOT A *WARNING* OF SOME KIND.

IT WAS JUST...

...THE *WEATHER*.

WE'RE NOT HANDLING THIS VERY WELL, ARE WE?

WE'RE BOTH COMING IN A LITTLE HOT.

PLEASE, MEDUSA. WE ARE *NOT* ENEMIES.

LET ME HELP YOU.

LET ME FIND OUT WHAT IT IS MAGNETO WANTS.

AT THIS POINT, ALL HE'S DONE IS SEND A *SPY*.

OF COURSE, I MUST TAKE *SOME* ACTION, IF ONLY TO PROTECT THE INTERESTS OF NEW ATTILAN.

AS YOU SAID, MAGNE[TO] SENT A *SPY* ATTILAN.

THE LEAST I CAN DO...

VERY WELL, STORM.

I'LL WAIT TO HEAR FROM YOU BEFORE MAKING ANY *DRASTIC* RESPONSE.

IF, HOWEVER, MAGNETO DOES ANYTHING ELSE, I'LL HAVE NO CHOICE BUT TO RESPOND IN KIND.

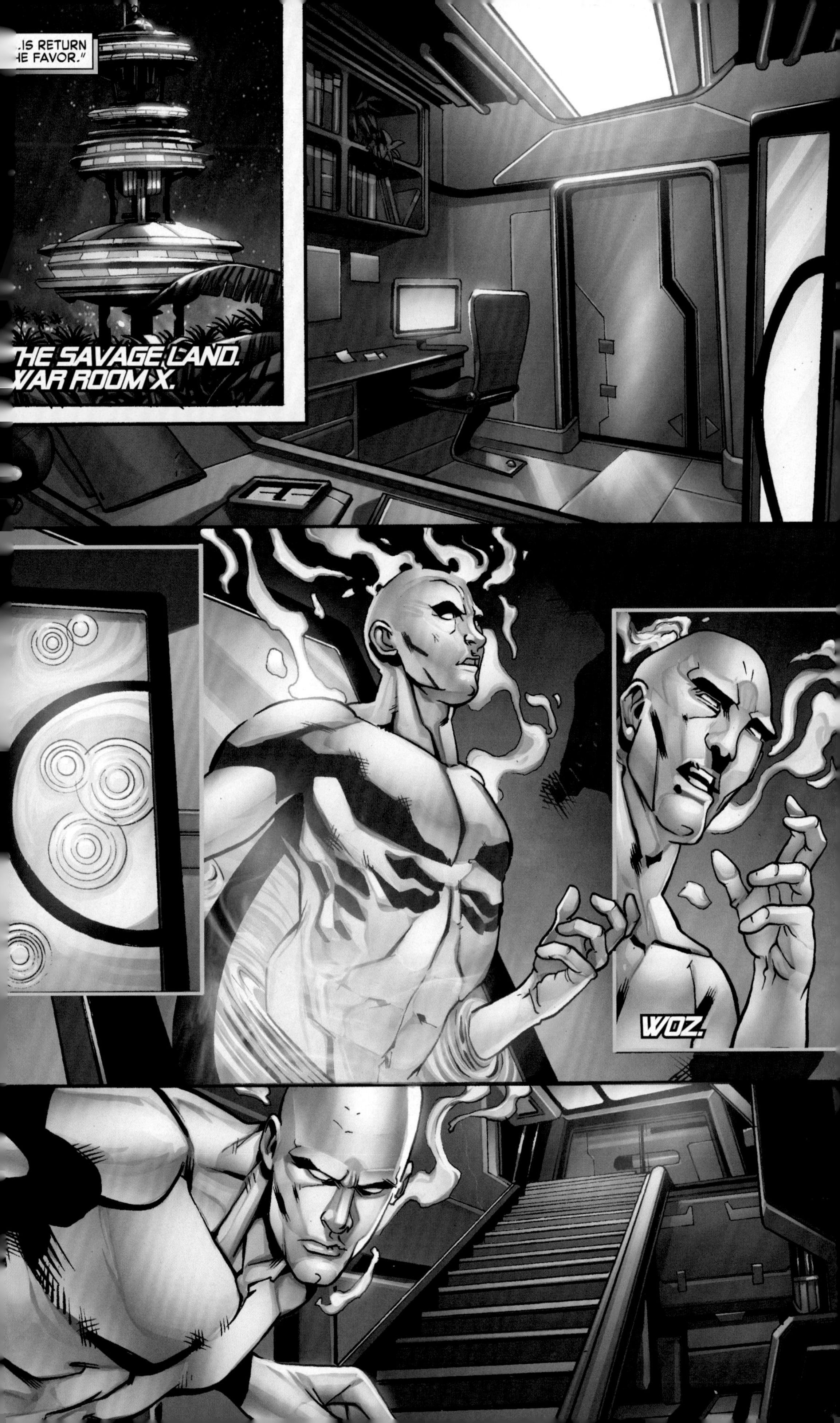
...IS RETURN
...HE FAVOR."
THE SAVAGE LAND.
WAR ROOM X.
WOZ.

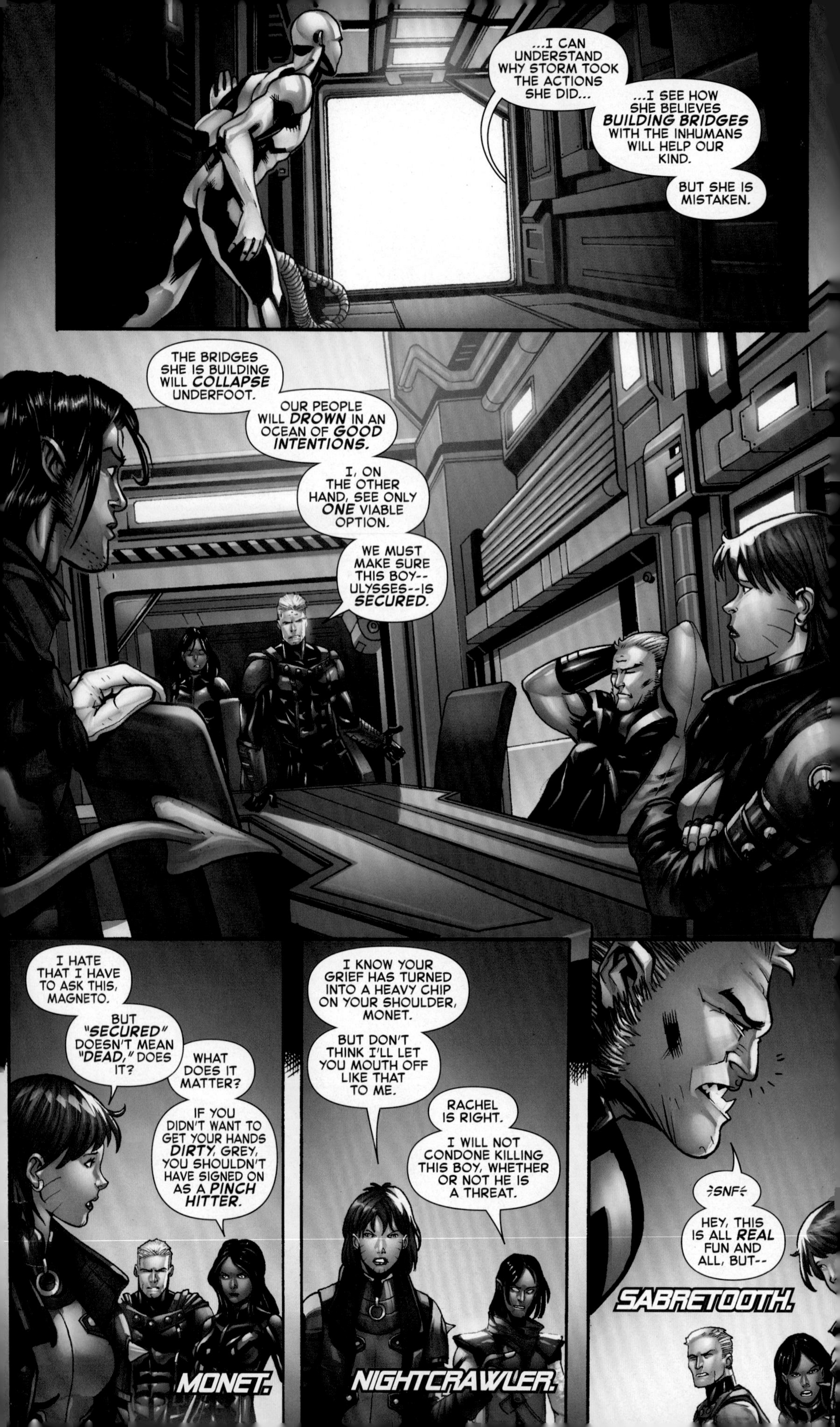
...I CAN UNDERSTAND WHY STORM TOOK THE ACTIONS SHE DID...
...I SEE HOW SHE BELIEVES BUILDING BRIDGES WITH THE INHUMANS WILL HELP OUR KIND.
BUT SHE IS MISTAKEN.
THE BRIDGES SHE IS BUILDING WILL COLLAPSE UNDERFOOT.
OUR PEOPLE WILL DROWN IN AN OCEAN OF GOOD INTENTIONS.
I, ON THE OTHER HAND, SEE ONLY ONE VIABLE OPTION.
WE MUST MAKE SURE THIS BOY--ULYSSES--IS SECURED.
I HATE THAT I HAVE TO ASK THIS, MAGNETO.
BUT "SECURED" DOESN'T MEAN "DEAD," DOES IT?
WHAT DOES IT MATTER?
IF YOU DIDN'T WANT TO GET YOUR HANDS DIRTY, GREY, YOU SHOULDN'T HAVE SIGNED ON AS A PINCH HITTER.
MONET.
I KNOW YOUR GRIEF HAS TURNED INTO A HEAVY CHIP ON YOUR SHOULDER, MONET.
BUT DON'T THINK I'LL LET YOU MOUTH OFF LIKE THAT TO ME.
RACHEL IS RIGHT.
I WILL NOT CONDONE KILLING THIS BOY, WHETHER OR NOT HE IS A THREAT.
NIGHTCRAWLER.
SNF
HEY, THIS IS ALL REAL FUN AND ALL, BUT--
SABRETOOTH.

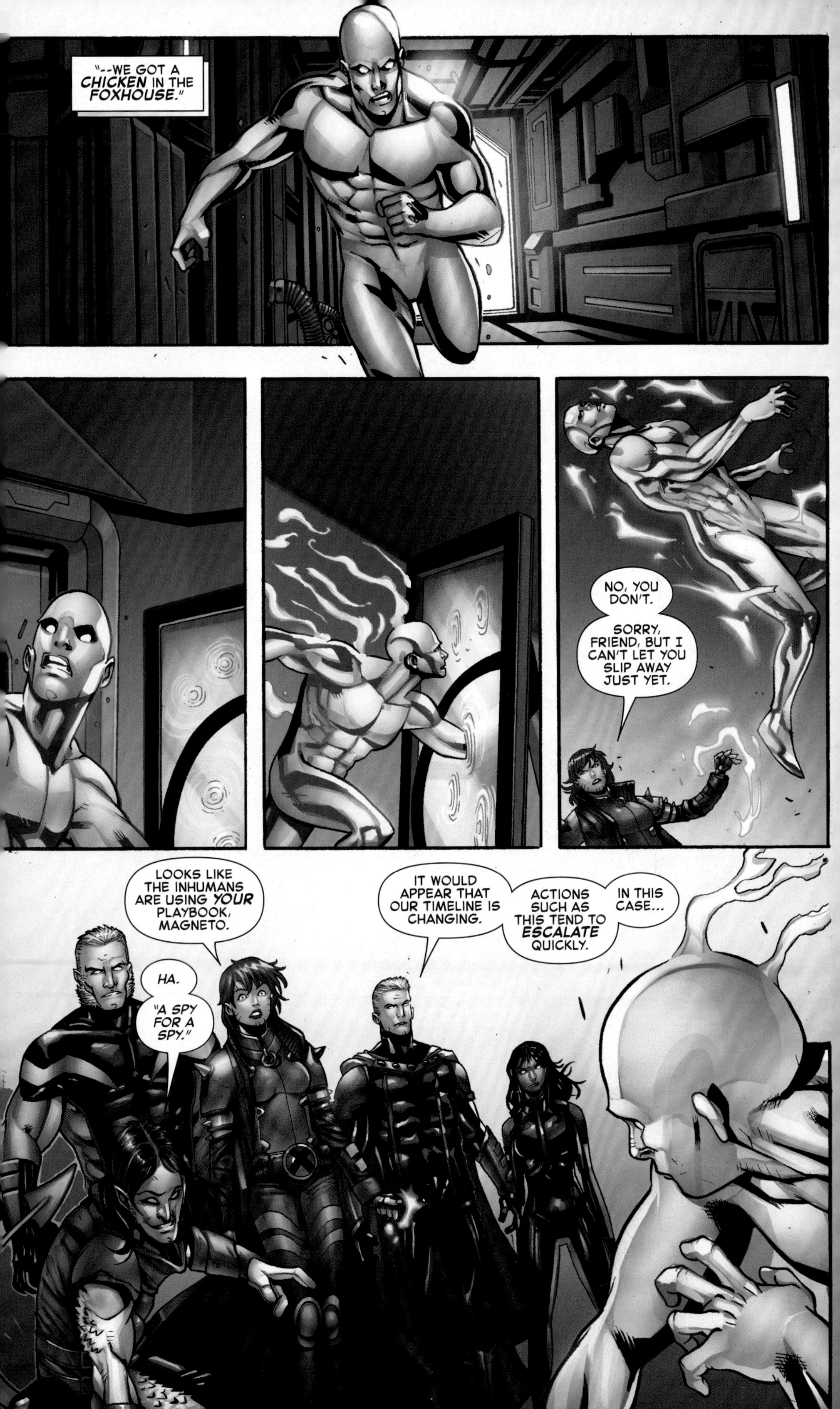
"--WE GOT A CHICKEN IN THE FOXHOUSE."
NO, YOU DON'T.
SORRY, FRIEND, BUT I CAN'T LET YOU SLIP AWAY JUST YET.
LOOKS LIKE THE INHUMANS ARE USING YOUR PLAYBOOK, MAGNETO.
HA.
"A SPY FOR A SPY."
IT WOULD APPEAR THAT OUR TIMELINE IS CHANGING.
ACTIONS SUCH AS THIS TEND TO ESCALATE QUICKLY.
IN THIS CASE...

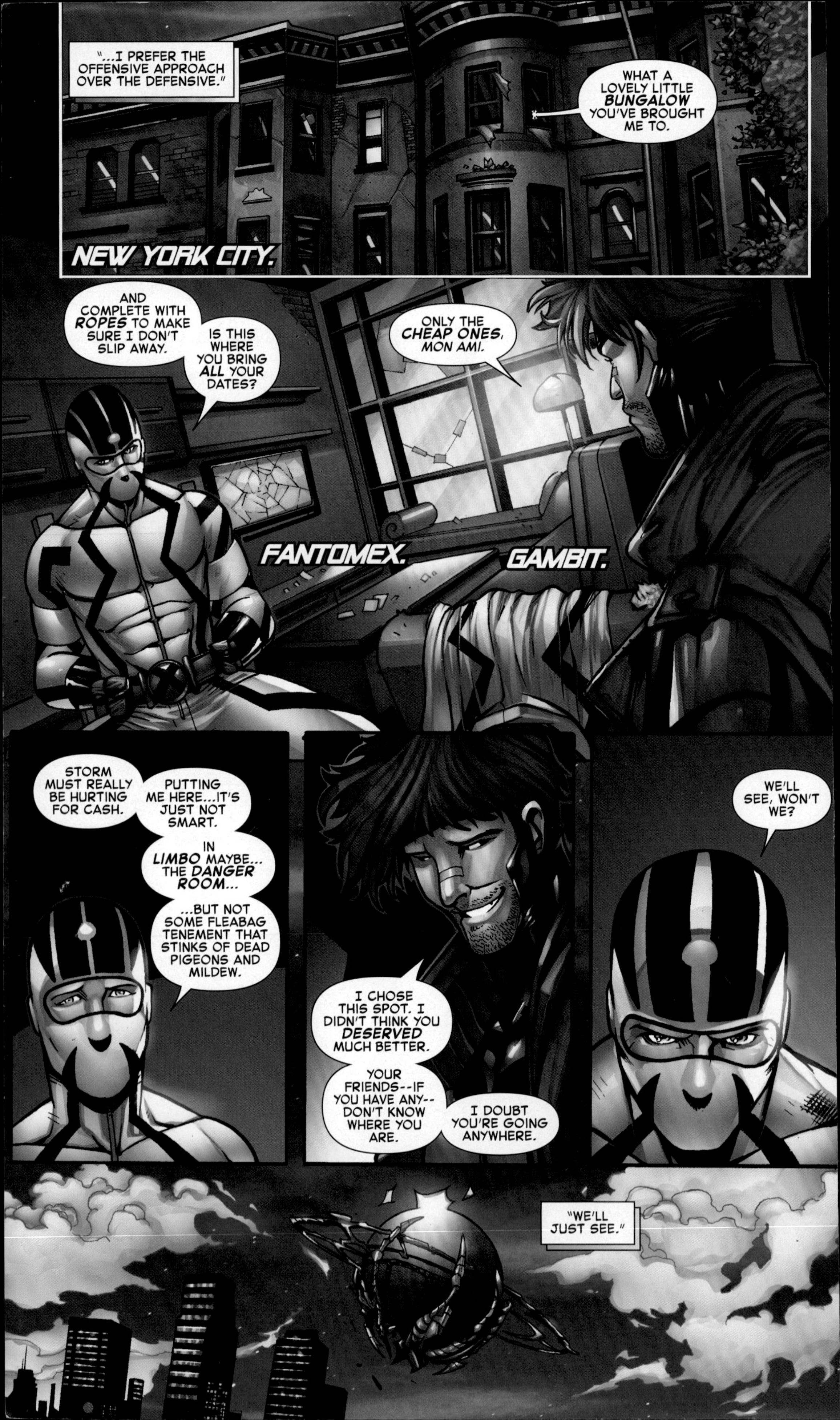
"...I PREFER THE OFFENSIVE APPROACH OVER THE DEFENSIVE."
WHAT A LOVELY LITTLE BUNGALOW YOU'VE BROUGHT ME TO.
NEW YORK CITY.
AND COMPLETE WITH ROPES TO MAKE SURE I DON'T SLIP AWAY.
IS THIS WHERE YOU BRING ALL YOUR DATES?
ONLY THE CHEAP ONES, MON AMI.
FANTOMEX.
GAMBIT.
STORM MUST REALLY BE HURTING FOR CASH.
PUTTING ME HERE...IT'S JUST NOT SMART.
IN LIMBO MAYBE... THE DANGER ROOM...
...BUT NOT SOME FLEABAG TENEMENT THAT STINKS OF DEAD PIGEONS AND MILDEW.
I CHOSE THIS SPOT. I DIDN'T THINK YOU DESERVED MUCH BETTER.
YOUR FRIENDS--IF YOU HAVE ANY--DON'T KNOW WHERE YOU ARE.
I DOUBT YOU'RE GOING ANYWHERE.
WE'LL SEE, WON'T WE?
"WE'LL JUST SEE."

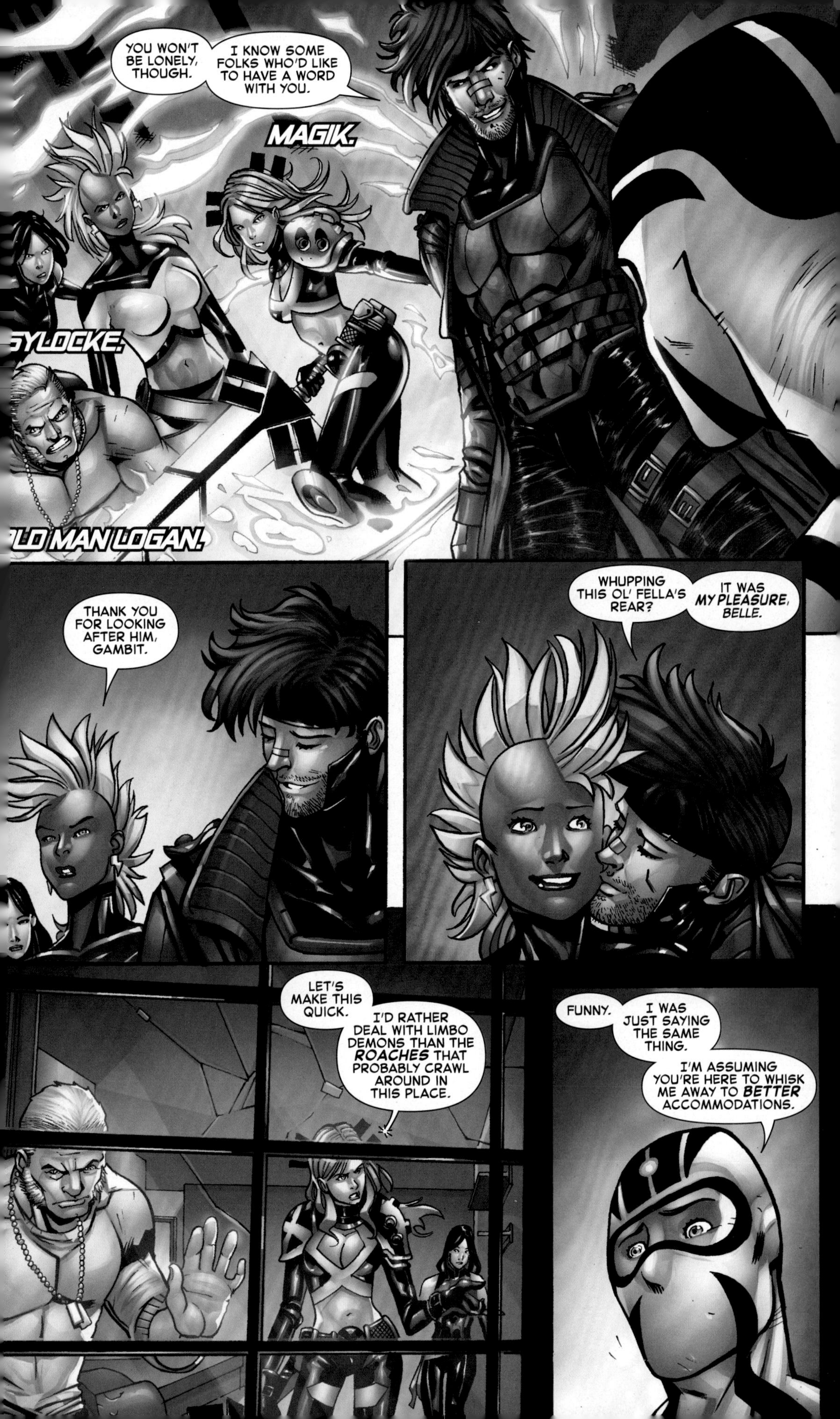
YOU WON'T BE LONELY, THOUGH.
I KNOW SOME FOLKS WHO'D LIKE TO HAVE A WORD WITH YOU.
MAGIK.
PSYLOCKE.
OLD MAN LOGAN.
THANK YOU FOR LOOKING AFTER HIM, GAMBIT.
WHUPPING THIS OL' FELLA'S REAR?
IT WAS MY PLEASURE, BELLE.
LET'S MAKE THIS QUICK.
I'D RATHER DEAL WITH LIMBO DEMONS THAN THE ROACHES THAT PROBABLY CRAWL AROUND IN THIS PLACE.
FUNNY.
I WAS JUST SAYING THE SAME THING.
I'M ASSUMING YOU'RE HERE TO WHISK ME AWAY TO BETTER ACCOMMODATIONS.

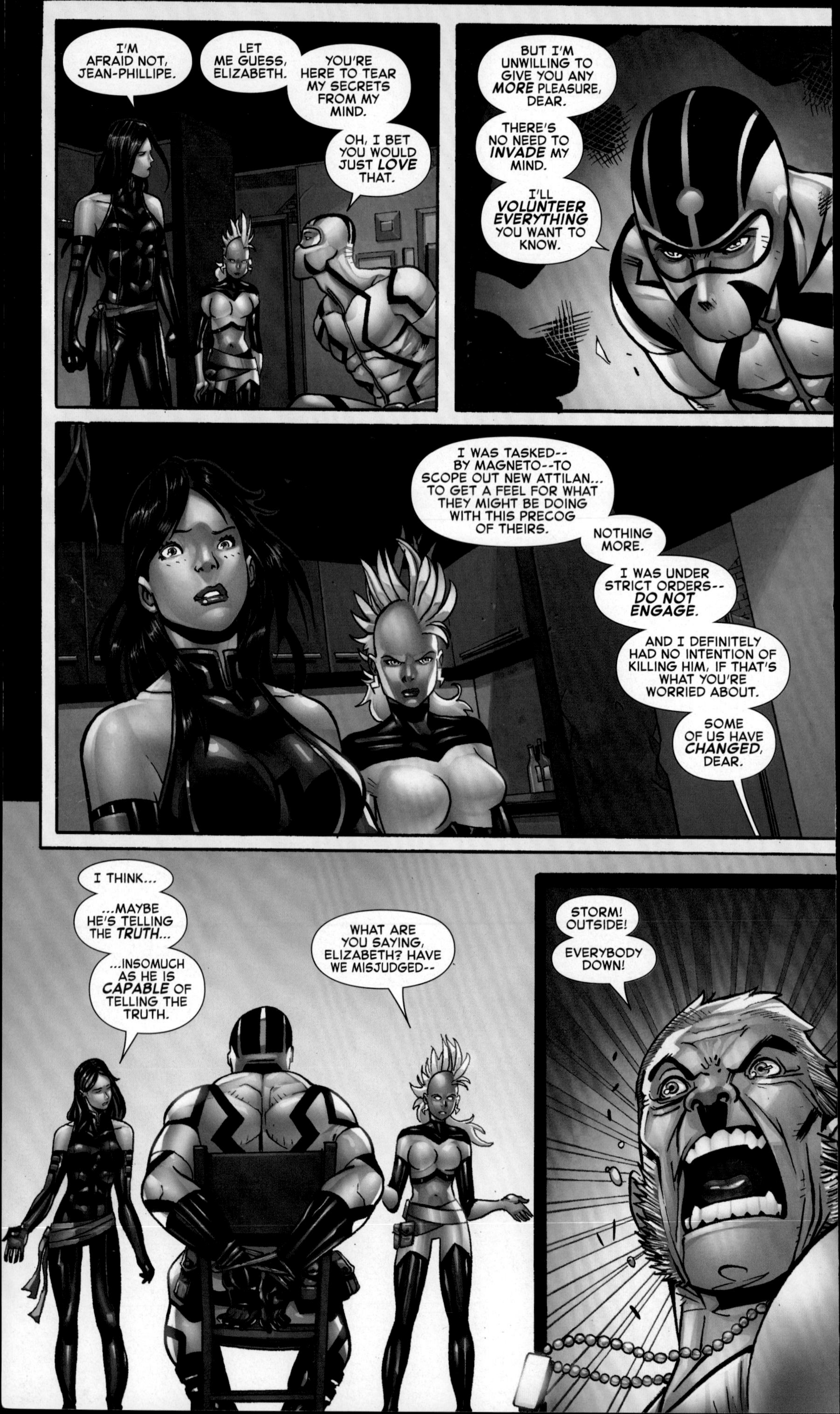
I'M AFRAID NOT, JEAN-PHILLIPE.
LET ME GUESS, ELIZABETH.
YOU'RE HERE TO TEAR MY SECRETS FROM MY MIND.
OH, I BET YOU WOULD JUST *LOVE* THAT.
BUT I'M UNWILLING TO GIVE YOU ANY *MORE* PLEASURE, DEAR.
THERE'S NO NEED TO *INVADE* MY MIND.
I'LL *VOLUNTEER EVERYTHING* YOU WANT TO KNOW.
I WAS TASKED-- BY MAGNETO--TO SCOPE OUT NEW ATTILAN... TO GET A FEEL FOR WHAT THEY MIGHT BE DOING WITH THIS PRECOG OF THEIRS.
NOTHING MORE.
I WAS UNDER STRICT ORDERS-- *DO NOT ENGAGE*.
AND I DEFINITELY HAD NO INTENTION OF KILLING HIM, IF THAT'S WHAT YOU'RE WORRIED ABOUT.
SOME OF US HAVE *CHANGED*, DEAR.
I THINK...
...MAYBE HE'S TELLING THE *TRUTH*...
...INSOMUCH AS HE IS *CAPABLE* OF TELLING THE TRUTH.
WHAT ARE YOU SAYING, ELIZABETH? HAVE WE MISJUDGED--
STORM! OUTSIDE!
EVERYBODY DOWN!

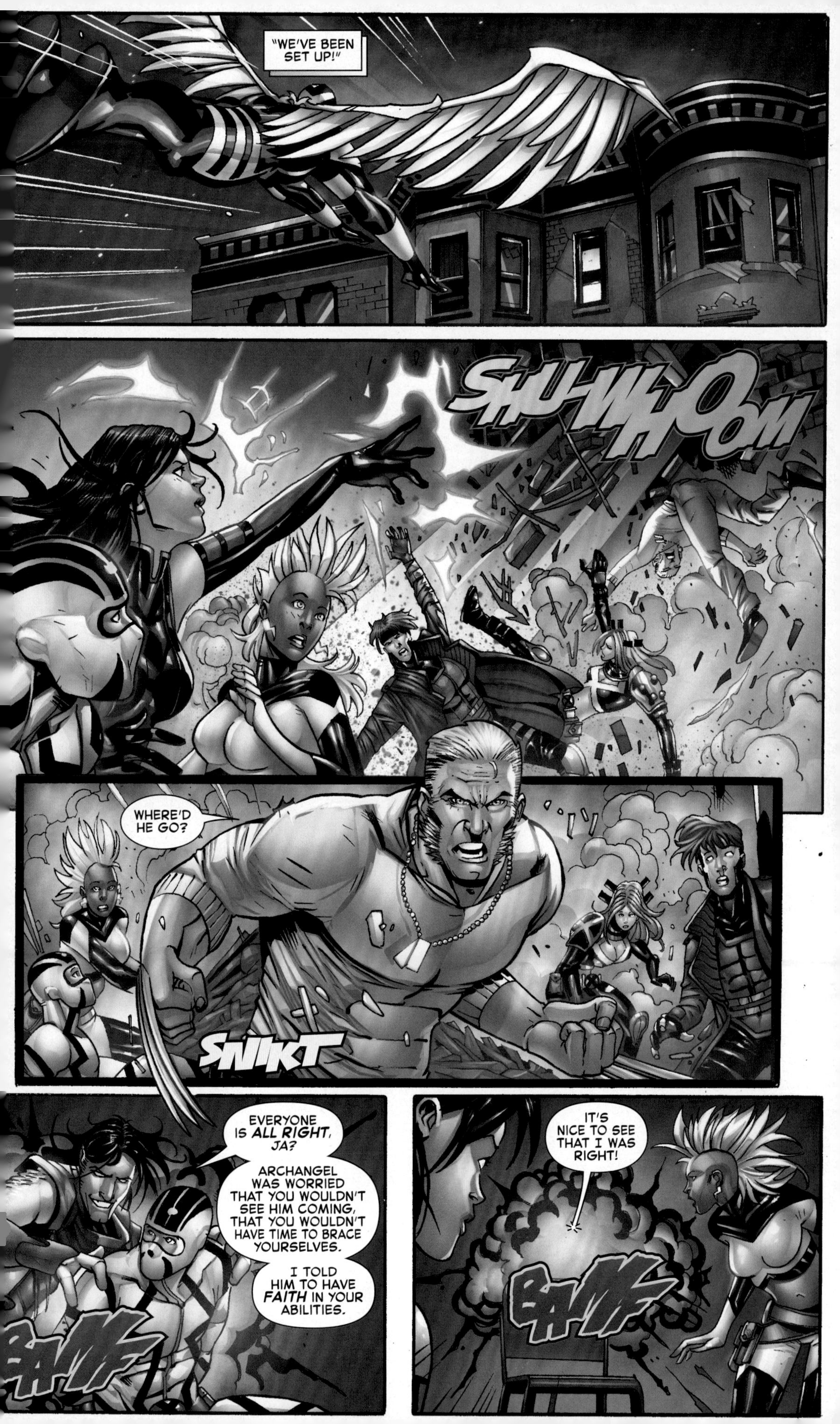
"WE'VE BEEN SET UP!"
SHU-WHOOM
WHERE'D HE GO?
SNIKT
EVERYONE IS *ALL RIGHT*, JA?
ARCHANGEL WAS WORRIED THAT YOU WOULDN'T SEE HIM COMING, THAT YOU WOULDN'T HAVE TIME TO BRACE YOURSELVES.
I TOLD HIM TO HAVE *FAITH* IN YOUR ABILITIES.
BAMF
IT'S NICE TO SEE THAT I WAS RIGHT!
BAMF

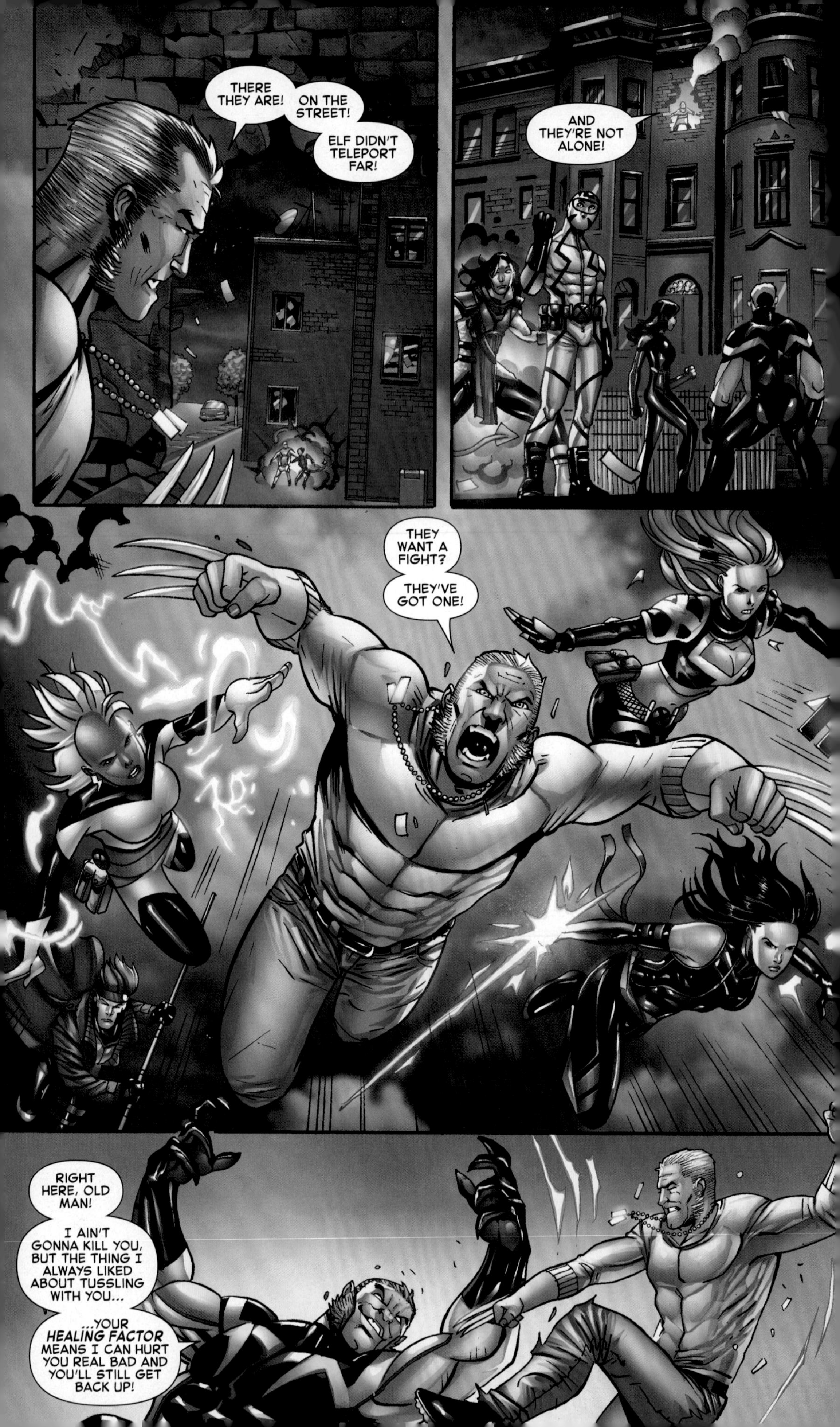
THERE THEY ARE!
ON THE STREET!
ELF DIDN'T TELEPORT FAR!
AND THEY'RE NOT ALONE!
THEY WANT A FIGHT?
THEY'VE GOT ONE!
RIGHT HERE, OLD MAN!
I AIN'T GONNA KILL YOU, BUT THE THING I ALWAYS LIKED ABOUT TUSSLING WITH YOU...
...YOUR *HEALING FACTOR* MEANS I CAN HURT YOU REAL BAD AND YOU'LL STILL GET BACK UP!

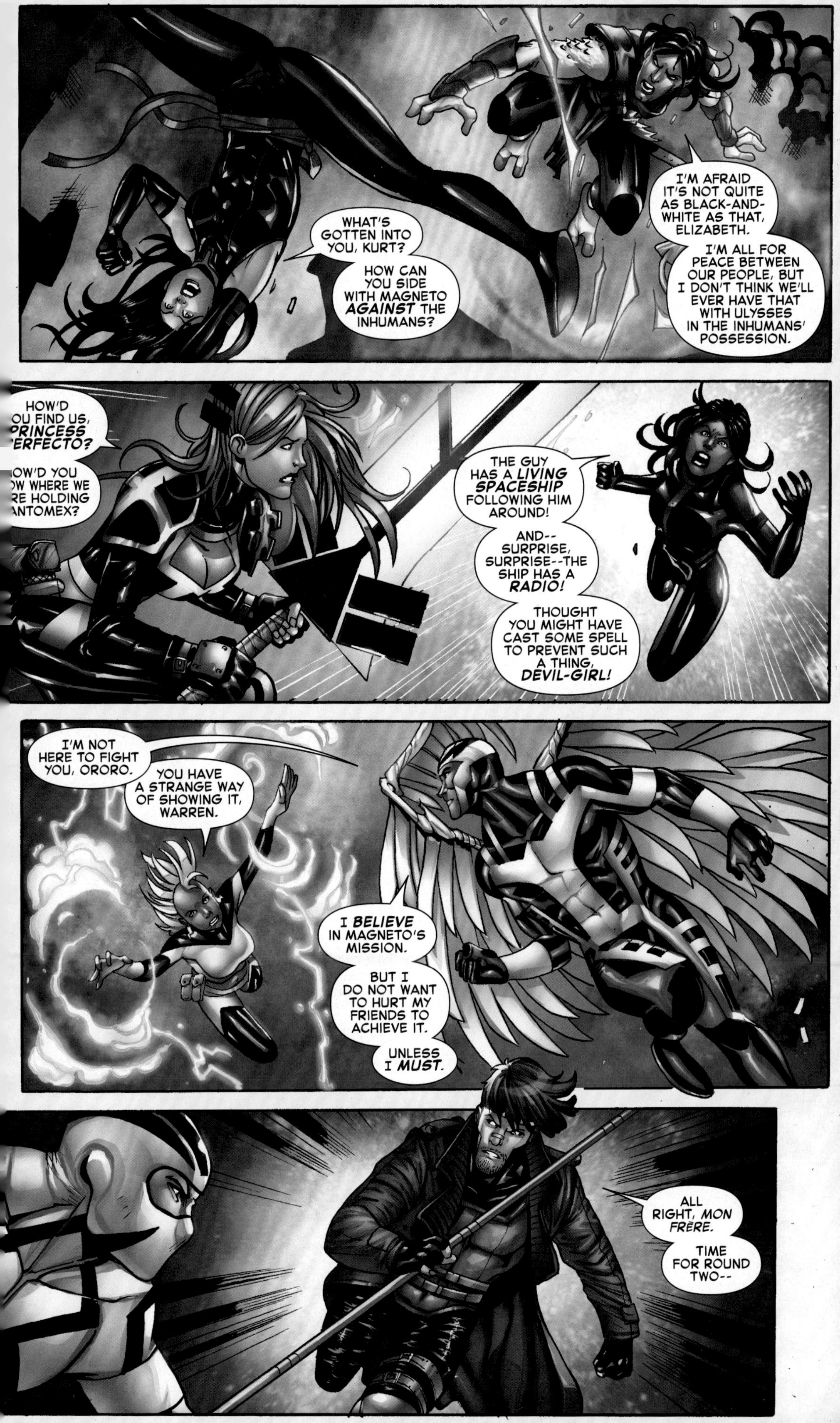
WHAT'S GOTTEN INTO YOU, KURT?
HOW CAN YOU SIDE WITH MAGNETO AGAINST THE INHUMANS?
I'M AFRAID IT'S NOT QUITE AS BLACK-AND-WHITE AS THAT, ELIZABETH.
I'M ALL FOR PEACE BETWEEN OUR PEOPLE, BUT I DON'T THINK WE'LL EVER HAVE THAT WITH ULYSSES IN THE INHUMANS' POSSESSION.
HOW'D OU FIND US, PRINCESS ERFECTO?
OW'D YOU OW WHERE WE RE HOLDING ANTOMEX?
THE GUY HAS A LIVING SPACESHIP FOLLOWING HIM AROUND!
AND-- SURPRISE, SURPRISE--THE SHIP HAS A RADIO!
THOUGHT YOU MIGHT HAVE CAST SOME SPELL TO PREVENT SUCH A THING, DEVIL-GIRL!
I'M NOT HERE TO FIGHT YOU, ORORO.
YOU HAVE A STRANGE WAY OF SHOWING IT, WARREN.
I BELIEVE IN MAGNETO'S MISSION.
BUT I DO NOT WANT TO HURT MY FRIENDS TO ACHIEVE IT.
UNLESS I MUST.
ALL RIGHT, MON FRÈRE.
TIME FOR ROUND TWO--

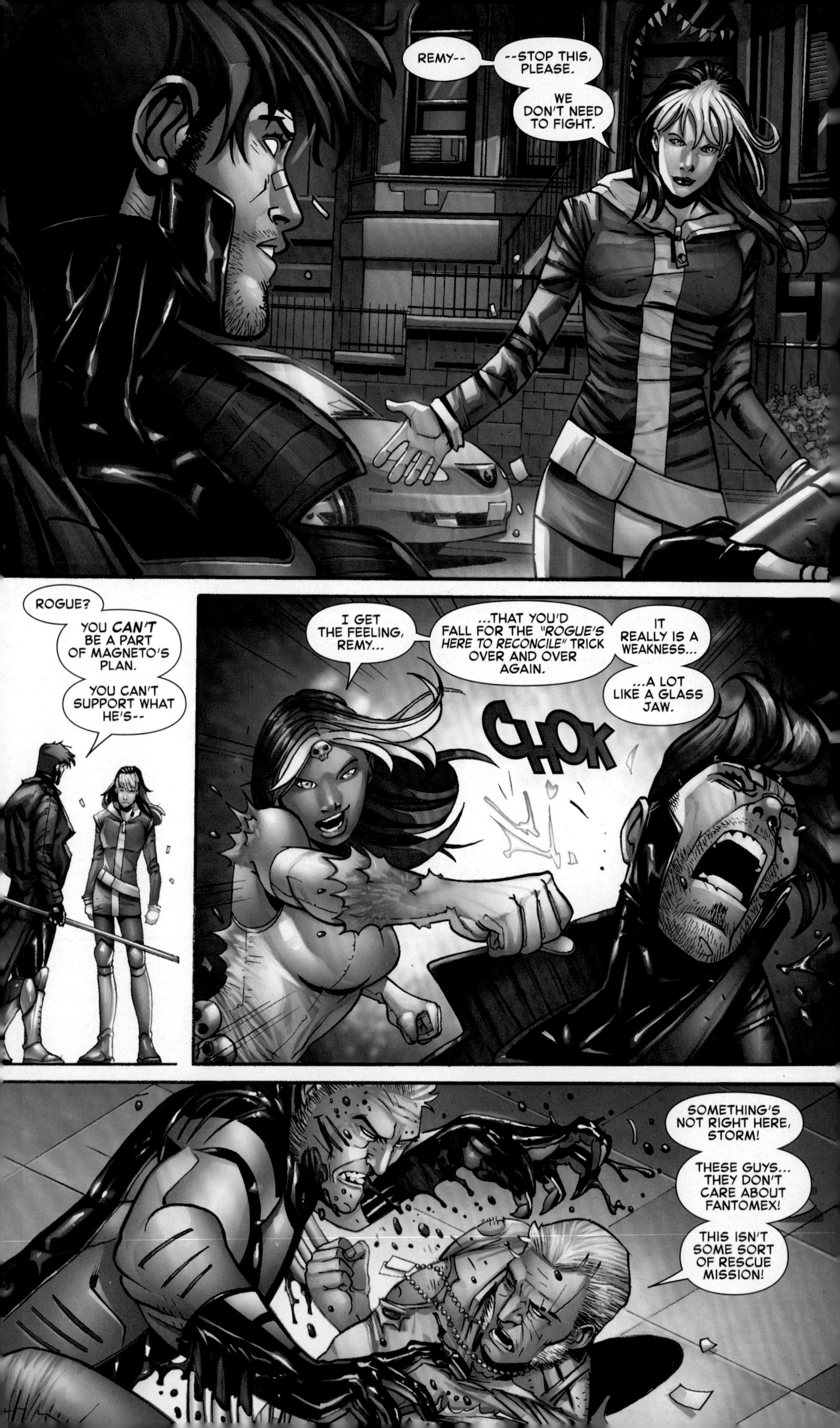
REMY--
--STOP THIS, PLEASE.
WE DON'T NEED TO FIGHT.
ROGUE?
YOU *CAN'T* BE A PART OF MAGNETO'S PLAN.
YOU CAN'T SUPPORT WHAT HE'S--
I GET THE FEELING, REMY...
...THAT YOU'D FALL FOR THE *"ROGUE'S HERE TO RECONCILE"* TRICK OVER AND OVER AGAIN.
IT REALLY IS A WEAKNESS...
...A LOT LIKE A GLASS JAW.
CHOK
SOMETHING'S NOT RIGHT HERE, STORM!
THESE GUYS... THEY DON'T CARE ABOUT FANTOMEX!
THIS ISN'T SOME SORT OF RESCUE MISSION!

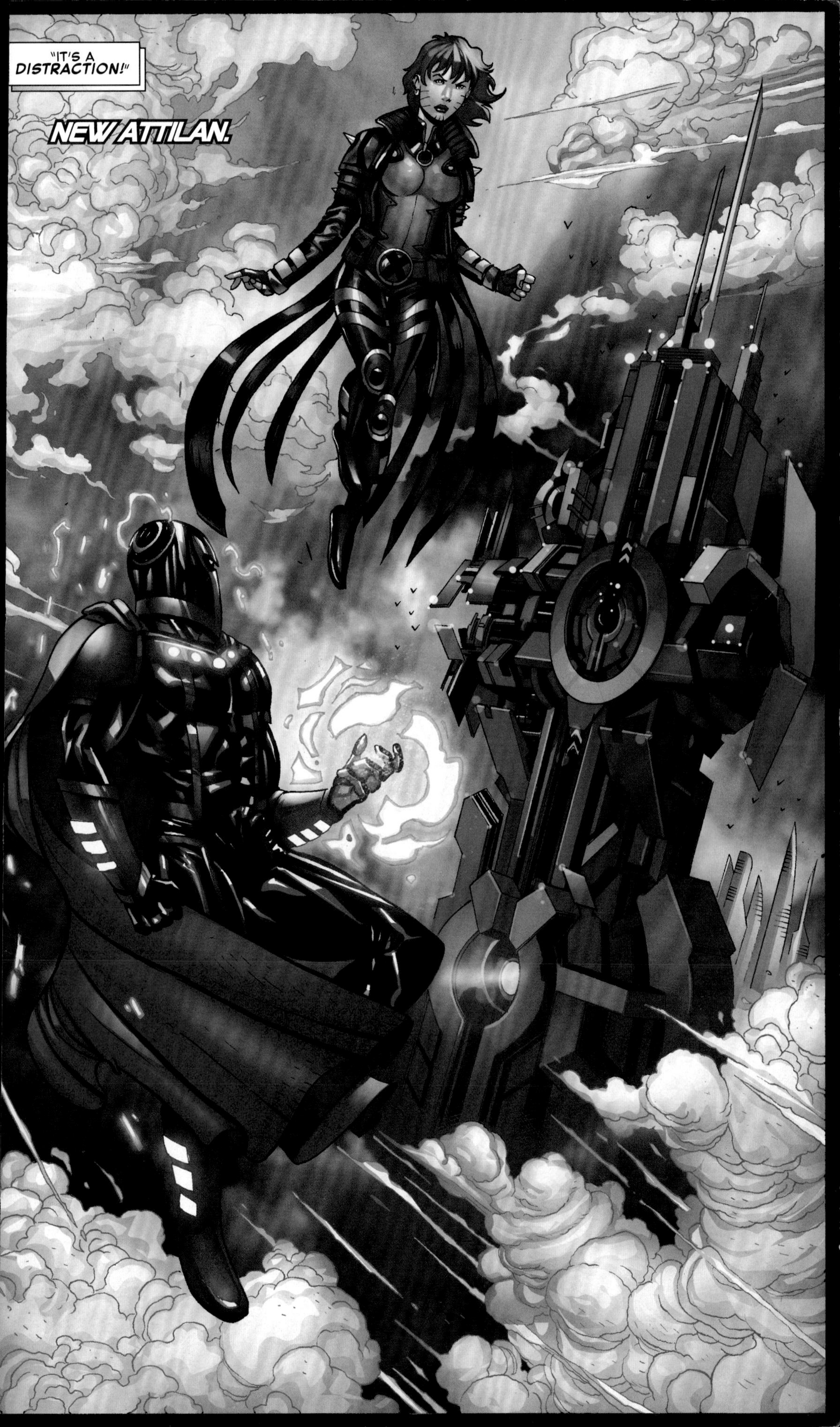
"IT'S A DISTRACTION!"
NEW ATTILAN.

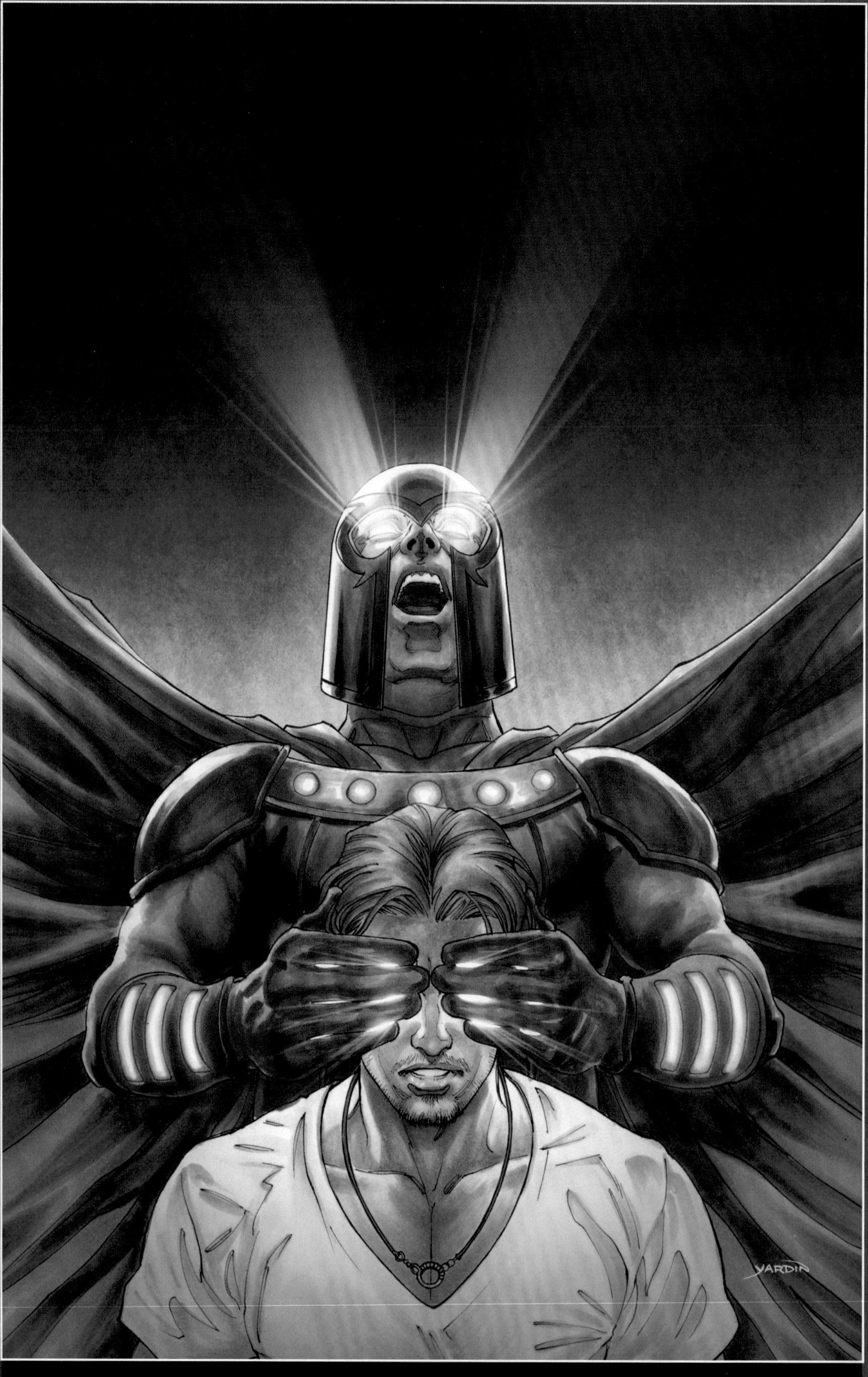
YARDIN

IV

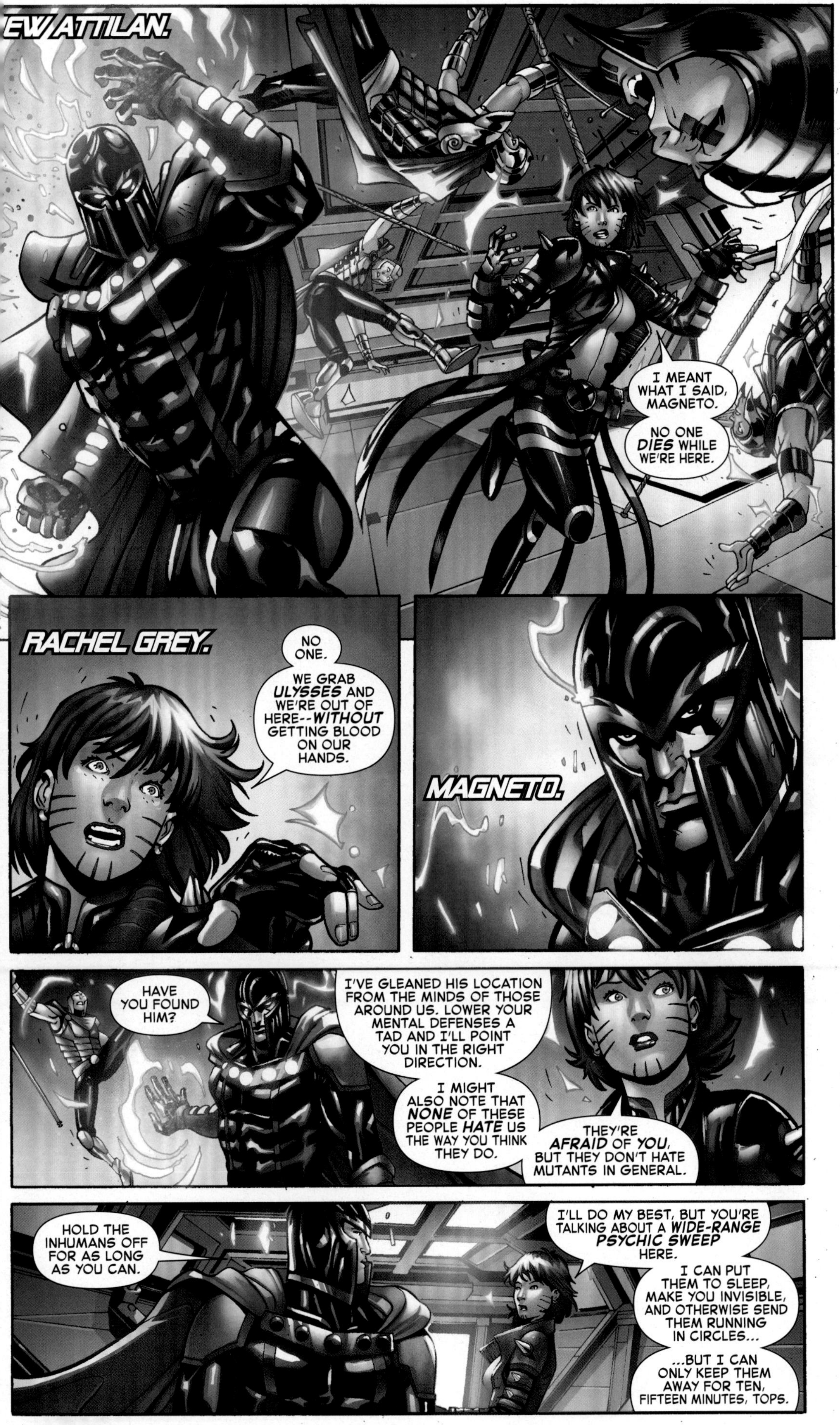
EW ATTILAN.
I MEANT WHAT I SAID, MAGNETO.
NO ONE DIES WHILE WE'RE HERE.
RACHEL GREY.
NO ONE.
WE GRAB ULYSSES AND WE'RE OUT OF HERE--WITHOUT GETTING BLOOD ON OUR HANDS.
MAGNETO.
HAVE YOU FOUND HIM?
I'VE GLEANED HIS LOCATION FROM THE MINDS OF THOSE AROUND US. LOWER YOUR MENTAL DEFENSES A TAD AND I'LL POINT YOU IN THE RIGHT DIRECTION.
I MIGHT ALSO NOTE THAT NONE OF THESE PEOPLE HATE US THE WAY YOU THINK THEY DO.
THEY'RE AFRAID OF YOU, BUT THEY DON'T HATE MUTANTS IN GENERAL.
HOLD THE INHUMANS OFF FOR AS LONG AS YOU CAN.
I'LL DO MY BEST, BUT YOU'RE TALKING ABOUT A WIDE-RANGE PSYCHIC SWEEP HERE.
I CAN PUT THEM TO SLEEP, MAKE YOU INVISIBLE, AND OTHERWISE SEND THEM RUNNING IN CIRCLES...
...BUT I CAN ONLY KEEP THEM AWAY FOR TEN, FIFTEEN MINUTES, TOPS.

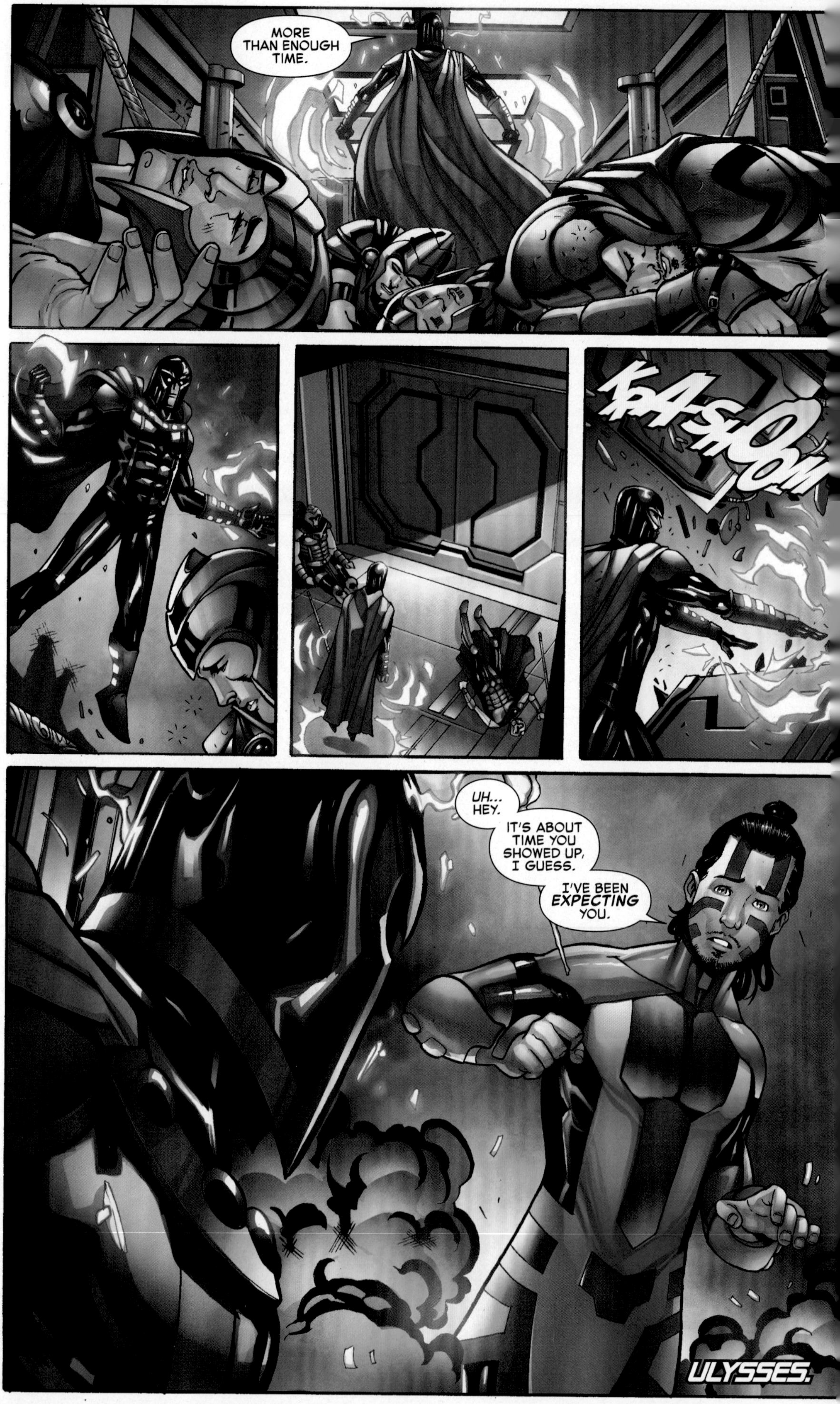
MORE THAN ENOUGH TIME.
KA-SHOOM
UH... HEY.
IT'S ABOUT TIME YOU SHOWED UP, I GUESS.
I'VE BEEN EXPECTING YOU.
ULYSSES.

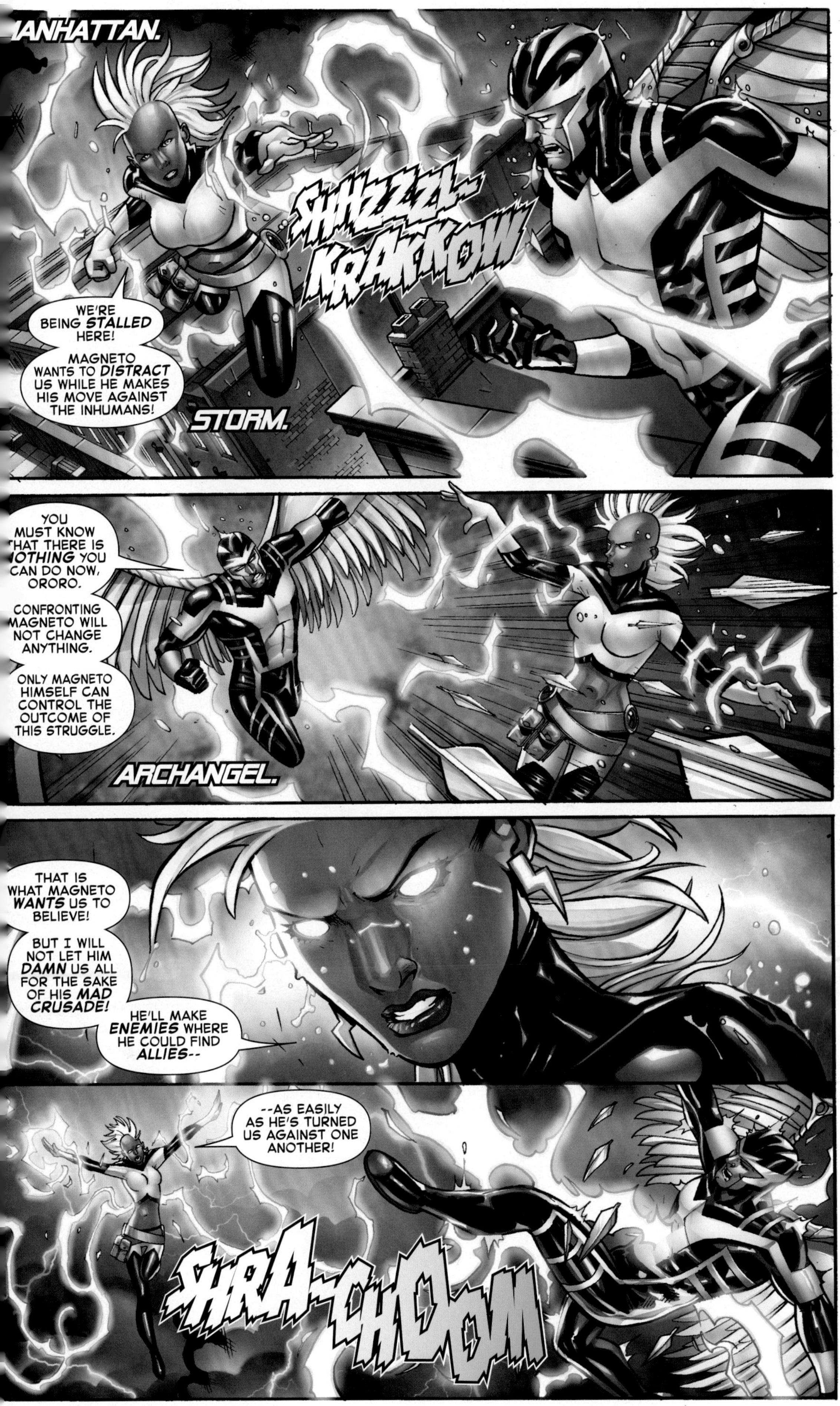

MANHATTAN.
SHHZZZL-KRAKKOW
WE'RE BEING STALLED HERE!
MAGNETO WANTS TO DISTRACT US WHILE HE MAKES HIS MOVE AGAINST THE INHUMANS!
STORM.
YOU MUST KNOW THAT THERE IS NOTHING YOU CAN DO NOW, ORORO.
CONFRONTING MAGNETO WILL NOT CHANGE ANYTHING.
ONLY MAGNETO HIMSELF CAN CONTROL THE OUTCOME OF THIS STRUGGLE.
ARCHANGEL.
THAT IS WHAT MAGNETO WANTS US TO BELIEVE!
BUT I WILL NOT LET HIM DAMN US ALL FOR THE SAKE OF HIS MAD CRUSADE!
HE'LL MAKE ENEMIES WHERE HE COULD FIND ALLIES--
--AS EASILY AS HE'S TURNED US AGAINST ONE ANOTHER!
SHRA-CHOOOM

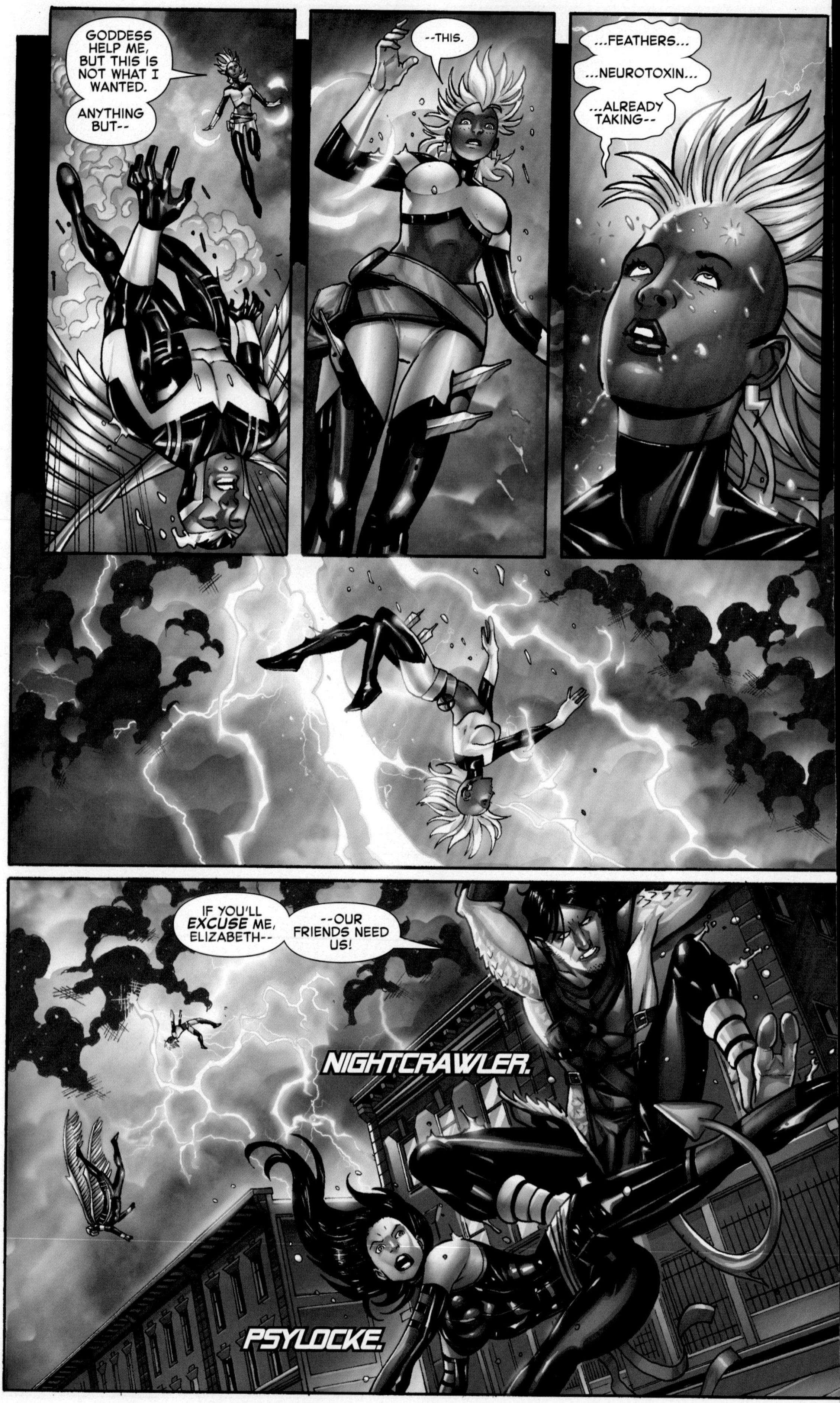
GODDESS HELP ME, BUT THIS IS NOT WHAT I WANTED.
ANYTHING BUT--
--THIS.
...FEATHERS...
...NEUROTOXIN...
...ALREADY TAKING--
IF YOU'LL EXCUSE ME, ELIZABETH--
--OUR FRIENDS NEED US!
NIGHTCRAWLER.
PSYLOCKE.

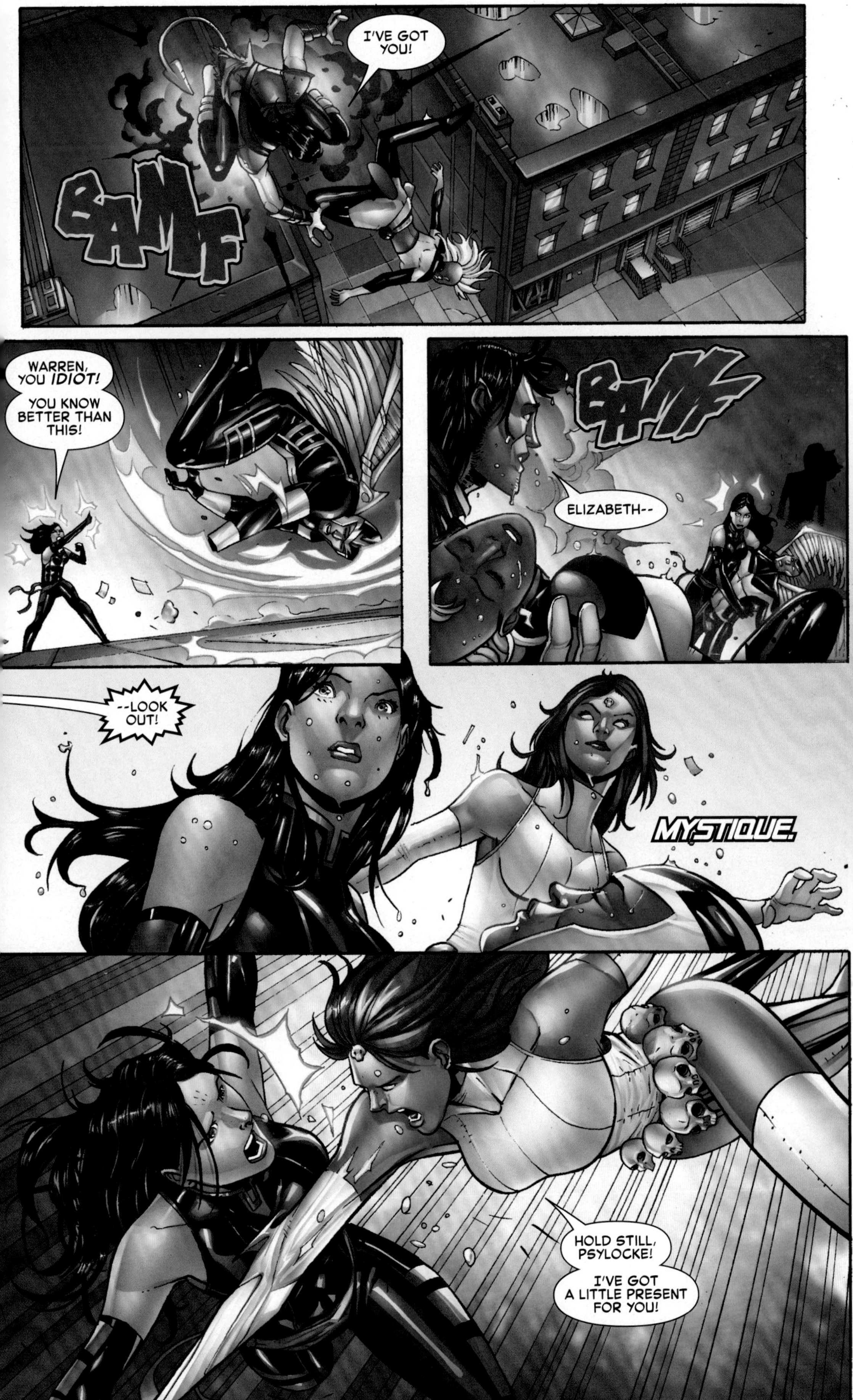
I'VE GOT YOU!
BAMF
WARREN, YOU *IDIOT!*
YOU KNOW BETTER THAN THIS!
BAMF
ELIZABETH--
--LOOK OUT!
MYSTIQUE.
HOLD STILL, PSYLOCKE!
I'VE GOT A LITTLE PRESENT FOR YOU!

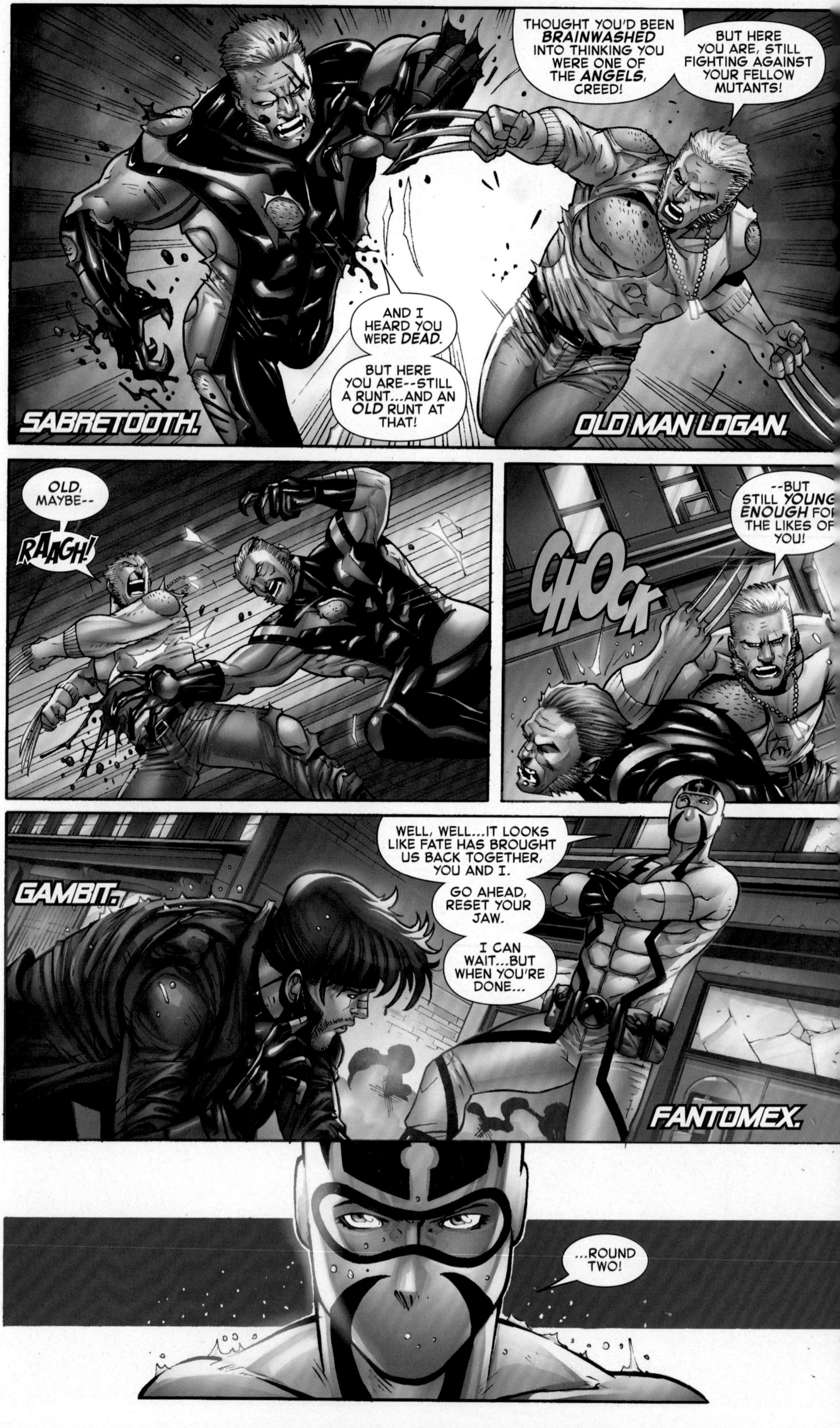
SABRETOOTH.
THOUGHT YOU'D BEEN BRAINWASHED INTO THINKING YOU WERE ONE OF THE ANGELS, CREED!
BUT HERE YOU ARE, STILL FIGHTING AGAINST YOUR FELLOW MUTANTS!
OLD MAN LOGAN.
AND I HEARD YOU WERE DEAD.
BUT HERE YOU ARE--STILL A RUNT...AND AN OLD RUNT AT THAT!
OLD, MAYBE--
RAAGH!
CHOCK
--BUT STILL YOUNG ENOUGH FOR THE LIKES OF YOU!
GAMBIT.
WELL, WELL...IT LOOKS LIKE FATE HAS BROUGHT US BACK TOGETHER, YOU AND I.
GO AHEAD, RESET YOUR JAW.
I CAN WAIT...BUT WHEN YOU'RE DONE...
FANTOMEX.
...ROUND TWO!

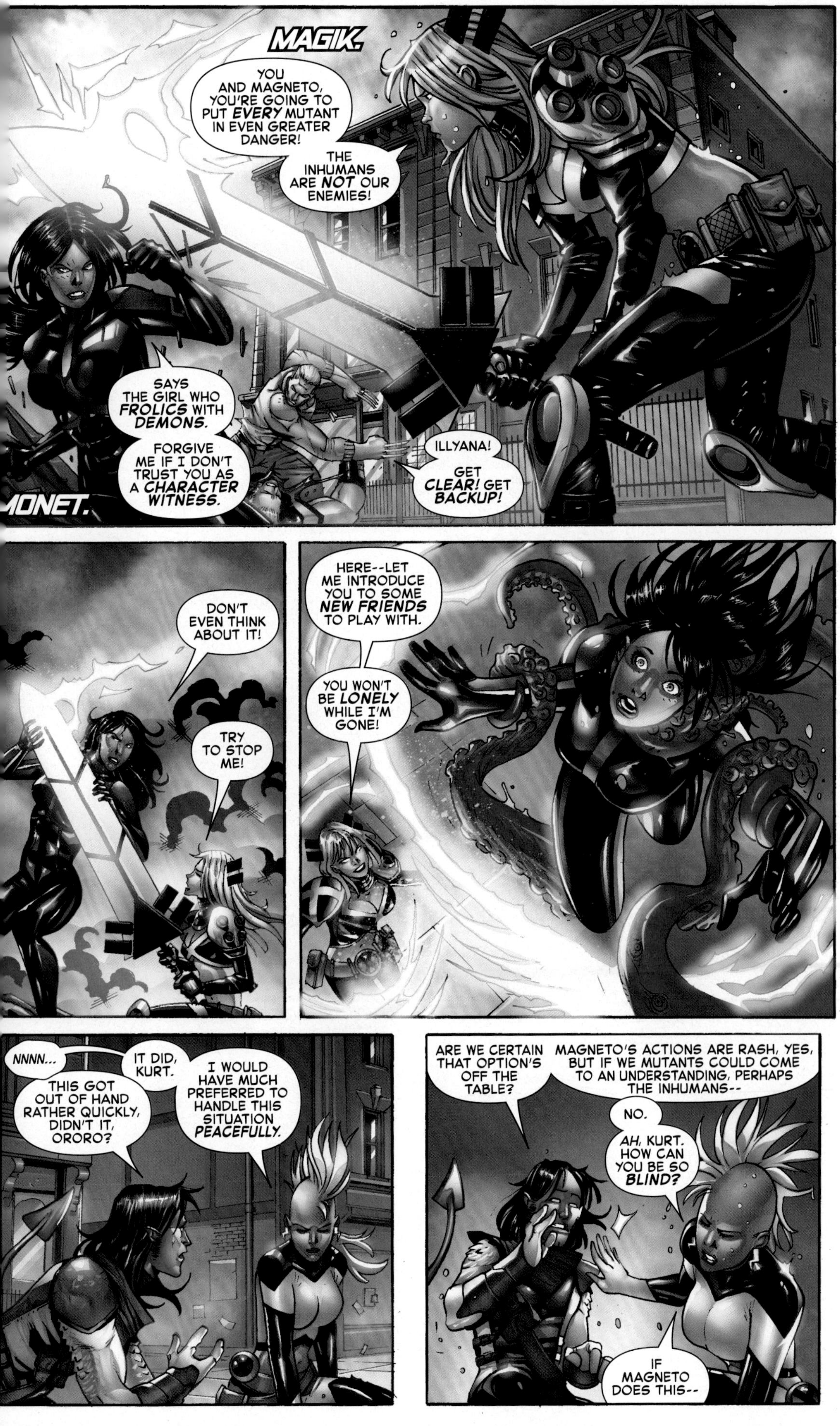
MAGIK.
YOU AND MAGNETO, YOU'RE GOING TO PUT EVERY MUTANT IN EVEN GREATER DANGER!
THE INHUMANS ARE NOT OUR ENEMIES!
SAYS THE GIRL WHO FROLICS WITH DEMONS.
FORGIVE ME IF I DON'T TRUST YOU AS A CHARACTER WITNESS.
ILLYANA!
GET CLEAR! GET BACKUP!
MONET.
DON'T EVEN THINK ABOUT IT!
TRY TO STOP ME!
HERE--LET ME INTRODUCE YOU TO SOME NEW FRIENDS TO PLAY WITH.
YOU WON'T BE LONELY WHILE I'M GONE!
NNNN...
THIS GOT OUT OF HAND RATHER QUICKLY, DIDN'T IT, ORORO?
IT DID, KURT.
I WOULD HAVE MUCH PREFERRED TO HANDLE THIS SITUATION PEACEFULLY.
ARE WE CERTAIN THAT OPTION'S OFF THE TABLE?
MAGNETO'S ACTIONS ARE RASH, YES, BUT IF WE MUTANTS COULD COME TO AN UNDERSTANDING, PERHAPS THE INHUMANS--
NO.
AH, KURT. HOW CAN YOU BE SO BLIND?
IF MAGNETO DOES THIS--

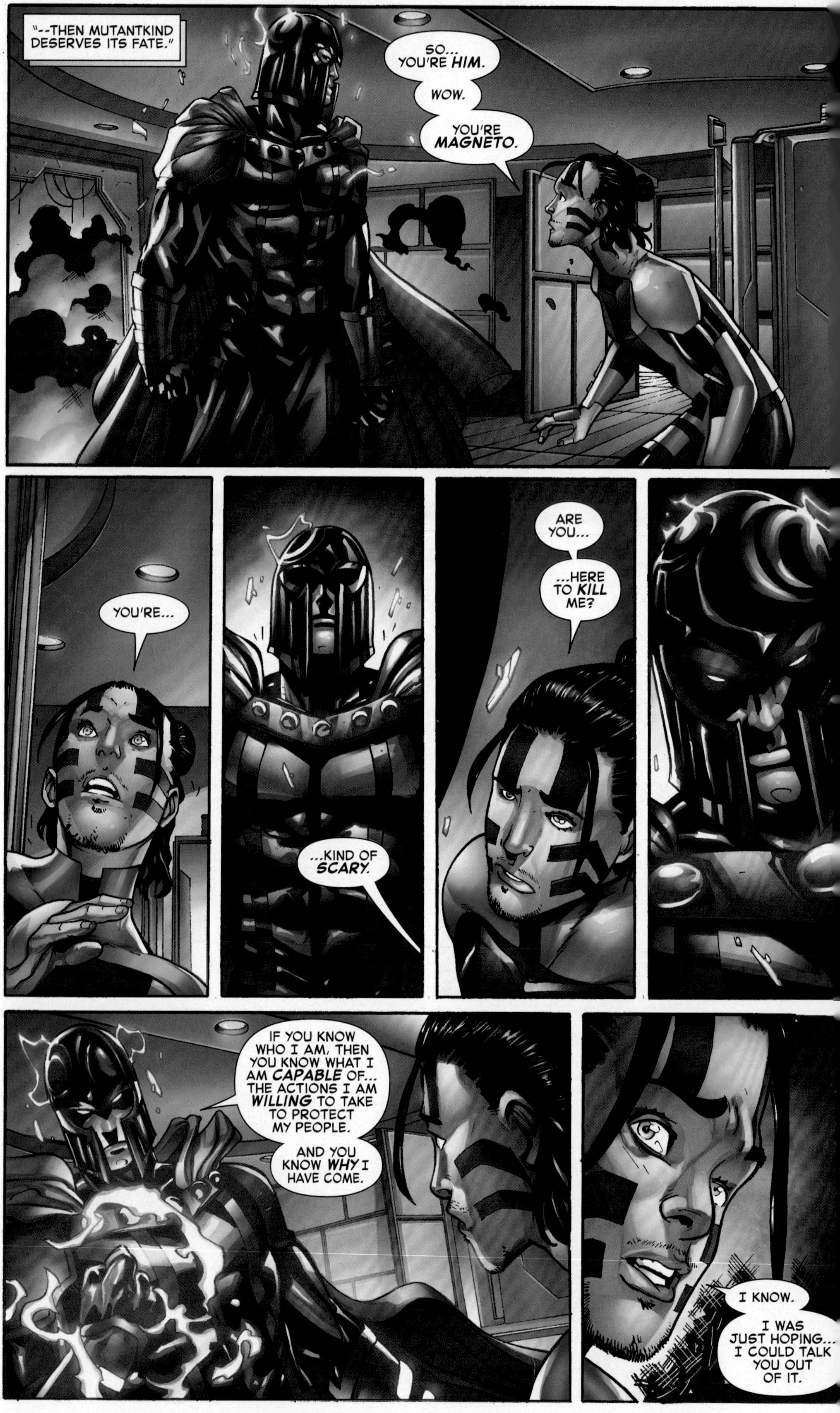
"--THEN MUTANTKIND DESERVES ITS FATE."
SO... YOU'RE HIM.
WOW.
YOU'RE MAGNETO.
YOU'RE...
...KIND OF SCARY.
ARE YOU...
...HERE TO KILL ME?
IF YOU KNOW WHO I AM, THEN YOU KNOW WHAT I AM CAPABLE OF... THE ACTIONS I AM WILLING TO TAKE TO PROTECT MY PEOPLE.
AND YOU KNOW WHY I HAVE COME.
I KNOW.
I WAS JUST HOPING... I COULD TALK YOU OUT OF IT.

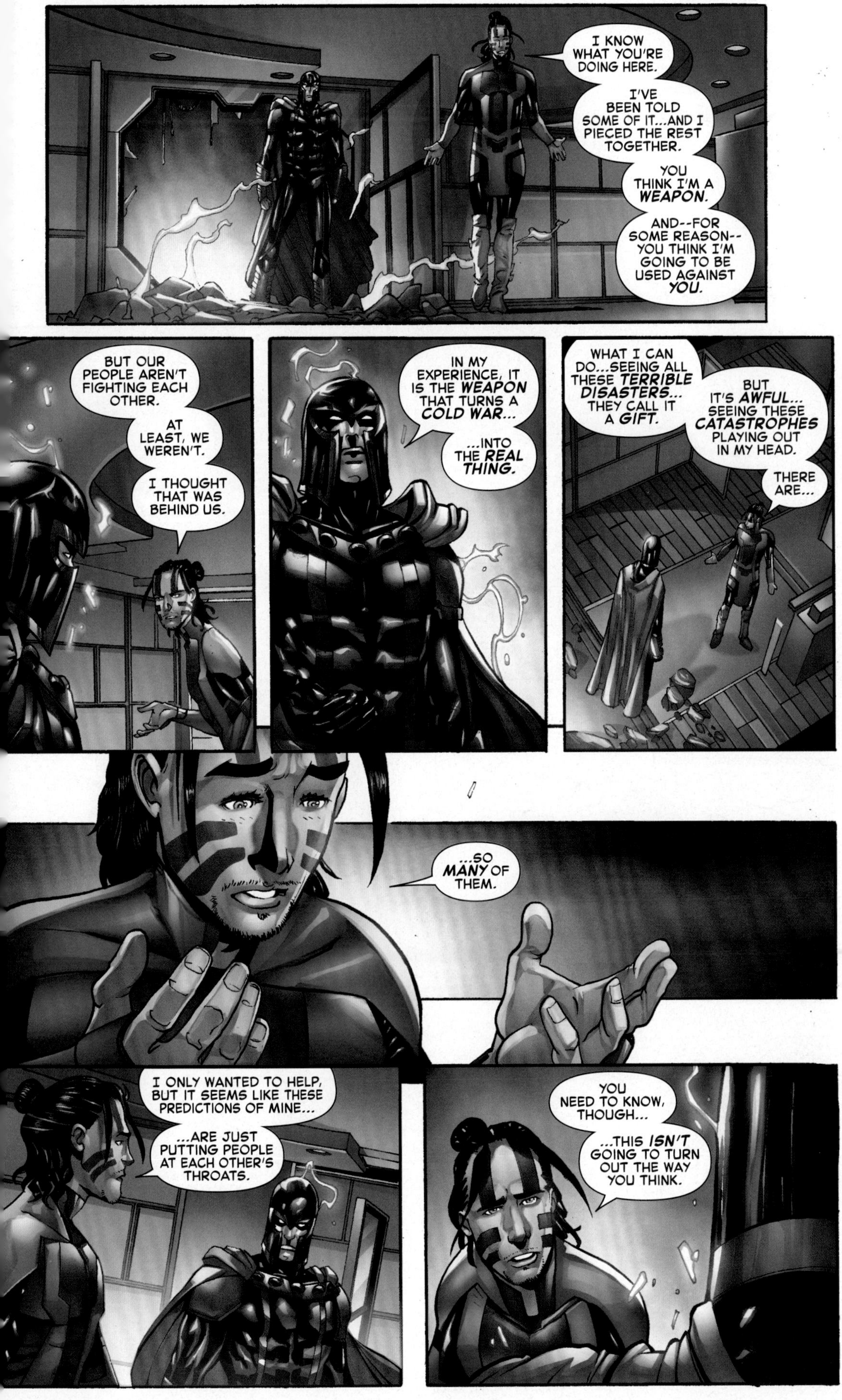
I KNOW WHAT YOU'RE DOING HERE.
I'VE BEEN TOLD SOME OF IT...AND I PIECED THE REST TOGETHER.
YOU THINK I'M A WEAPON.
AND--FOR SOME REASON--YOU THINK I'M GOING TO BE USED AGAINST YOU.
BUT OUR PEOPLE AREN'T FIGHTING EACH OTHER.
AT LEAST, WE WEREN'T.
I THOUGHT THAT WAS BEHIND US.
IN MY EXPERIENCE, IT IS THE WEAPON THAT TURNS A COLD WAR...
...INTO THE REAL THING.
WHAT I CAN DO...SEEING ALL THESE TERRIBLE DISASTERS... THEY CALL IT A GIFT.
BUT IT'S AWFUL... SEEING THESE CATASTROPHES PLAYING OUT IN MY HEAD.
THERE ARE...
...SO MANY OF THEM.
I ONLY WANTED TO HELP, BUT IT SEEMS LIKE THESE PREDICTIONS OF MINE...
...ARE JUST PUTTING PEOPLE AT EACH OTHER'S THROATS.
YOU NEED TO KNOW, THOUGH...
...THIS ISN'T GOING TO TURN OUT THE WAY YOU THINK.

"IT WILL BE MUCH, MUCH WORSE."

ALL THOSE TIMES I WANTED TO SEE YOU DEAD, CREED...BUT HERE WE ARE.

I DON'T *WANT* TO CUT YOU DOWN...BUT IF YOU AND YOURS DON'T STOP WHAT YOU'RE DOING, THAT'S HOW IT'LL BE!

RAAAAARGH!

WE'RE ON *BORROWED TIME* NOW!

THE WITCH WILL BE BACK WITH THE CAVALRY ANY MINUTE!

LET'S HOPE WE GAVE MAGNETO THE BREATHING ROOM HE NEEDED!

WHEN MAGNETO TAKES OUR CHOICES FROM US, KURT, WHERE WILL WE BE THEN?

WHOSE SIDE ARE YOU GOING TO TAKE?

OUR DECISIO WERE MADE FO LONG AGO, STO AND NOT B MAGNETO.

NO PREDICTIO IS GOING TO CHANG THAT NOW

WE HAVE BE READY W THOSE DECIS YIELD THE RESULTS

"WHEN THAT HAPPENS, I'LL BE ON THE SAME *'SIDE'* I'VE ALWAYS BEEN ON."

AACK!

BAMF

KURT! WHAT ARE YOU--

I'LL NOT LET YOU *MURDER* ANOTHER MUTANT, MYSTIQUE!

THERE ARE *TOO FEW* OF US LEFT!

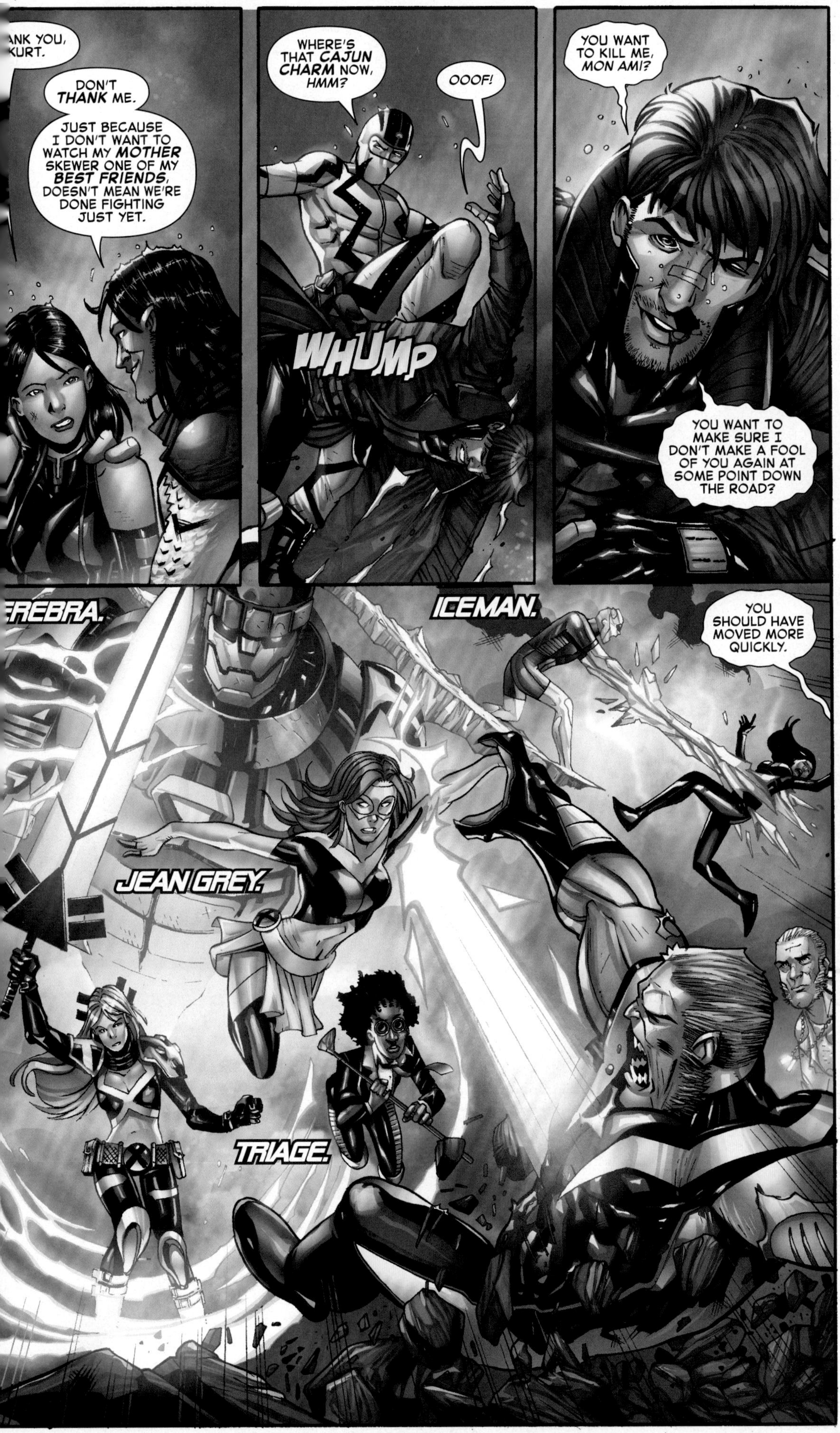

ANK YOU, KURT.
DON'T THANK ME.
JUST BECAUSE I DON'T WANT TO WATCH MY MOTHER SKEWER ONE OF MY BEST FRIENDS, DOESN'T MEAN WE'RE DONE FIGHTING JUST YET.
WHERE'S THAT CAJUN CHARM NOW, HMM?
OOOF!
WHUMP
YOU WANT TO KILL ME, MON AMI?
YOU WANT TO MAKE SURE I DON'T MAKE A FOOL OF YOU AGAIN AT SOME POINT DOWN THE ROAD?
EREBRA.
ICEMAN.
YOU SHOULD HAVE MOVED MORE QUICKLY.
JEAN GREY.
TRIAGE.

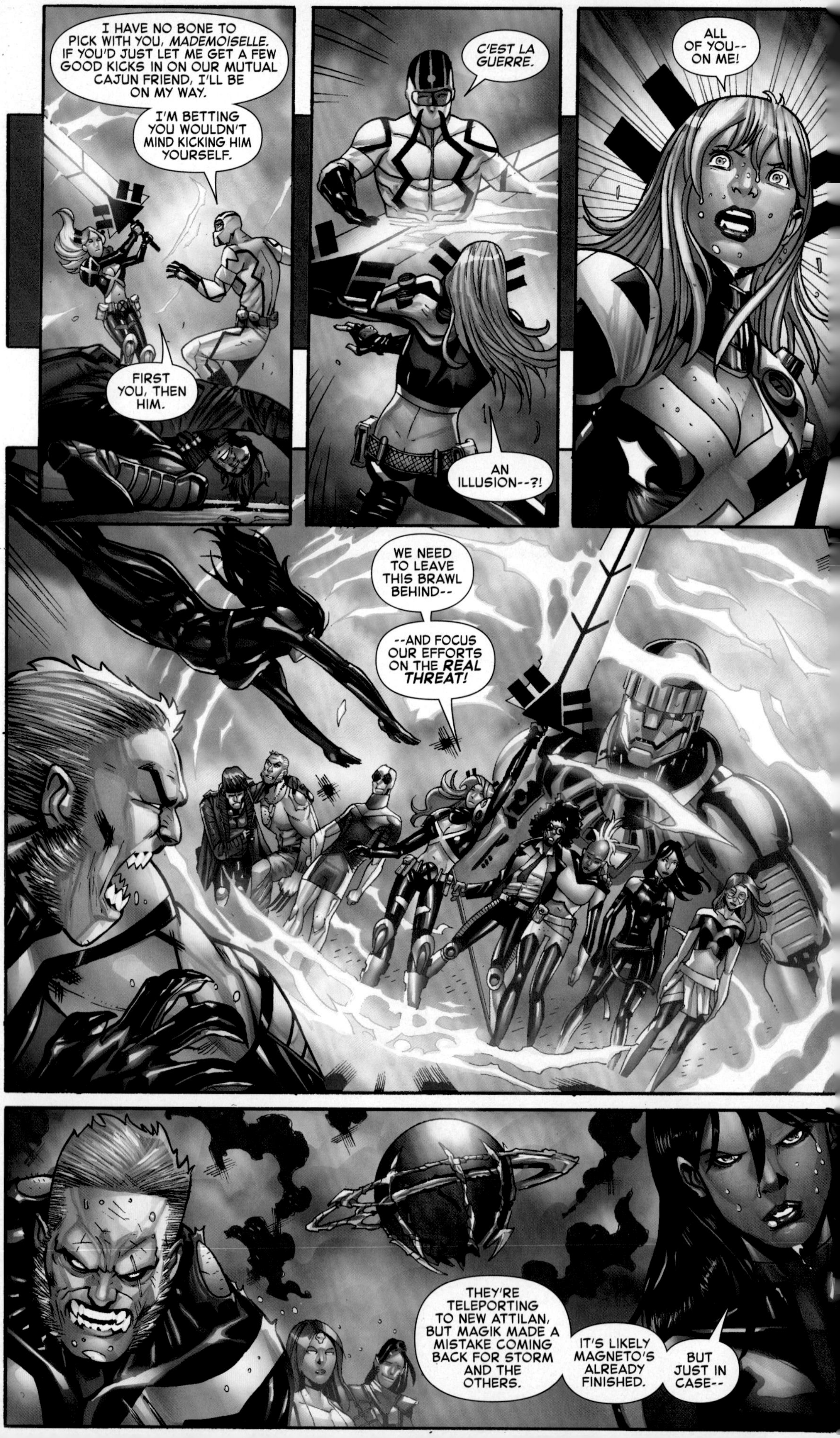
I HAVE NO BONE TO PICK WITH YOU, *MADEMOISELLE*. IF YOU'D JUST LET ME GET A FEW GOOD KICKS IN ON OUR MUTUAL CAJUN FRIEND, I'LL BE ON MY WAY.
I'M BETTING YOU WOULDN'T MIND KICKING HIM YOURSELF.
FIRST YOU, THEN HIM.
C'EST LA GUERRE.
AN ILLUSION--?!
ALL OF YOU-- ON ME!
WE NEED TO LEAVE THIS BRAWL BEHIND--
--AND FOCUS OUR EFFORTS ON THE ***REAL THREAT!***
THEY'RE TELEPORTING TO NEW ATTILAN, BUT MAGIK MADE A MISTAKE COMING BACK FOR STORM AND THE OTHERS.
IT'S LIKELY MAGNETO'S ALREADY FINISHED.
BUT JUST IN CASE--

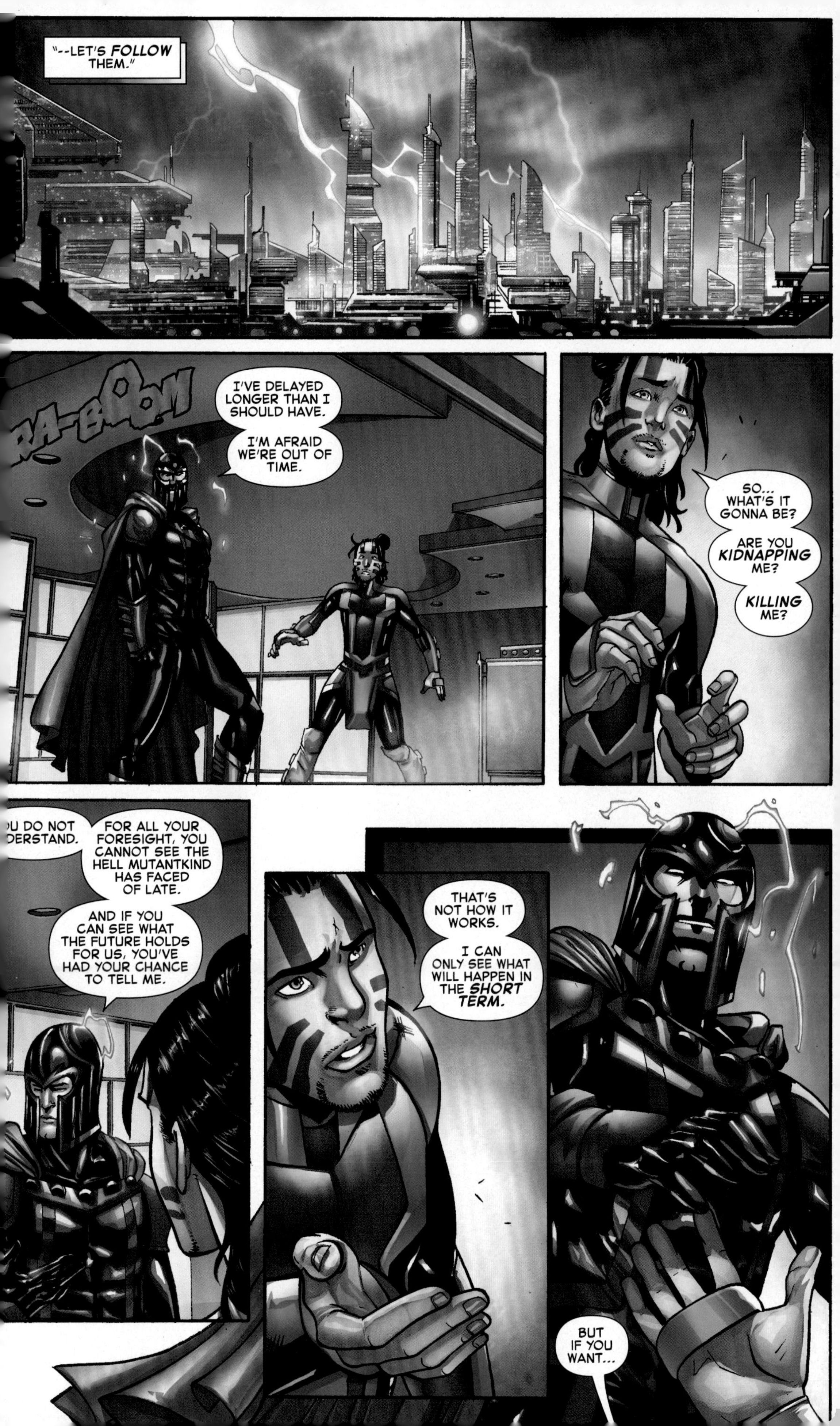
"--LET'S FOLLOW THEM."
KRA-BOOM
I'VE DELAYED LONGER THAN I SHOULD HAVE.
I'M AFRAID WE'RE OUT OF TIME.
SO... WHAT'S IT GONNA BE?
ARE YOU KIDNAPPING ME?
KILLING ME?
YOU DO NOT UNDERSTAND.
FOR ALL YOUR FORESIGHT, YOU CANNOT SEE THE HELL MUTANTKIND HAS FACED OF LATE.
AND IF YOU CAN SEE WHAT THE FUTURE HOLDS FOR US, YOU'VE HAD YOUR CHANCE TO TELL ME.
THAT'S NOT HOW IT WORKS.
I CAN ONLY SEE WHAT WILL HAPPEN IN THE SHORT TERM.
BUT IF YOU WANT...

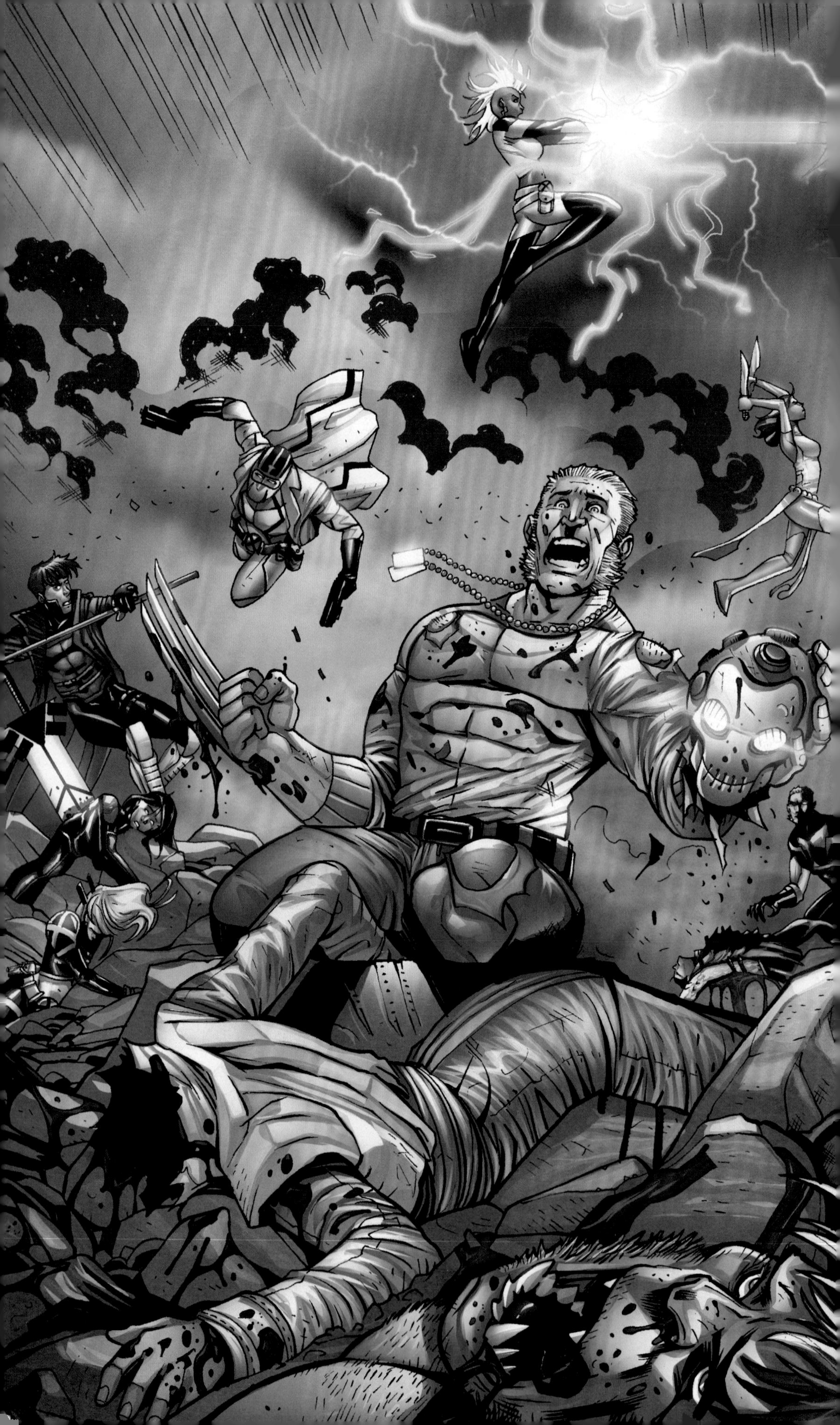

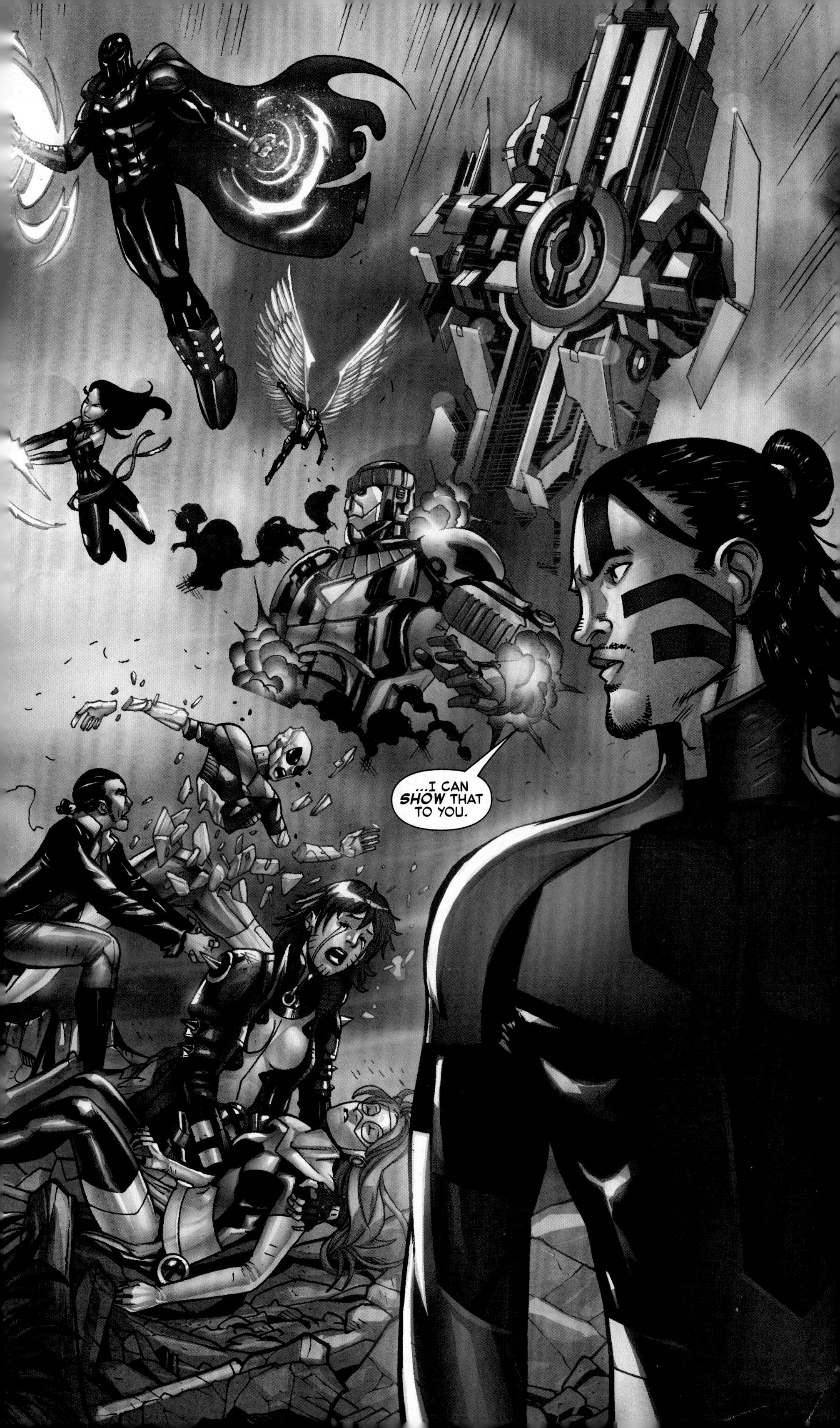
...I CAN SHOW THAT TO YOU.

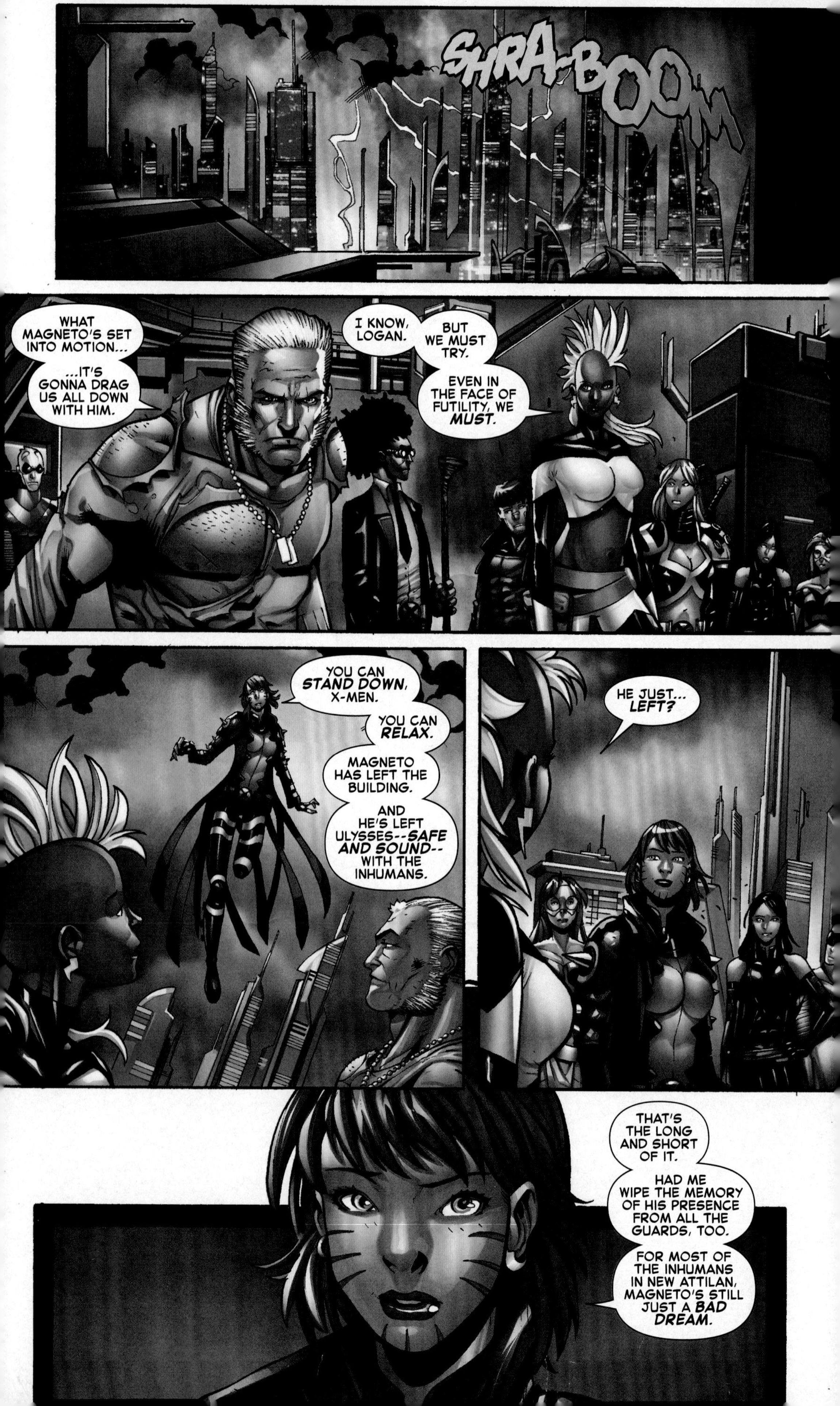
SHRA-BOOM
WHAT MAGNETO'S SET INTO MOTION...
...IT'S GONNA DRAG US ALL DOWN WITH HIM.
I KNOW, LOGAN.
BUT WE MUST TRY.
EVEN IN THE FACE OF FUTILITY, WE MUST.
YOU CAN STAND DOWN, X-MEN.
YOU CAN RELAX.
MAGNETO HAS LEFT THE BUILDING.
AND HE'S LEFT ULYSSES--SAFE AND SOUND--WITH THE INHUMANS.
HE JUST... LEFT?
THAT'S THE LONG AND SHORT OF IT.
HAD ME WIPE THE MEMORY OF HIS PRESENCE FROM ALL THE GUARDS, TOO.
FOR MOST OF THE INHUMANS IN NEW ATTILAN, MAGNETO'S STILL JUST A BAD DREAM.

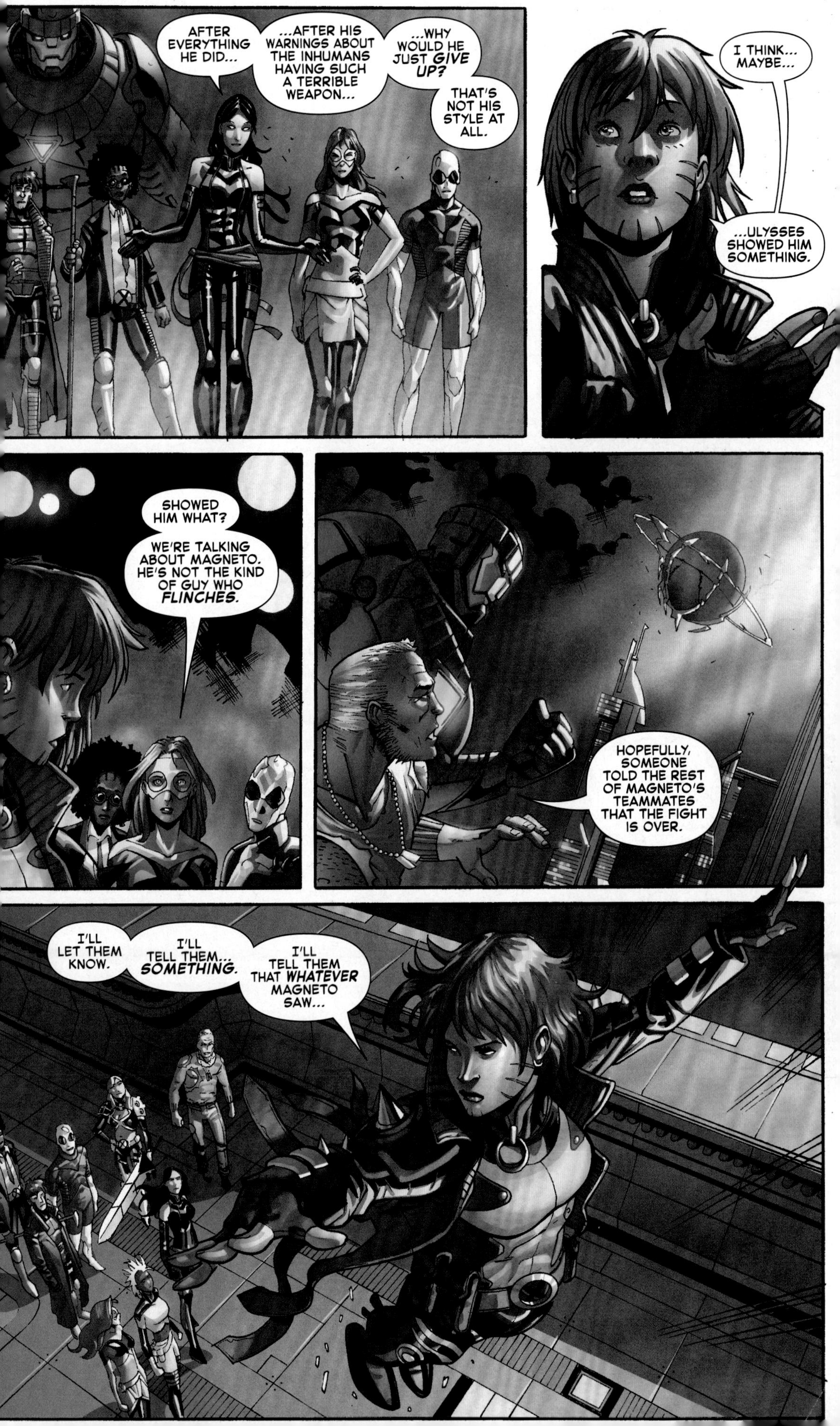
AFTER EVERYTHING HE DID...
...AFTER HIS WARNINGS ABOUT THE INHUMANS HAVING SUCH A TERRIBLE WEAPON...
...WHY WOULD HE JUST GIVE UP?
THAT'S NOT HIS STYLE AT ALL.
I THINK... MAYBE...
...ULYSSES SHOWED HIM SOMETHING.
SHOWED HIM WHAT?
WE'RE TALKING ABOUT MAGNETO. HE'S NOT THE KIND OF GUY WHO FLINCHES.
HOPEFULLY, SOMEONE TOLD THE REST OF MAGNETO'S TEAMMATES THAT THE FIGHT IS OVER.
I'LL LET THEM KNOW.
I'LL TELL THEM... SOMETHING.
I'LL TELL THEM THAT WHATEVER MAGNETO SAW...

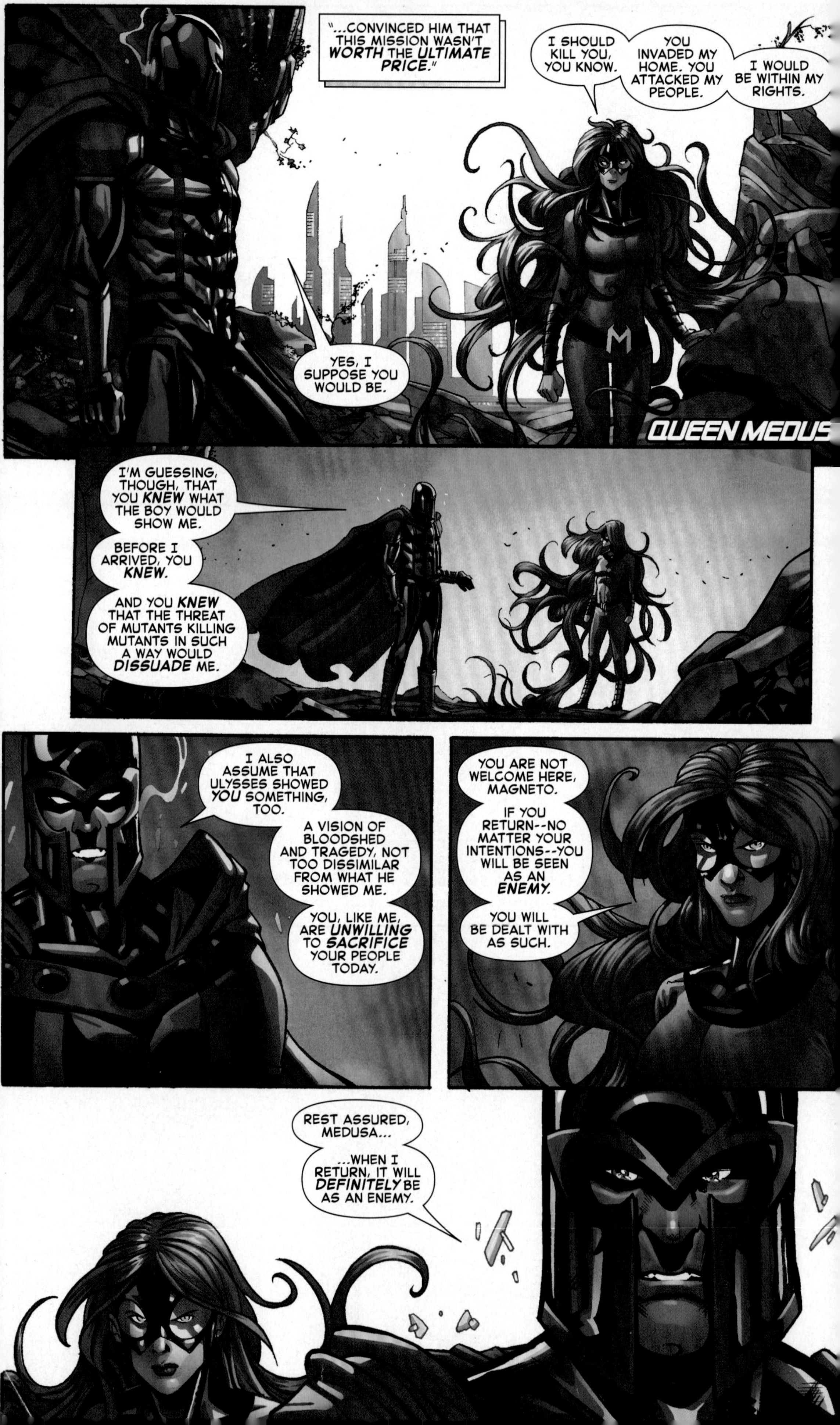

"...CONVINCED HIM THAT THIS MISSION WASN'T WORTH THE ULTIMATE PRICE."
I SHOULD KILL YOU, YOU KNOW.
YOU INVADED MY HOME. YOU ATTACKED MY PEOPLE.
I WOULD BE WITHIN MY RIGHTS.
YES, I SUPPOSE YOU WOULD BE.
QUEEN MEDUS
I'M GUESSING, THOUGH, THAT YOU KNEW WHAT THE BOY WOULD SHOW ME.
BEFORE I ARRIVED, YOU KNEW.
AND YOU KNEW THAT THE THREAT OF MUTANTS KILLING MUTANTS IN SUCH A WAY WOULD DISSUADE ME.
I ALSO ASSUME THAT ULYSSES SHOWED YOU SOMETHING, TOO.
A VISION OF BLOODSHED AND TRAGEDY, NOT TOO DISSIMILAR FROM WHAT HE SHOWED ME.
YOU, LIKE ME, ARE UNWILLING TO SACRIFICE YOUR PEOPLE TODAY.
YOU ARE NOT WELCOME HERE, MAGNETO.
IF YOU RETURN--NO MATTER YOUR INTENTIONS--YOU WILL BE SEEN AS AN ENEMY.
YOU WILL BE DEALT WITH AS SUCH.
REST ASSURED, MEDUSA...
...WHEN I RETURN, IT WILL DEFINITELY BE AS AN ENEMY.

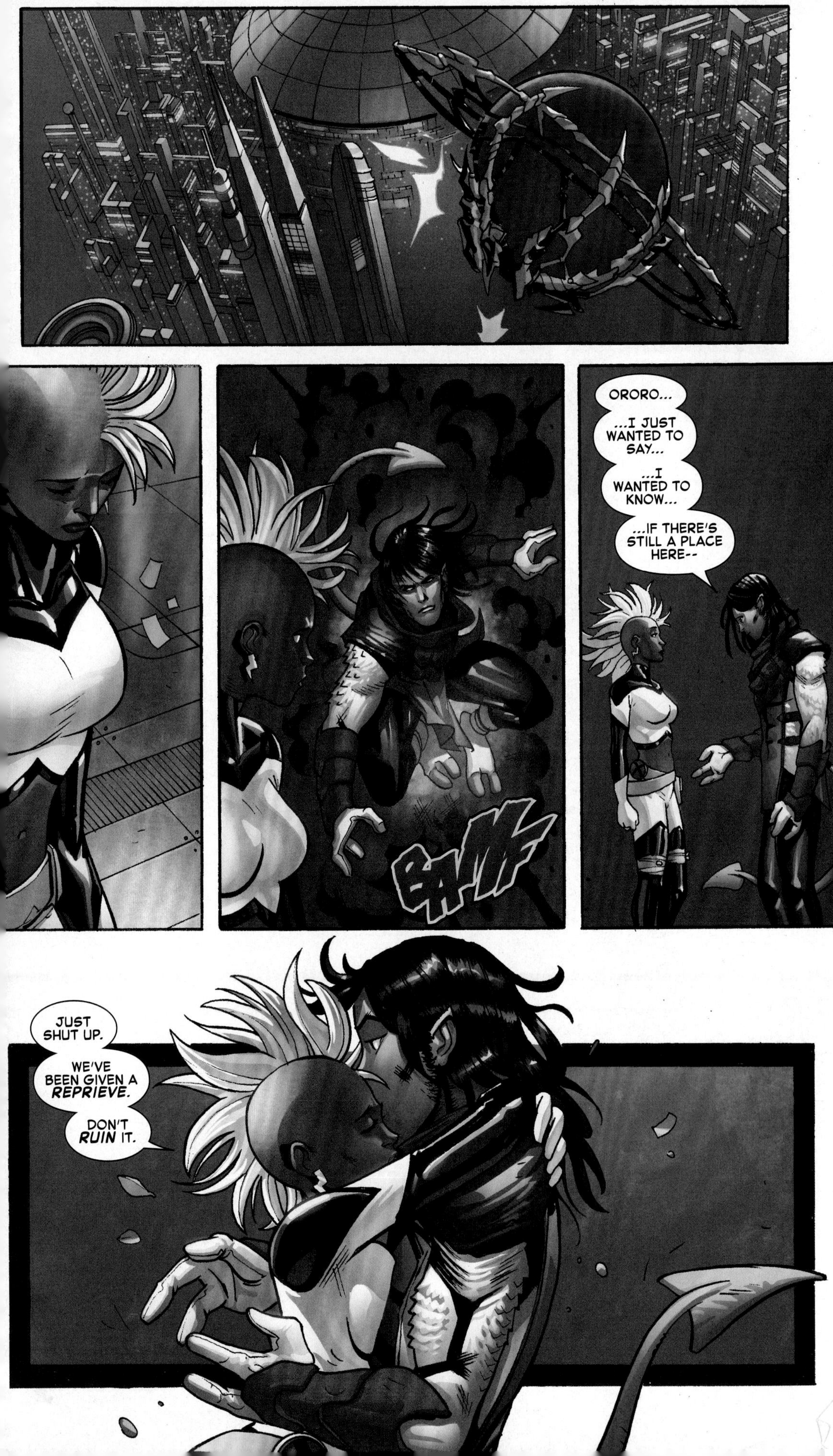
BAMF
ORORO...
...I JUST WANTED TO SAY...
...I WANTED TO KNOW...
...IF THERE'S STILL A PLACE HERE--
JUST SHUT UP.
WE'VE BEEN GIVEN A *REPRIEVE*.
DON'T *RUIN* IT.

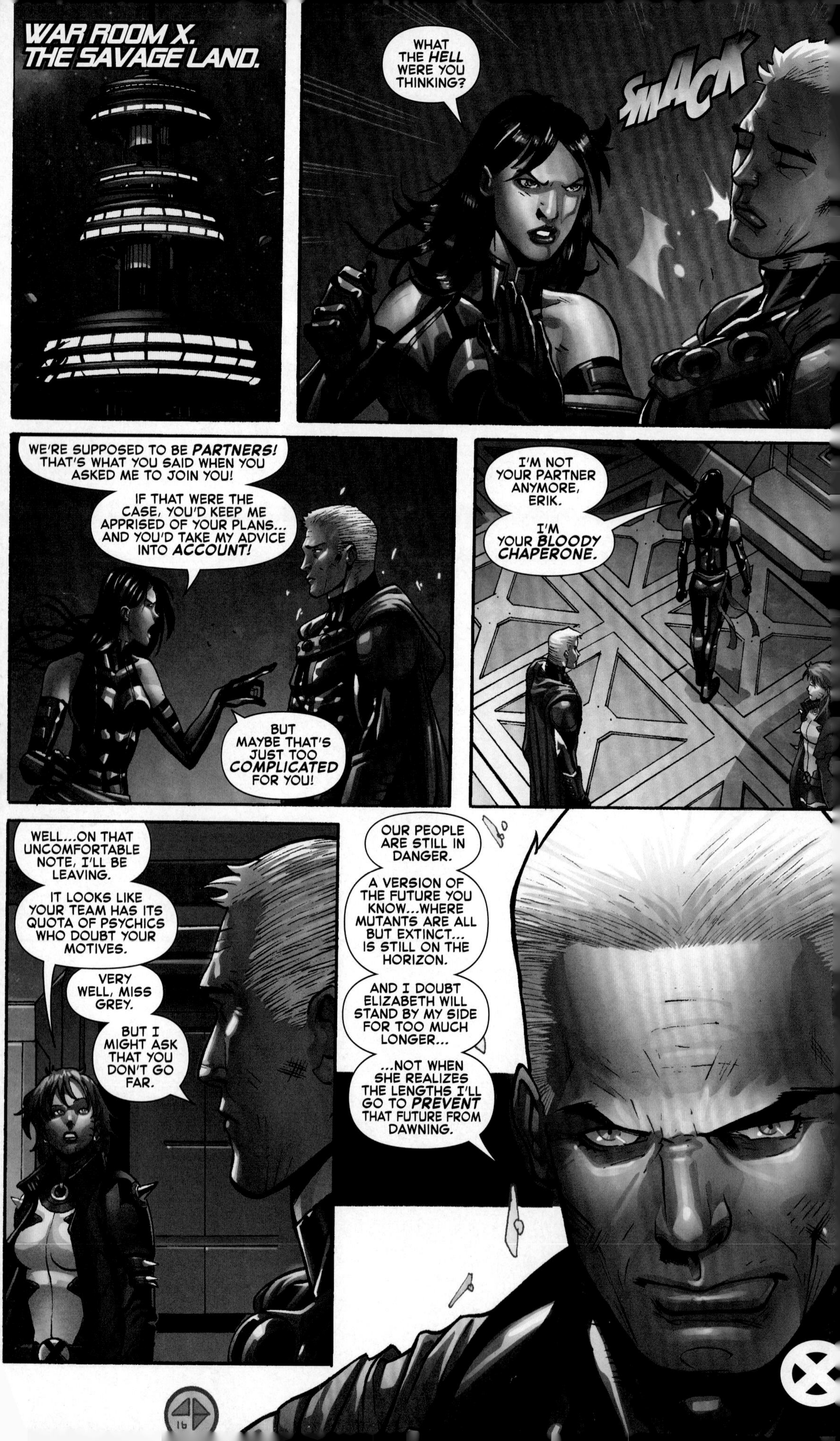

WAR ROOM X. THE SAVAGE LAND.
WHAT THE HELL WERE YOU THINKING?
SMACK
WE'RE SUPPOSED TO BE PARTNERS! THAT'S WHAT YOU SAID WHEN YOU ASKED ME TO JOIN YOU!
IF THAT WERE THE CASE, YOU'D KEEP ME APPRISED OF YOUR PLANS... AND YOU'D TAKE MY ADVICE INTO ACCOUNT!
BUT MAYBE THAT'S JUST TOO COMPLICATED FOR YOU!
I'M NOT YOUR PARTNER ANYMORE, ERIK.
I'M YOUR BLOODY CHAPERONE.
WELL...ON THAT UNCOMFORTABLE NOTE, I'LL BE LEAVING.
IT LOOKS LIKE YOUR TEAM HAS ITS QUOTA OF PSYCHICS WHO DOUBT YOUR MOTIVES.
VERY WELL, MISS GREY.
BUT I MIGHT ASK THAT YOU DON'T GO FAR.
OUR PEOPLE ARE STILL IN DANGER.
A VERSION OF THE FUTURE YOU KNOW...WHERE MUTANTS ARE ALL BUT EXTINCT... IS STILL ON THE HORIZON.
AND I DOUBT ELIZABETH WILL STAND BY MY SIDE FOR TOO MUCH LONGER...
...NOT WHEN SHE REALIZES THE LENGTHS I'LL GO TO PREVENT THAT FUTURE FROM DAWNING.

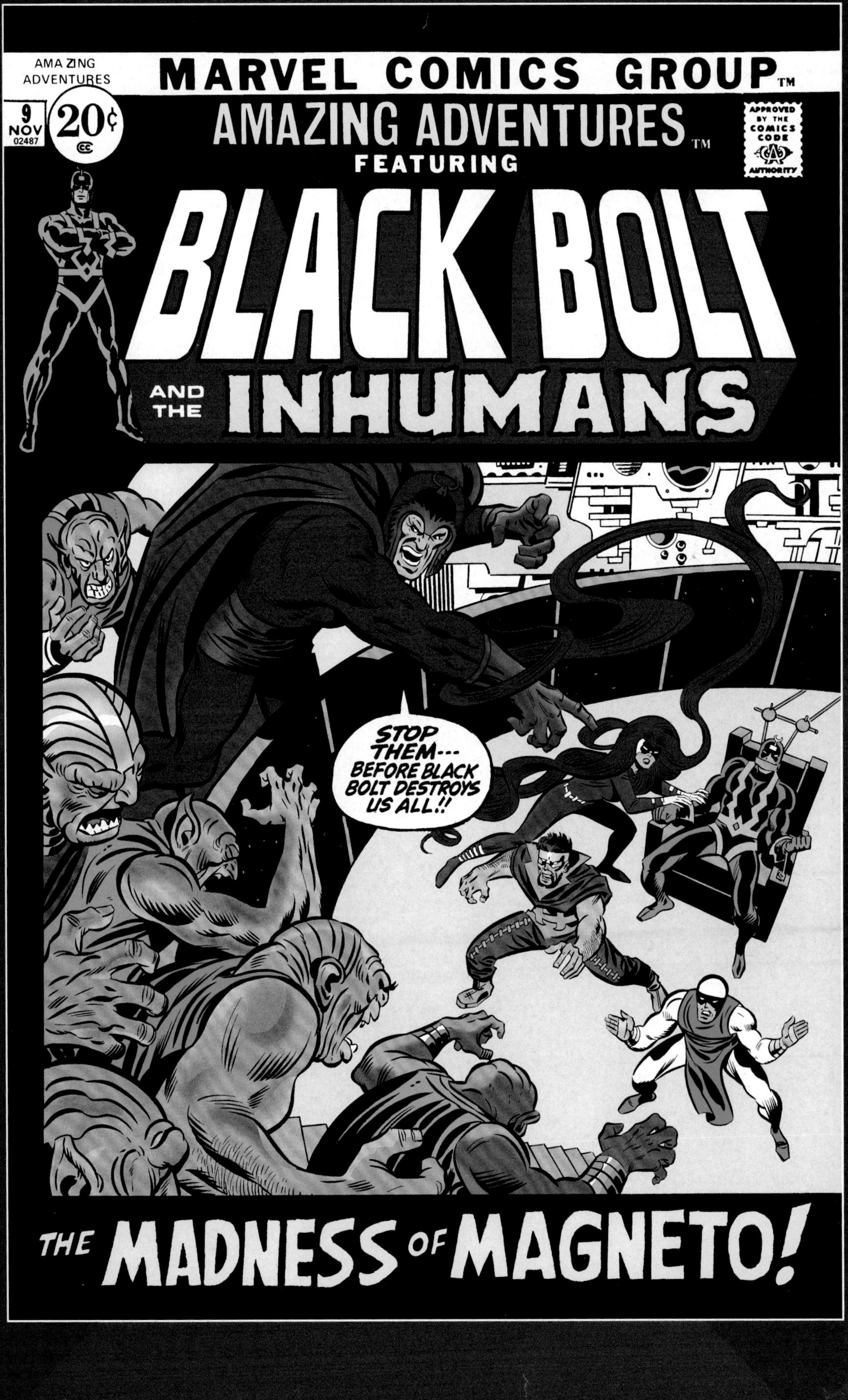
AMAZING ADVENTURES
MARVEL COMICS GROUP™
9 NOV 02487
20¢
AMAZING ADVENTURES™
FEATURING
APPROVED BY THE COMICS CODE AUTHORITY
BLACK BOLT
AND THE INHUMANS
STOP THEM--- BEFORE BLACK BOLT DESTROYS US ALL!!
THE MADNESS OF MAGNETO!

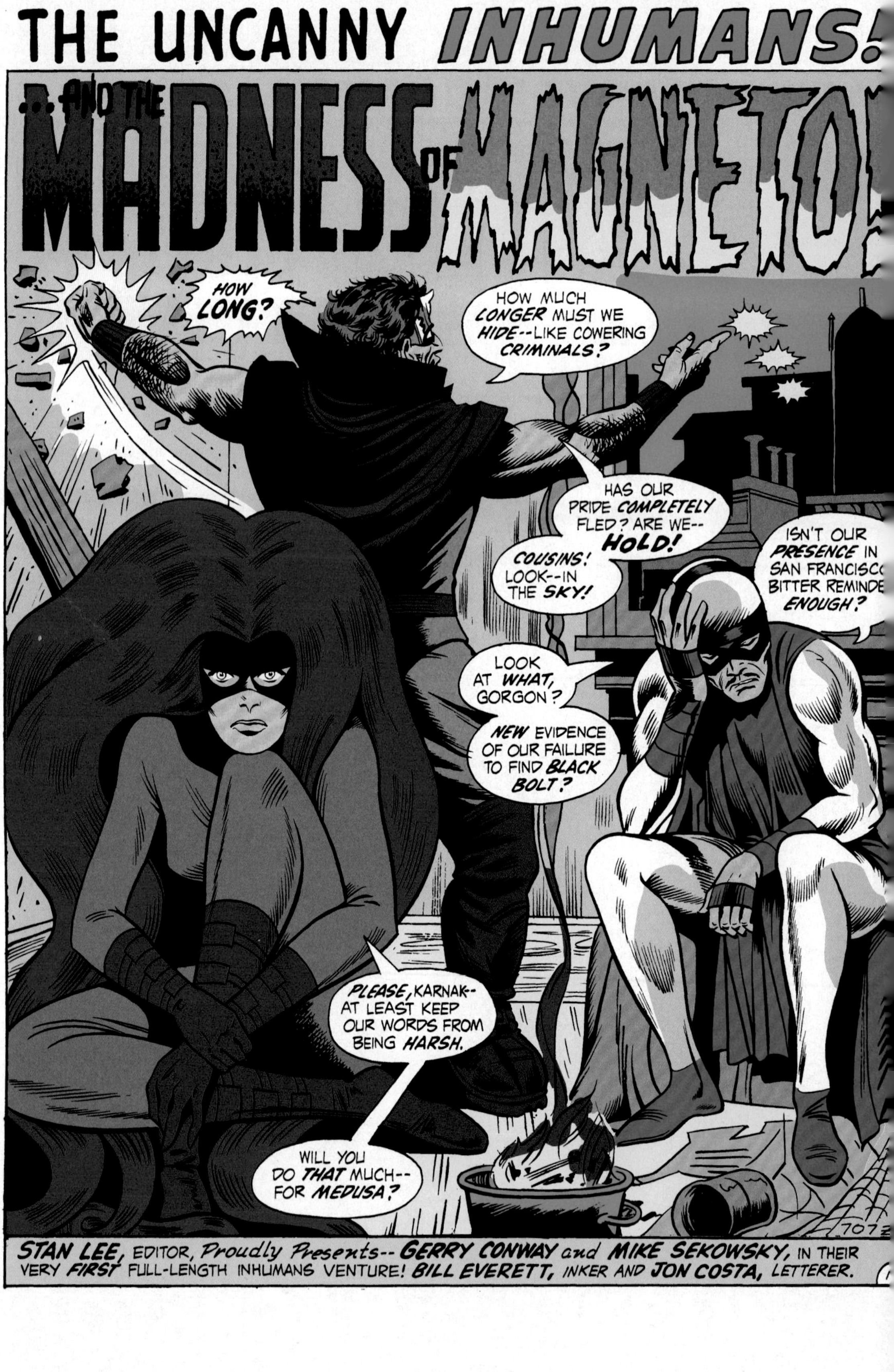
THE UNCANNY INHUMANS!
...AND THE MADNESS OF MAGNETO!
HOW LONG?
HOW MUCH LONGER MUST WE HIDE--LIKE COWERING CRIMINALS?
HAS OUR PRIDE COMPLETELY FLED? ARE WE-- HOLD!
COUSINS! LOOK--IN THE SKY!
ISN'T OUR PRESENCE IN SAN FRANCISC BITTER REMINDE ENOUGH?
LOOK AT WHAT, GORGON?
NEW EVIDENCE OF OUR FAILURE TO FIND BLACK BOLT?
PLEASE, KARNAK--AT LEAST KEEP OUR WORDS FROM BEING HARSH.
WILL YOU DO THAT MUCH--FOR MEDUSA?
STAN LEE, EDITOR, Proudly Presents-- GERRY CONWAY and MIKE SEKOWSKY, IN THEIR VERY FIRST FULL-LENGTH INHUMANS VENTURE! BILL EVERETT, INKER AND JON COSTA, LETTERER.

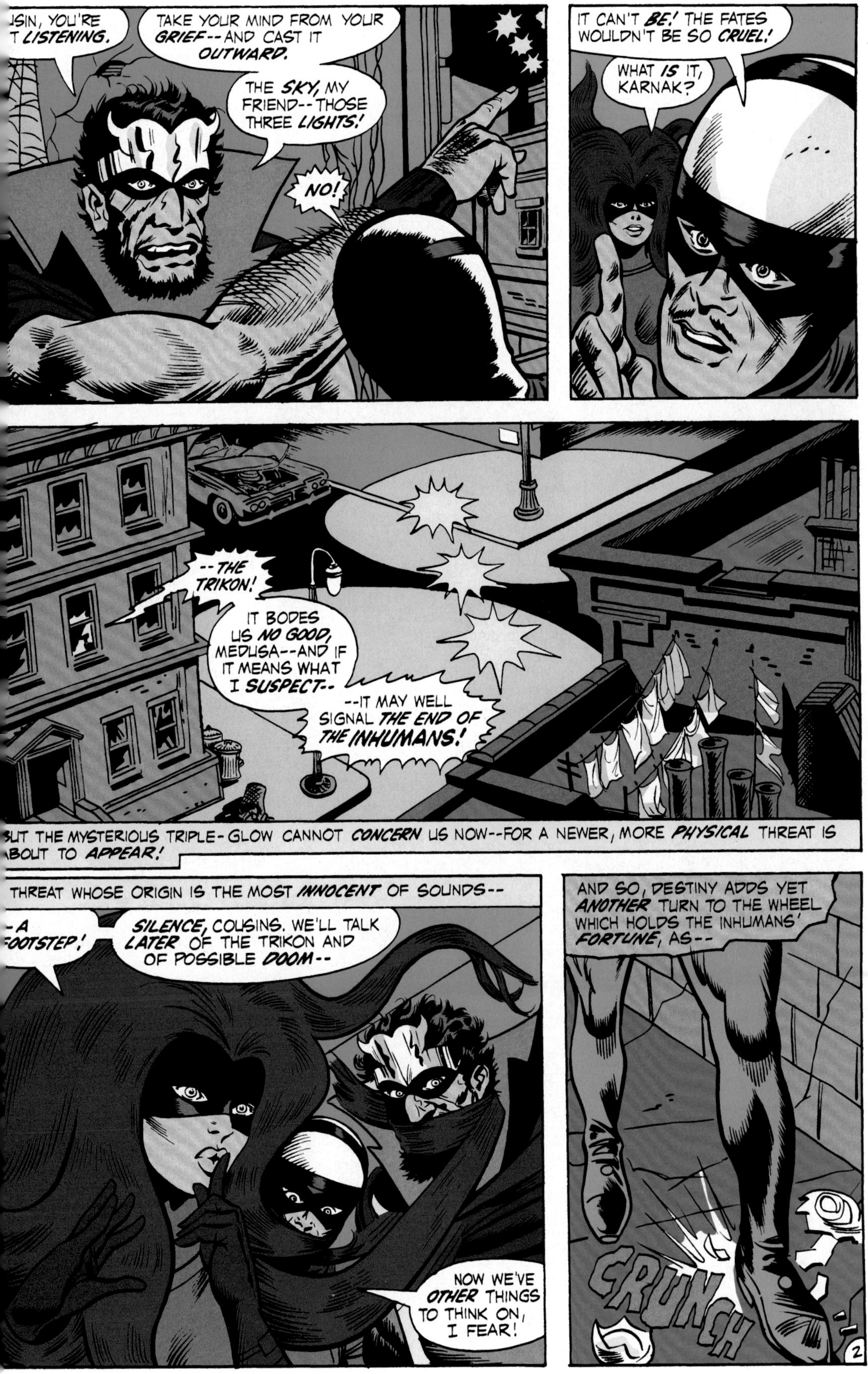

USIN, YOU'RE
T LISTENING.
TAKE YOUR MIND FROM YOUR GRIEF--AND CAST IT OUTWARD.
THE SKY, MY FRIEND--THOSE THREE LIGHTS!
NO!
IT CAN'T BE! THE FATES WOULDN'T BE SO CRUEL!
WHAT IS IT, KARNAK?
--THE TRIKON!
IT BODES US NO GOOD, MEDUSA--AND IF IT MEANS WHAT I SUSPECT--
--IT MAY WELL SIGNAL THE END OF THE INHUMANS!
BUT THE MYSTERIOUS TRIPLE-GLOW CANNOT CONCERN US NOW--FOR A NEWER, MORE PHYSICAL THREAT IS ABOUT TO APPEAR!
THREAT WHOSE ORIGIN IS THE MOST INNOCENT OF SOUNDS--
--A FOOTSTEP!
SILENCE, COUSINS. WE'LL TALK LATER OF THE TRIKON AND OF POSSIBLE DOOM--
NOW WE'VE OTHER THINGS TO THINK ON, I FEAR!
AND SO, DESTINY ADDS YET ANOTHER TURN TO THE WHEEL WHICH HOLDS THE INHUMANS' FORTUNE, AS--
CRUNCH
2

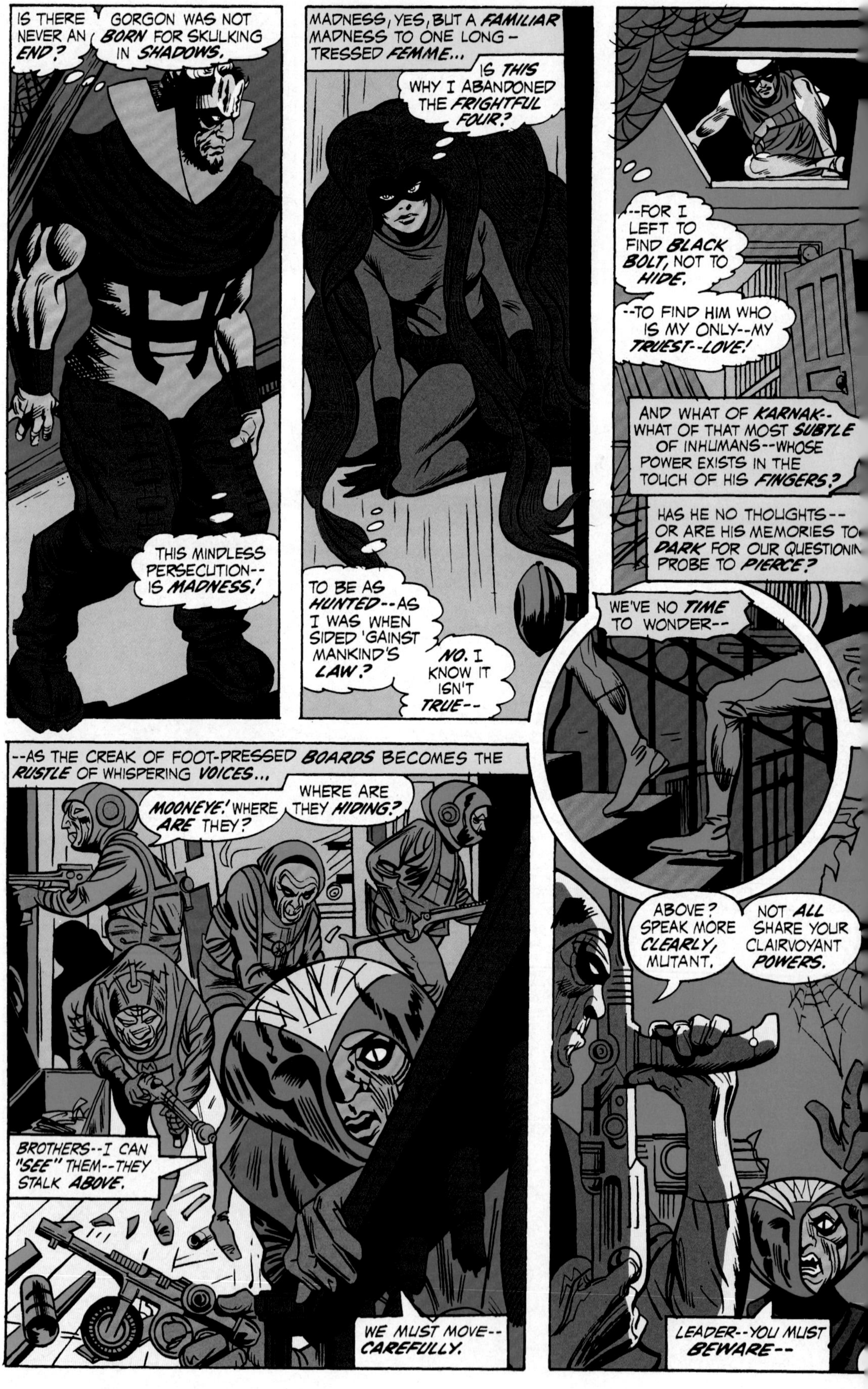
IS THERE NEVER AN END?
GORGON WAS NOT BORN FOR SKULKING IN SHADOWS.
THIS MINDLESS PERSECUTION--IS MADNESS!
MADNESS, YES, BUT A FAMILIAR MADNESS TO ONE LONG-TRESSED FEMME...
IS THIS WHY I ABANDONED THE FRIGHTFUL FOUR?
TO BE AS HUNTED--AS I WAS WHEN SIDED 'GAINST MANKIND'S LAW?
NO. I KNOW IT ISN'T TRUE--
--FOR I LEFT TO FIND BLACK BOLT, NOT TO HIDE.
--TO FIND HIM WHO IS MY ONLY--MY TRUEST--LOVE!
AND WHAT OF KARNAK--WHAT OF THAT MOST SUBTLE OF INHUMANS--WHOSE POWER EXISTS IN THE TOUCH OF HIS FINGERS?
HAS HE NO THOUGHTS--OR ARE HIS MEMORIES TO DARK FOR OUR QUESTIONIN PROBE TO PIERCE?
WE'VE NO TIME TO WONDER--
--AS THE CREAK OF FOOT-PRESSED BOARDS BECOMES THE RUSTLE OF WHISPERING VOICES...
MOONEYE! WHERE ARE THEY?
WHERE ARE THEY HIDING?
BROTHERS--I CAN "SEE" THEM--THEY STALK ABOVE.
WE MUST MOVE--CAREFULLY.
ABOVE? SPEAK MORE CLEARLY, MUTANT.
NOT ALL SHARE YOUR CLAIRVOYANT POWERS.
LEADER--YOU MUST BEWARE--

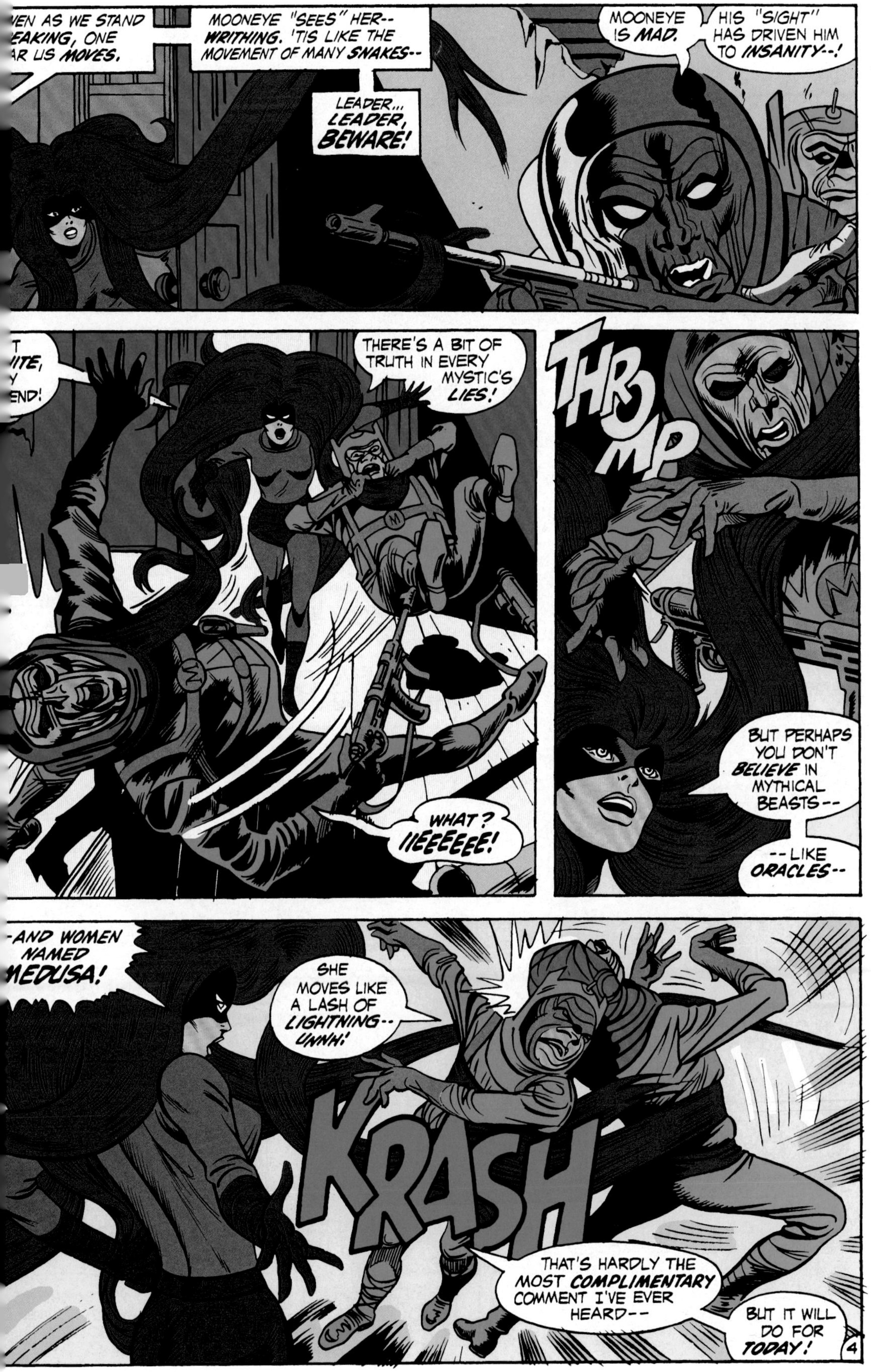
VEN AS WE STAND
EAKING, ONE
AR US MOVES.
MOONEYE "SEES" HER-- WRITHING. 'TIS LIKE THE MOVEMENT OF MANY SNAKES--
LEADER... LEADER, BEWARE!
MOONEYE IS MAD.
HIS "SIGHT" HAS DRIVEN HIM TO INSANITY--!
THERE'S A BIT OF TRUTH IN EVERY MYSTIC'S LIES!
WHAT? IIEEEEEE!
THBOMP
BUT PERHAPS YOU DON'T BELIEVE IN MYTHICAL BEASTS--
--LIKE ORACLES--
-AND WOMEN NAMED MEDUSA!
SHE MOVES LIKE A LASH OF LIGHTNING-- UNNH!
KRASH
THAT'S HARDLY THE MOST COMPLIMENTARY COMMENT I'VE EVER HEARD--
BUT IT WILL DO FOR TODAY!
4

DOWN *THIS* WAY.

PERHA— WE MA— SURROU— THAT--TH— AMAZO—

MEDUSA SEEKS A *DIVERSION*...

...THEN, IT'S GORGON'S PLACE... TO *DIVERT*!

I THINK *NOT*, SMALL ONE--

I DON'T KNOW *WHO* YOU ARE-- *WHAT* YOU ARE--

--NOT IF GORGON MAY *SPEAK*!

--BUT MAN OR *MUTANT*--

CHROOM

--YOU'LL FEEL THE *POWER*--OF GORGON'S *HOOF*!

THROD

LORDS--WHAT A *PITY*.

WILL *NONE* BE AWAKE--TO ANSWE— GORGON'S *QUESTIONS*?

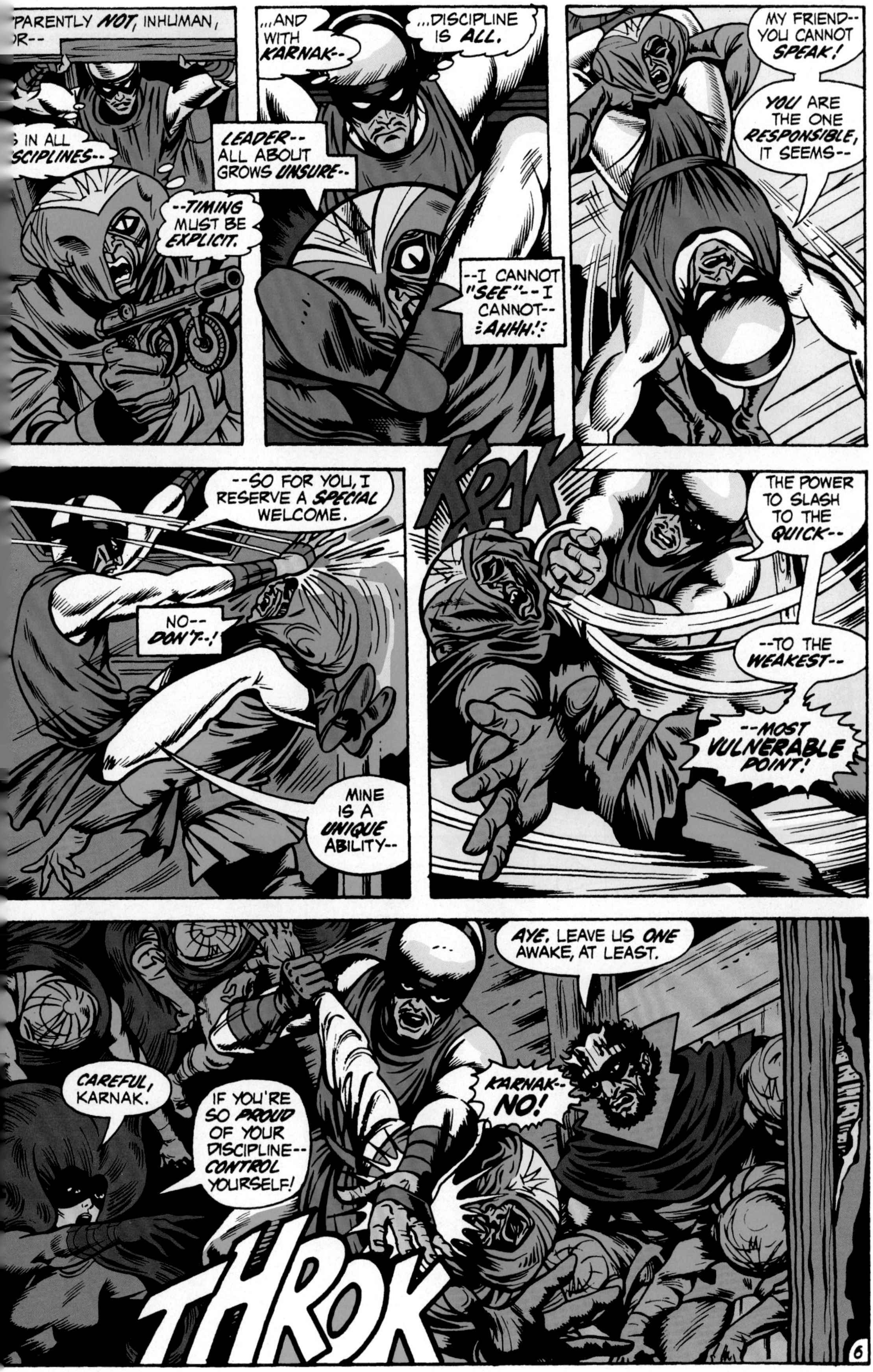

PARENTLY NOT, INHUMAN, OR--
S IN ALL SCIPLINES--
--TIMING MUST BE EXPLICIT.
...AND WITH KARNAK--
...DISCIPLINE IS ALL.
LEADER--ALL ABOUT GROWS UNSURE--
--I CANNOT "SEE"--I CANNOT-- AHHH!
MY FRIEND--YOU CANNOT SPEAK!
YOU ARE THE ONE RESPONSIBLE, IT SEEMS--
--SO FOR YOU, I RESERVE A SPECIAL WELCOME.
NO--DON'T--!
MINE IS A UNIQUE ABILITY--
KRAK
THE POWER TO SLASH TO THE QUICK--
--TO THE WEAKEST--
--MOST VULNERABLE POINT!
...
AYE, LEAVE US ONE AWAKE, AT LEAST.
CAREFUL, KARNAK.
IF YOU'RE SO PROUD OF YOUR DISCIPLINE--CONTROL YOURSELF!
KARNAK--NO!
THROK
6

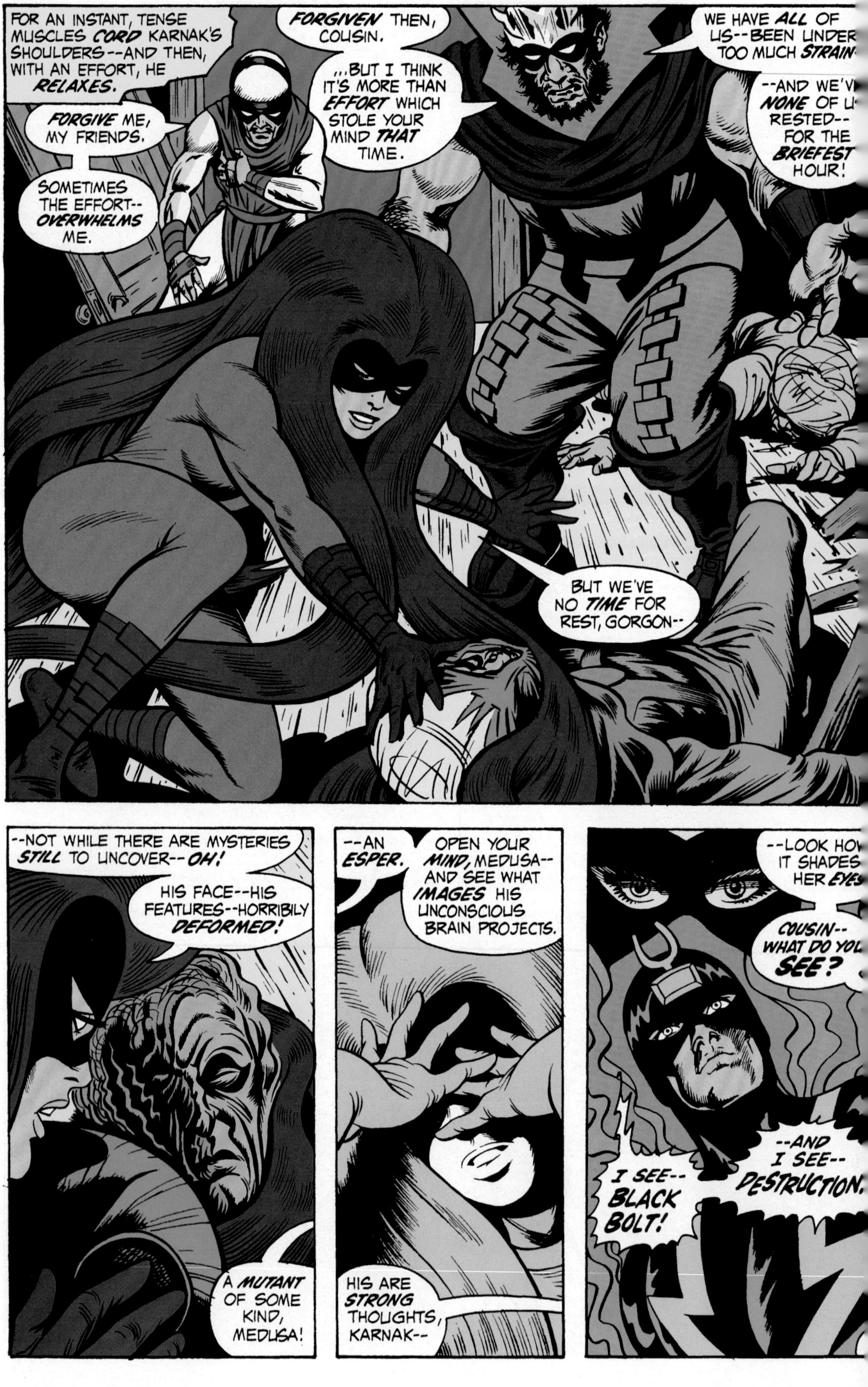
FOR AN INSTANT, TENSE MUSCLES CORD KARNAK'S SHOULDERS--AND THEN, WITH AN EFFORT, HE RELAXES.
FORGIVE ME, MY FRIENDS.
SOMETIMES THE EFFORT--OVERWHELMS ME.
FORGIVEN THEN, COUSIN.
...BUT I THINK IT'S MORE THAN EFFORT WHICH STOLE YOUR MIND THAT TIME.
WE HAVE ALL OF US--BEEN UNDER TOO MUCH STRAIN
--AND WE'VE NONE OF US RESTED--FOR THE BRIEFEST HOUR!
BUT WE'VE NO TIME FOR REST, GORGON--
--NOT WHILE THERE ARE MYSTERIES STILL TO UNCOVER--OH!
HIS FACE--HIS FEATURES--HORRIBLY DEFORMED!
A MUTANT OF SOME KIND, MEDUSA!
--AN ESPER.
OPEN YOUR MIND, MEDUSA--AND SEE WHAT IMAGES HIS UNCONSCIOUS BRAIN PROJECTS.
HIS ARE STRONG THOUGHTS, KARNAK--
--LOOK HOW IT SHADES HER EYES
COUSIN--WHAT DO YOU SEE?
I SEE--BLACK BOLT!
--AND I SEE--DESTRUCTION!

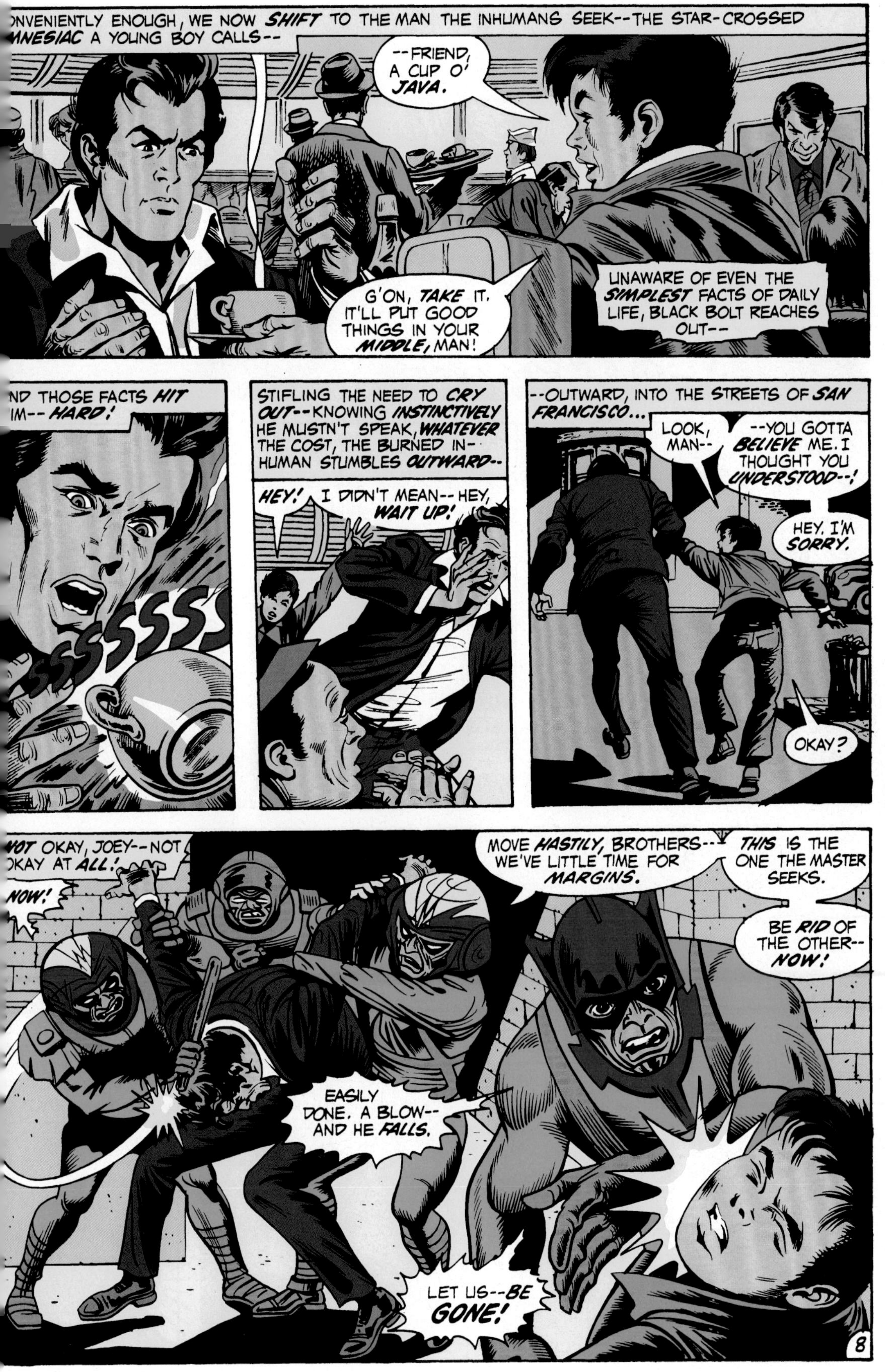
ONVENIENTLY ENOUGH, WE NOW SHIFT TO THE MAN THE INHUMANS SEEK--THE STAR-CROSSED MNESIAC A YOUNG BOY CALLS--
--FRIEND, A CUP O' JAVA.
G'ON, TAKE IT. IT'LL PUT GOOD THINGS IN YOUR MIDDLE, MAN!
UNAWARE OF EVEN THE SIMPLEST FACTS OF DAILY LIFE, BLACK BOLT REACHES OUT--
ND THOSE FACTS HIT IM-- HARD!
SSSSSSSSS
STIFLING THE NEED TO CRY OUT--KNOWING INSTINCTIVELY HE MUSTN'T SPEAK, WHATEVER THE COST, THE BURNED IN-HUMAN STUMBLES OUTWARD--
HEY! I DIDN'T MEAN--HEY, WAIT UP!
--OUTWARD, INTO THE STREETS OF SAN FRANCISCO...
LOOK, MAN--
--YOU GOTTA BELIEVE ME. I THOUGHT YOU UNDERSTOOD--!
HEY. I'M SORRY.
OKAY?
NOT OKAY, JOEY--NOT OKAY AT ALL!
NOW!
MOVE HASTILY, BROTHERS-- WE'VE LITTLE TIME FOR MARGINS.
THIS IS THE ONE THE MASTER SEEKS.
BE RID OF THE OTHER-- NOW!
EASILY DONE. A BLOW-- AND HE FALLS.
LET US--BE GONE!

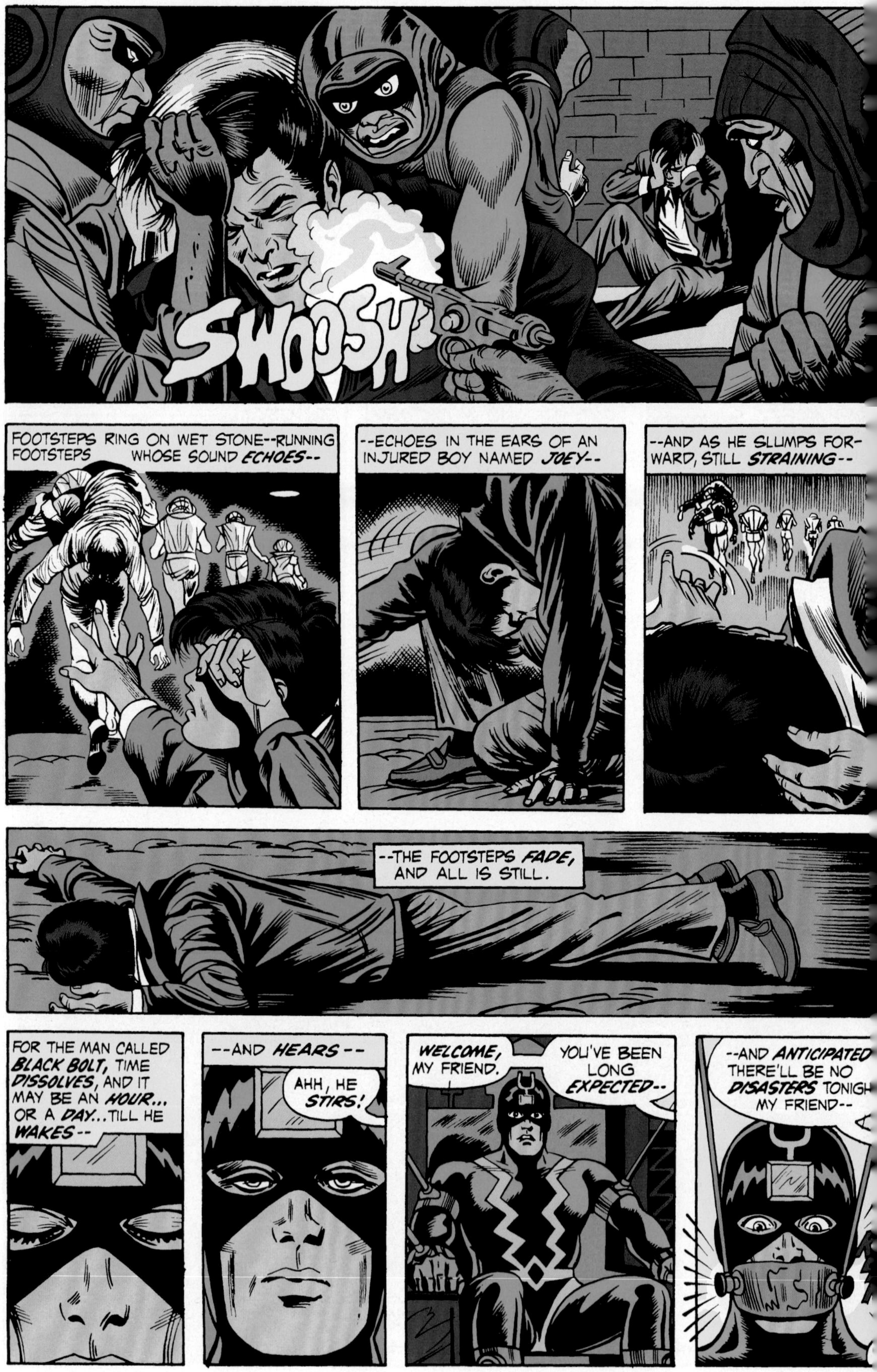
SWOOSH
FOOTSTEPS RING ON WET STONE--RUNNING FOOTSTEPS WHOSE SOUND ECHOES--
--ECHOES IN THE EARS OF AN INJURED BOY NAMED JOEY--
--AND AS HE SLUMPS FOR-WARD, STILL STRAINING--
--THE FOOTSTEPS FADE, AND ALL IS STILL.
FOR THE MAN CALLED BLACK BOLT, TIME DISSOLVES, AND IT MAY BE AN HOUR... OR A DAY...TILL HE WAKES--
--AND HEARS--
AHH, HE STIRS!
WELCOME, MY FRIEND.
YOU'VE BEEN LONG EXPECTED--
--AND ANTICIPATED
THERE'LL BE NO DISASTERS TONIGH
MY FRIEND--

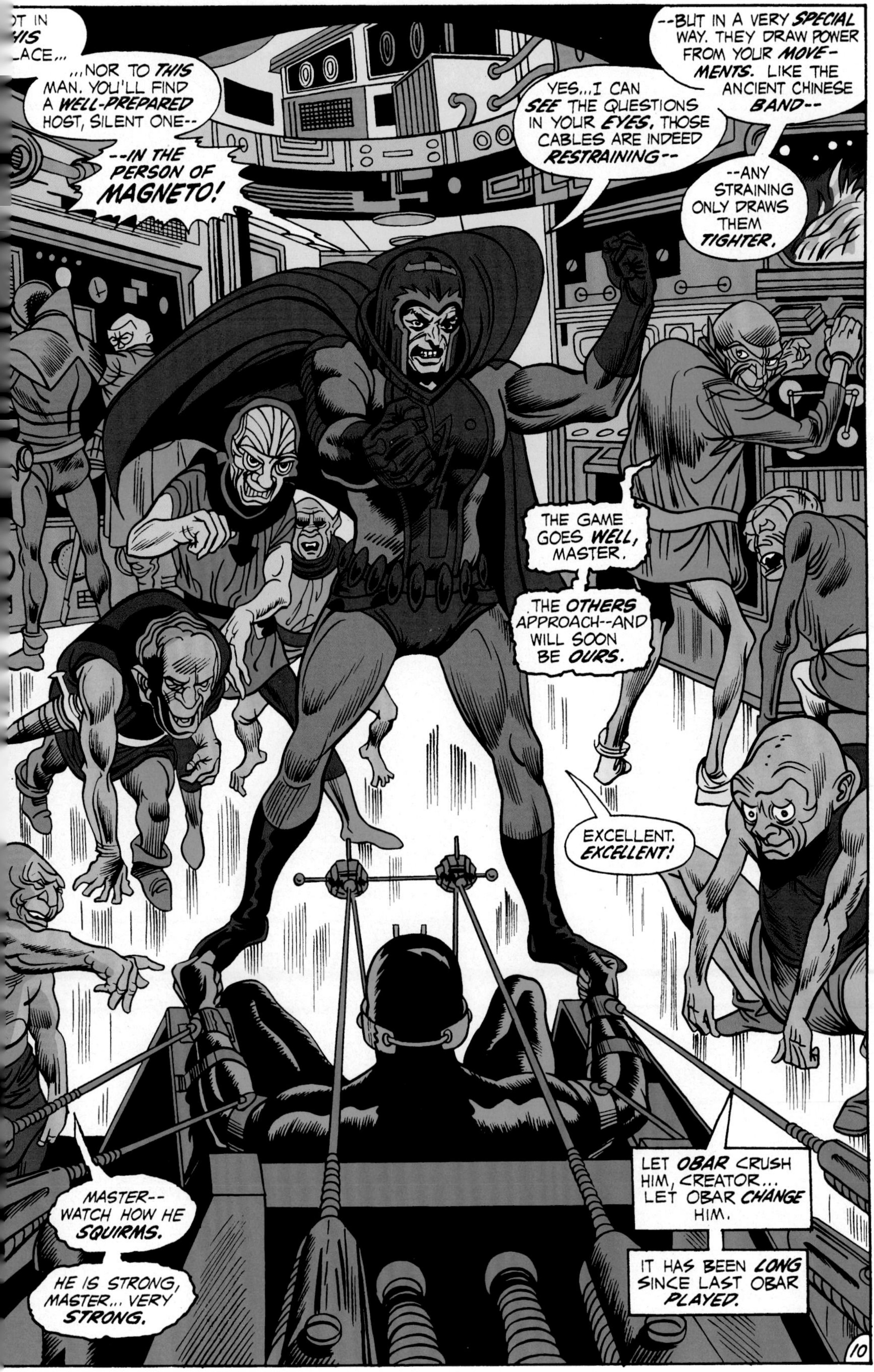

...NOR TO THIS MAN. YOU'LL FIND A WELL-PREPARED HOST, SILENT ONE--
--IN THE PERSON OF MAGNETO!
YES...I CAN SEE THE QUESTIONS IN YOUR EYES. THOSE CABLES ARE INDEED RESTRAINING--
--BUT IN A VERY SPECIAL WAY. THEY DRAW POWER FROM YOUR MOVE-MENTS. LIKE THE ANCIENT CHINESE BAND--
--ANY STRAINING ONLY DRAWS THEM TIGHTER.
THE GAME GOES WELL, MASTER.
THE OTHERS APPROACH--AND WILL SOON BE OURS.
EXCELLENT. EXCELLENT!
MASTER-- WATCH HOW HE SQUIRMS.
HE IS STRONG, MASTER... VERY STRONG.
LET OBAR CRUSH HIM, CREATOR... LET OBAR CHANGE HIM.
IT HAS BEEN LONG SINCE LAST OBAR PLAYED.
10

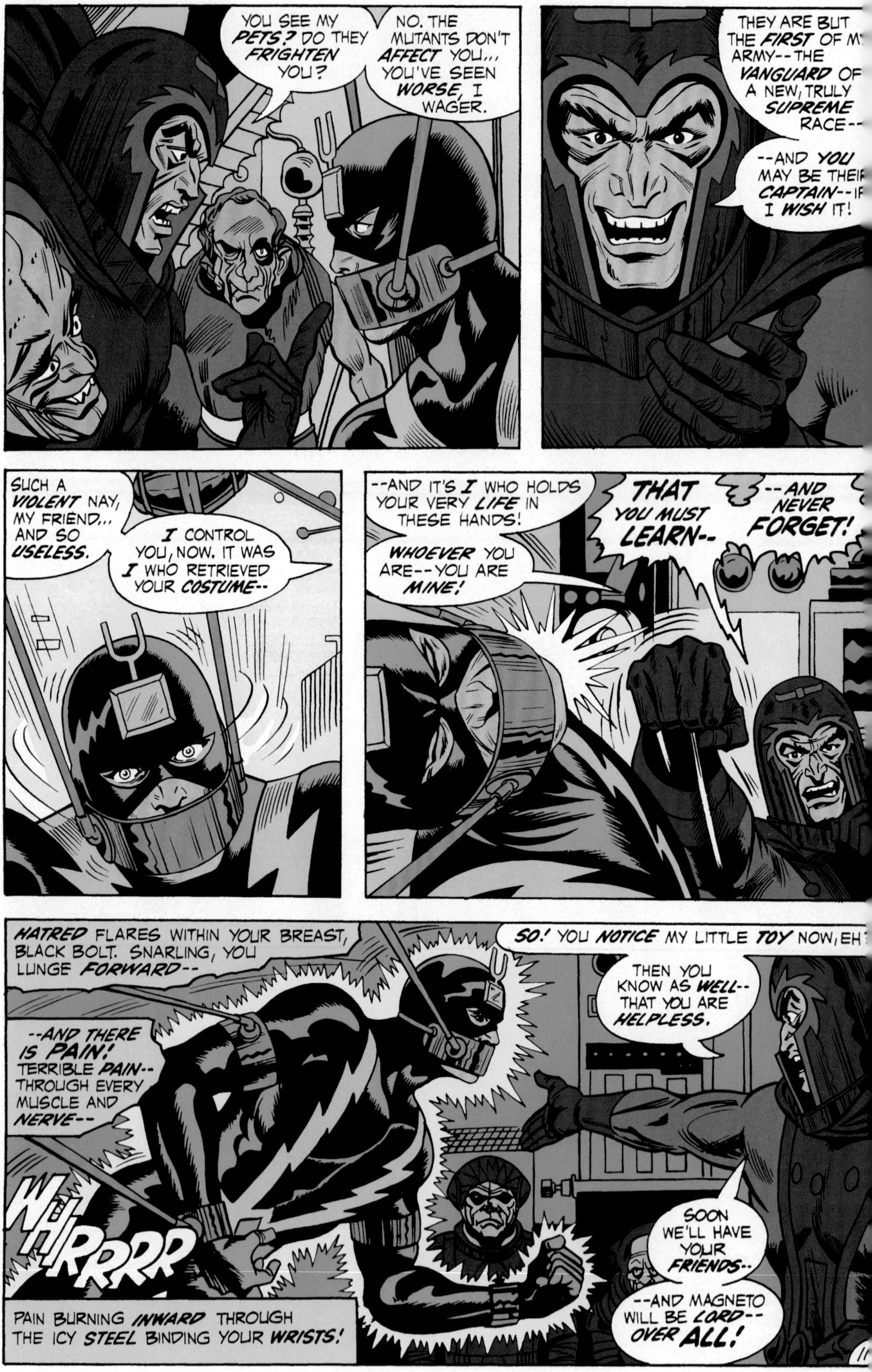
YOU SEE MY PETS? DO THEY FRIGHTEN YOU?
NO. THE MUTANTS DON'T AFFECT YOU... YOU'VE SEEN WORSE, I WAGER.
THEY ARE BUT THE FIRST OF MY ARMY--THE VANGUARD OF A NEW, TRULY SUPREME RACE--
--AND YOU MAY BE THEIR CAPTAIN--IF I WISH IT!
SUCH A VIOLENT NAY, MY FRIEND... AND SO USELESS.
I CONTROL YOU, NOW. IT WAS I WHO RETRIEVED YOUR COSTUME--
--AND IT'S I WHO HOLDS YOUR VERY LIFE IN THESE HANDS!
WHOEVER YOU ARE--YOU ARE MINE!
THAT YOU MUST LEARN--
--AND NEVER FORGET!
HATRED FLARES WITHIN YOUR BREAST, BLACK BOLT. SNARLING, YOU LUNGE FORWARD--
SO! YOU NOTICE MY LITTLE TOY NOW, EH?
THEN YOU KNOW AS WELL--THAT YOU ARE HELPLESS.
--AND THERE IS PAIN! TERRIBLE PAIN--THROUGH EVERY MUSCLE AND NERVE--
WHIRRRR
SOON WE'LL HAVE YOUR FRIENDS--
--AND MAGNETO WILL BE LORD--OVER ALL!
PAIN BURNING INWARD THROUGH THE ICY STEEL BINDING YOUR WRISTS!
11

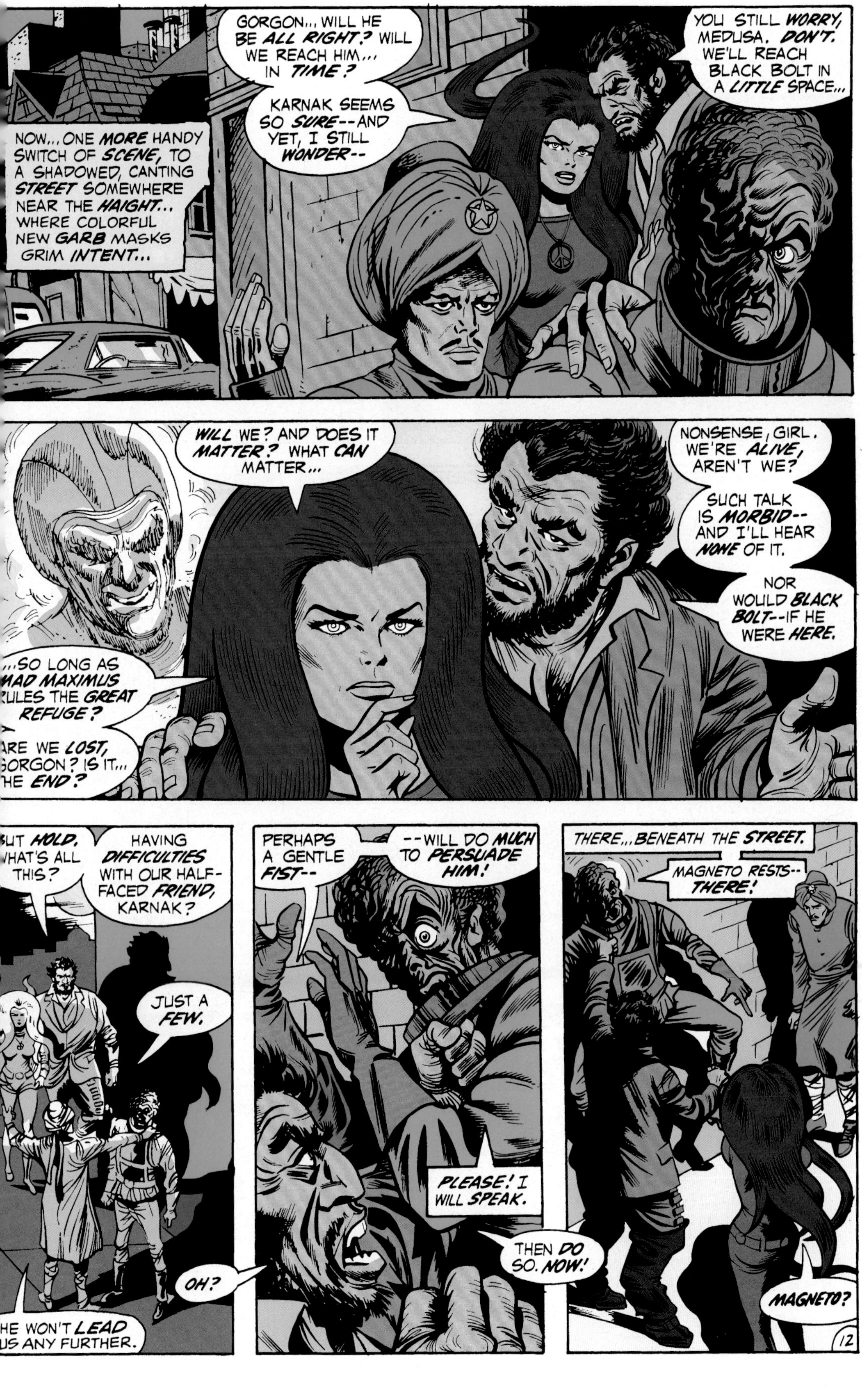
NOW... ONE MORE HANDY SWITCH OF SCENE, TO A SHADOWED, CANTING STREET SOMEWHERE NEAR THE HAIGHT... WHERE COLORFUL NEW GARB MASKS GRIM INTENT...
GORGON... WILL HE BE ALL RIGHT? WILL WE REACH HIM... IN TIME?
KARNAK SEEMS SO SURE--AND YET, I STILL WONDER--
YOU STILL WORRY, MEDUSA. DON'T. WE'LL REACH BLACK BOLT IN A LITTLE SPACE...
WILL WE? AND DOES IT MATTER? WHAT CAN MATTER...
...SO LONG AS MAD MAXIMUS RULES THE GREAT REFUGE?
ARE WE LOST, GORGON? IS IT... HE END?
NONSENSE, GIRL. WE'RE ALIVE, AREN'T WE?
SUCH TALK IS MORBID--AND I'LL HEAR NONE OF IT.
NOR WOULD BLACK BOLT--IF HE WERE HERE.
UT HOLD, WHAT'S ALL THIS?
HAVING DIFFICULTIES WITH OUR HALF-FACED FRIEND, KARNAK?
JUST A FEW.
OH?
HE WON'T LEAD US ANY FURTHER.
PERHAPS A GENTLE FIST--
--WILL DO MUCH TO PERSUADE HIM!
PLEASE! I WILL SPEAK.
THEN DO SO. NOW!
THERE... BENEATH THE STREET.
MAGNETO RESTS--THERE!
MAGNETO?

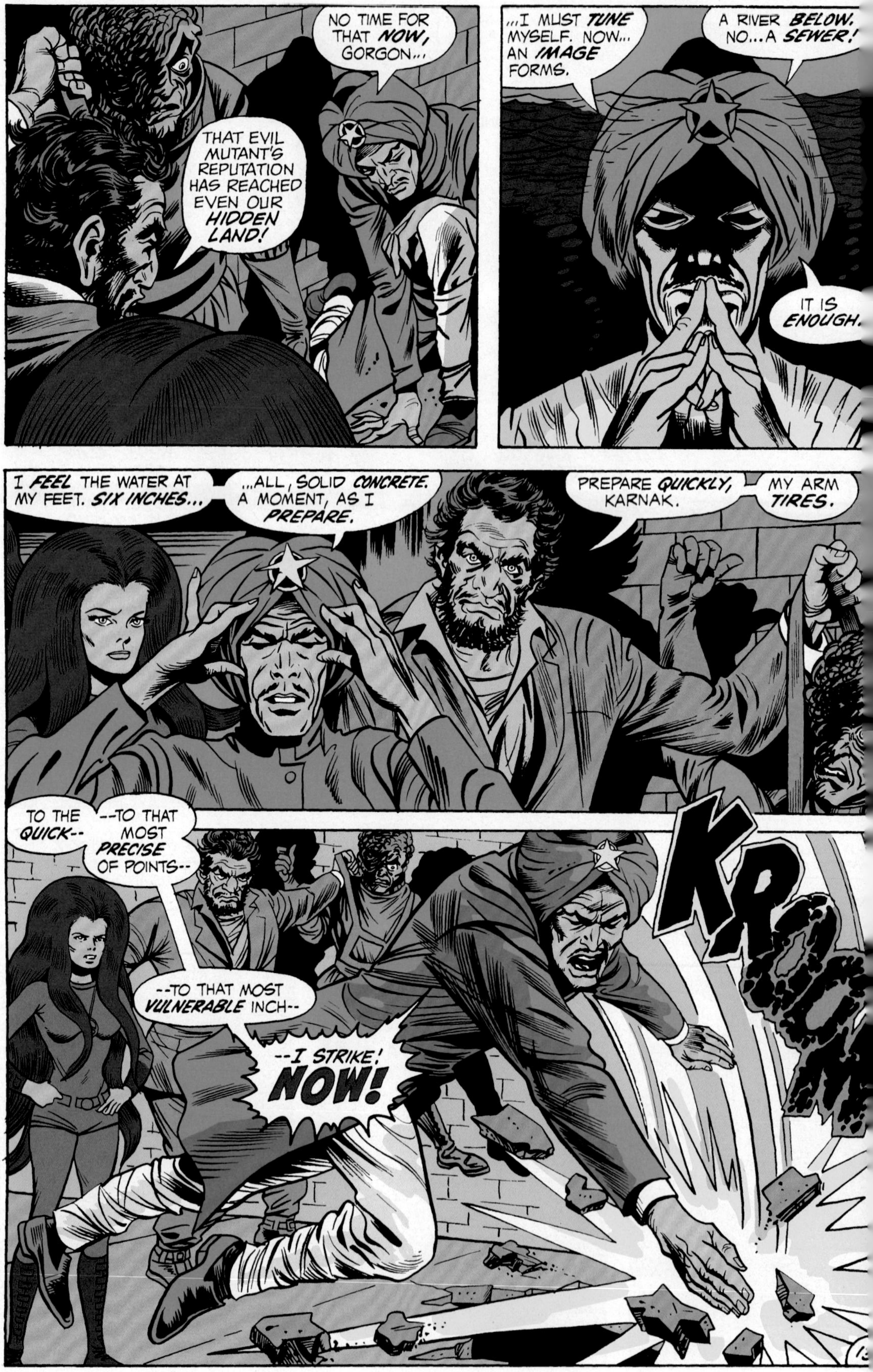
NO TIME FOR THAT NOW, GORGON...
THAT EVIL MUTANT'S REPUTATION HAS REACHED EVEN OUR HIDDEN LAND!
...I MUST TUNE MYSELF. NOW... AN IMAGE FORMS.
A RIVER BELOW. NO...A SEWER!
IT IS ENOUGH.
I FEEL THE WATER AT MY FEET. SIX INCHES...
...ALL, SOLID CONCRETE. A MOMENT, AS I PREPARE.
PREPARE QUICKLY, KARNAK.
MY ARM TIRES.
TO THE QUICK--
--TO THAT MOST PRECISE OF POINTS--
--TO THAT MOST VULNERABLE INCH--
--I STRIKE! NOW!
13

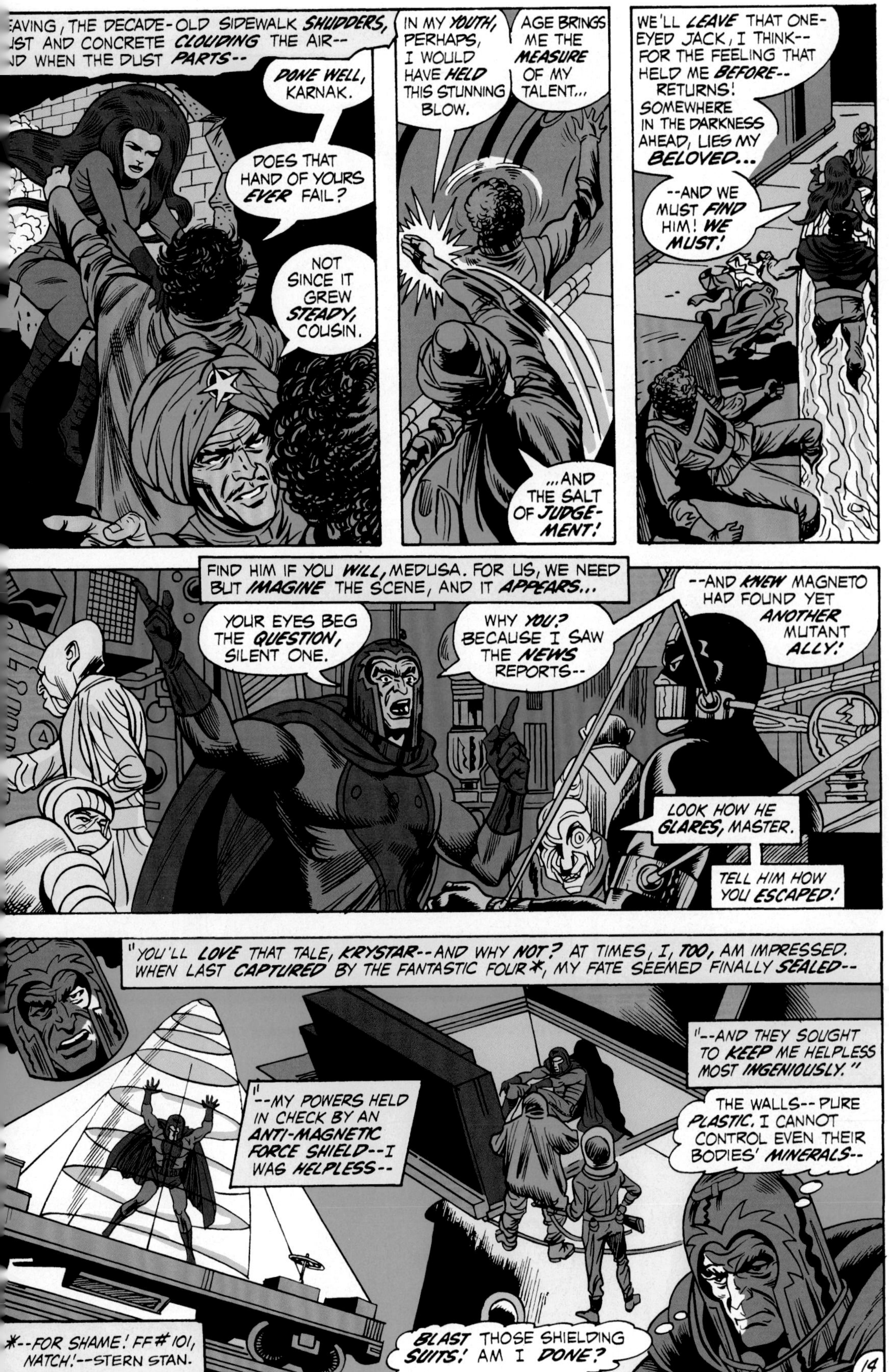

EAVING, THE DECADE-OLD SIDEWALK SHUDDERS, UST AND CONCRETE CLOUDING THE AIR-- ND WHEN THE DUST PARTS--
DONE WELL, KARNAK.
DOES THAT HAND OF YOURS EVER FAIL?
NOT SINCE IT GREW STEADY, COUSIN.
IN MY YOUTH, PERHAPS, I WOULD HAVE HELD THIS STUNNING BLOW.
AGE BRINGS ME THE MEASURE OF MY TALENT...
...AND THE SALT OF JUDGEMENT!
WE'LL LEAVE THAT ONE-EYED JACK, I THINK-- FOR THE FEELING THAT HELD ME BEFORE-- RETURNS! SOMEWHERE IN THE DARKNESS AHEAD, LIES MY BELOVED...
--AND WE MUST FIND HIM! WE MUST!
FIND HIM IF YOU WILL, MEDUSA. FOR US, WE NEED BUT IMAGINE THE SCENE, AND IT APPEARS...
YOUR EYES BEG THE QUESTION, SILENT ONE.
WHY YOU? BECAUSE I SAW THE NEWS REPORTS--
--AND KNEW MAGNETO HAD FOUND YET ANOTHER MUTANT ALLY!
LOOK HOW HE GLARES, MASTER.
TELL HIM HOW YOU ESCAPED!
"YOU'LL LOVE THAT TALE, KRYSTAR--AND WHY NOT? AT TIMES, I, TOO, AM IMPRESSED. WHEN LAST CAPTURED BY THE FANTASTIC FOUR*, MY FATE SEEMED FINALLY SEALED--
"--MY POWERS HELD IN CHECK BY AN ANTI-MAGNETIC FORCE SHIELD--I WAS HELPLESS--
"--AND THEY SOUGHT TO KEEP ME HELPLESS MOST INGENIOUSLY."
THE WALLS--PURE PLASTIC. I CANNOT CONTROL EVEN THEIR BODIES' MINERALS--
BLAST THOSE SHIELDING SUITS! AM I DONE?
*--FOR SHAME! FF #101, NATCH!--STERN STAN.
14

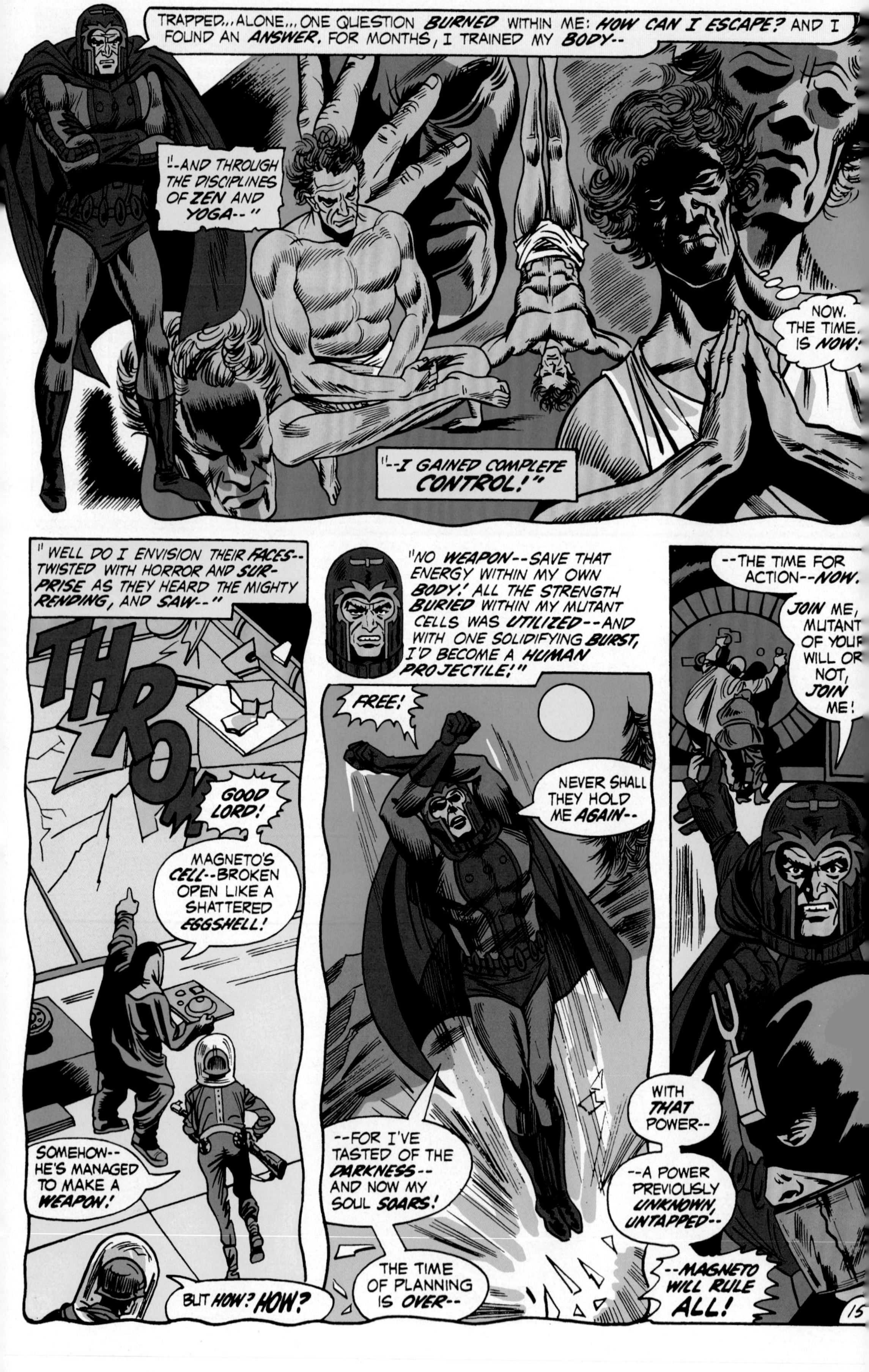
TRAPPED... ALONE... ONE QUESTION BURNED WITHIN ME: HOW CAN I ESCAPE? AND I FOUND AN ANSWER. FOR MONTHS, I TRAINED MY BODY--
"--AND THROUGH THE DISCIPLINES OF ZEN AND YOGA--"
"--I GAINED COMPLETE CONTROL!"
NOW. THE TIME. IS NOW!
"WELL DO I ENVISION THEIR FACES--TWISTED WITH HORROR AND SURPRISE AS THEY HEARD THE MIGHTY RENDING, AND SAW--"
THROOM
GOOD LORD!
MAGNETO'S CELL--BROKEN OPEN LIKE A SHATTERED EGGSHELL!
SOMEHOW--HE'S MANAGED TO MAKE A WEAPON!
BUT HOW? HOW?
"NO WEAPON--SAVE THAT ENERGY WITHIN MY OWN BODY! ALL THE STRENGTH BURIED WITHIN MY MUTANT CELLS WAS UTILIZED--AND WITH ONE SOLIDIFYING BURST, I'D BECOME A HUMAN PROJECTILE!"
FREE!
NEVER SHALL THEY HOLD ME AGAIN--
--FOR I'VE TASTED OF THE DARKNESS--AND NOW MY SOUL SOARS!
THE TIME OF PLANNING IS OVER--
--THE TIME FOR ACTION--NOW.
JOIN ME, MUTANT OF YOUR WILL OR NOT, JOIN ME!
WITH THAT POWER--
--A POWER PREVIOUSLY UNKNOWN, UNTAPPED--
--MAGNETO WILL RULE ALL!

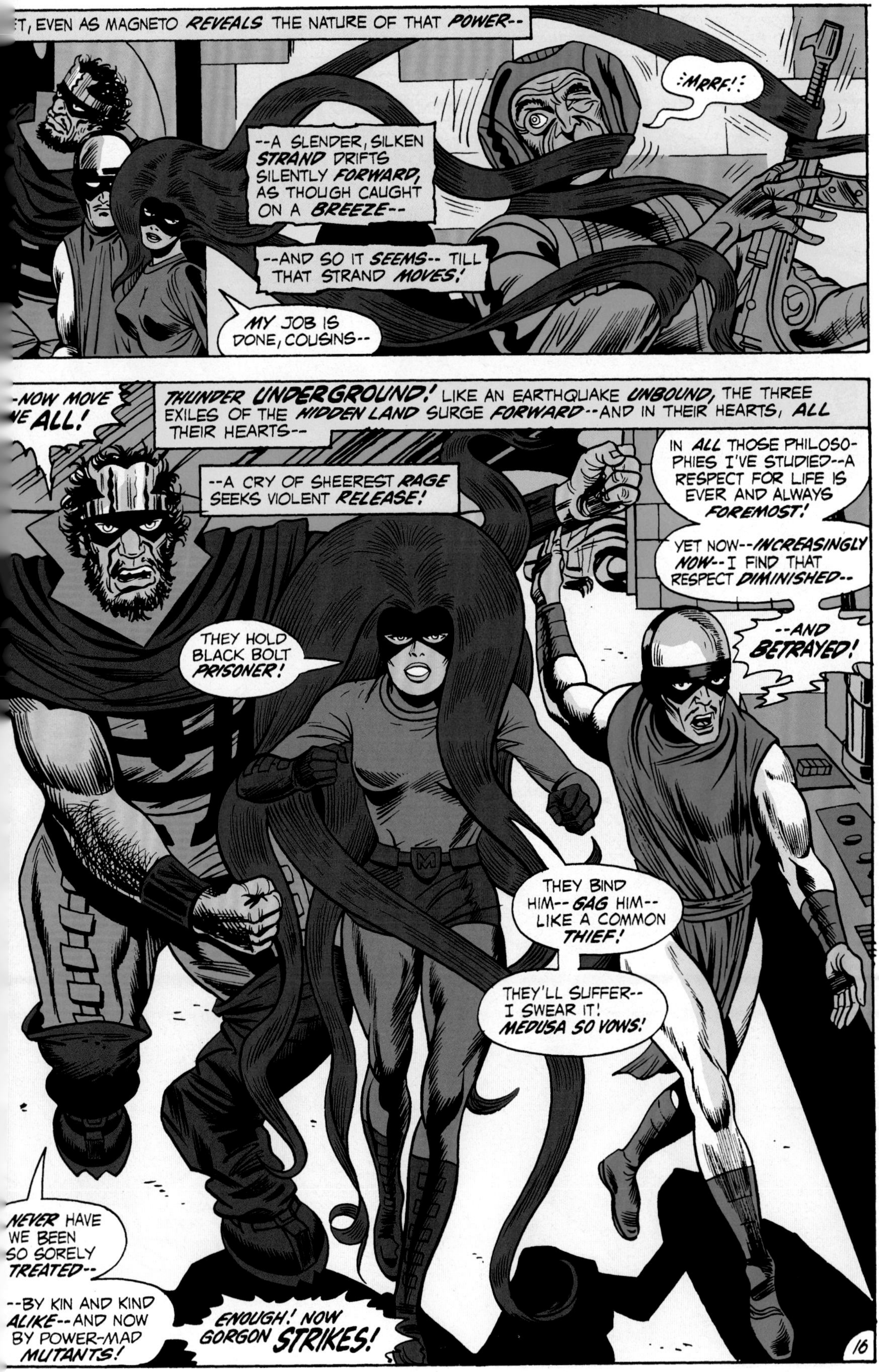

T, EVEN AS MAGNETO REVEALS THE NATURE OF THAT POWER--
:MRRF!:
--A SLENDER, SILKEN STRAND DRIFTS SILENTLY FORWARD, AS THOUGH CAUGHT ON A BREEZE--
--AND SO IT SEEMS-- TILL THAT STRAND MOVES!
MY JOB IS DONE, COUSINS--
-NOW MOVE WE ALL!
THUNDER UNDERGROUND! LIKE AN EARTHQUAKE UNBOUND, THE THREE EXILES OF THE HIDDEN LAND SURGE FORWARD--AND IN THEIR HEARTS, ALL THEIR HEARTS--
--A CRY OF SHEEREST RAGE SEEKS VIOLENT RELEASE!
IN ALL THOSE PHILOSOPHIES I'VE STUDIED--A RESPECT FOR LIFE IS EVER AND ALWAYS FOREMOST!
YET NOW--INCREASINGLY NOW--I FIND THAT RESPECT DIMINISHED--
--AND BETRAYED!
THEY HOLD BLACK BOLT PRISONER!
THEY BIND HIM--GAG HIM--LIKE A COMMON THIEF!
THEY'LL SUFFER--I SWEAR IT! MEDUSA SO VOWS!
NEVER HAVE WE BEEN SO SORELY TREATED--
--BY KIN AND KIND ALIKE--AND NOW BY POWER-MAD MUTANTS!
ENOUGH! NOW GORGON STRIKES!
16

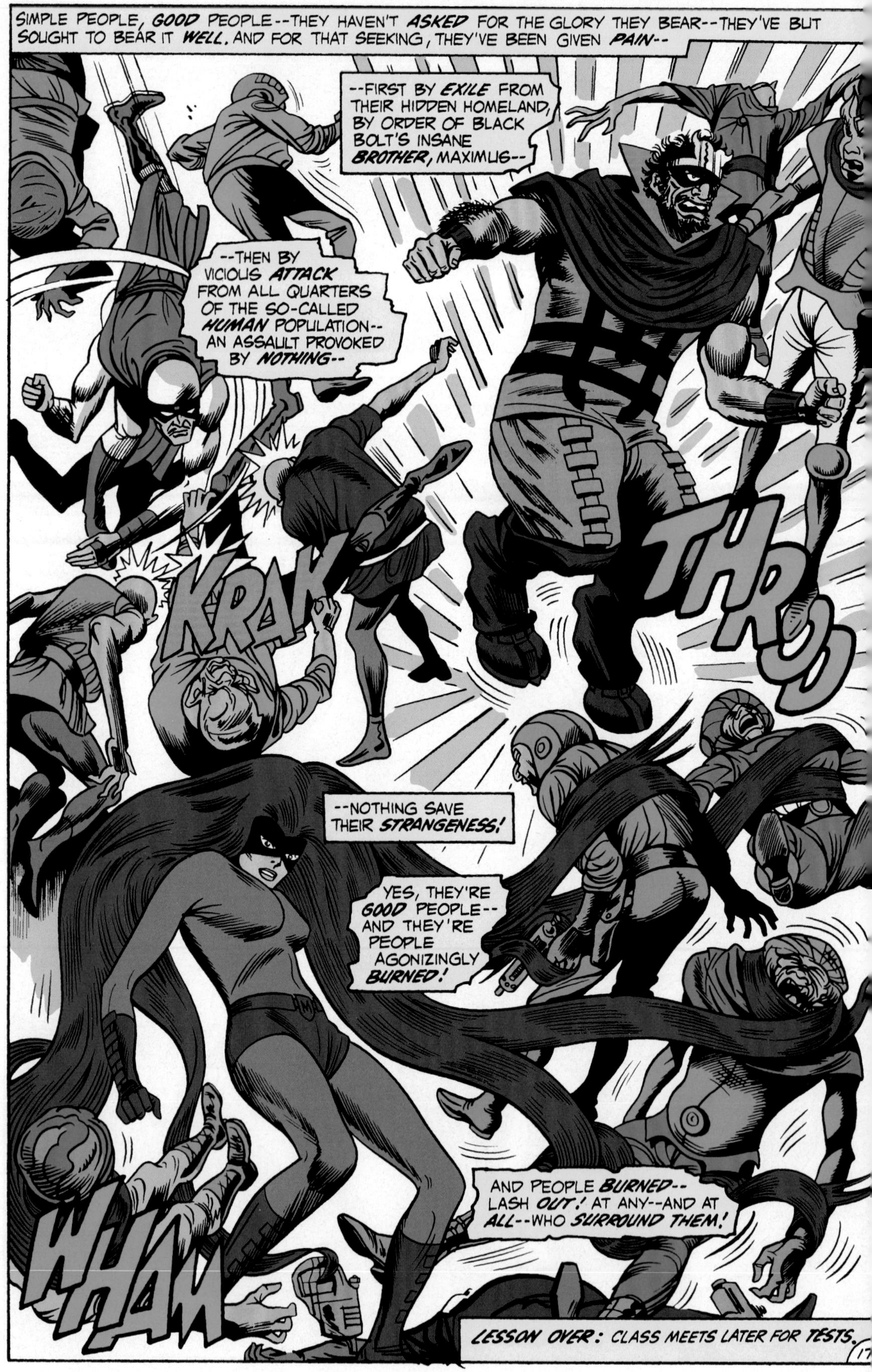
SIMPLE PEOPLE, GOOD PEOPLE--THEY HAVEN'T ASKED FOR THE GLORY THEY BEAR--THEY'VE BUT SOUGHT TO BEAR IT WELL. AND FOR THAT SEEKING, THEY'VE BEEN GIVEN PAIN--
--FIRST BY EXILE FROM THEIR HIDDEN HOMELAND, BY ORDER OF BLACK BOLT'S INSANE BROTHER, MAXIMUS--
--THEN BY VICIOUS ATTACK FROM ALL QUARTERS OF THE SO-CALLED HUMAN POPULATION-- AN ASSAULT PROVOKED BY NOTHING--
KRAK
THROD
--NOTHING SAVE THEIR STRANGENESS!
YES, THEY'RE GOOD PEOPLE-- AND THEY'RE PEOPLE AGONIZINGLY BURNED!
AND PEOPLE BURNED-- LASH OUT! AT ANY--AND AT ALL--WHO SURROUND THEM!
WHAM
LESSON OVER: CLASS MEETS LATER FOR TESTS.

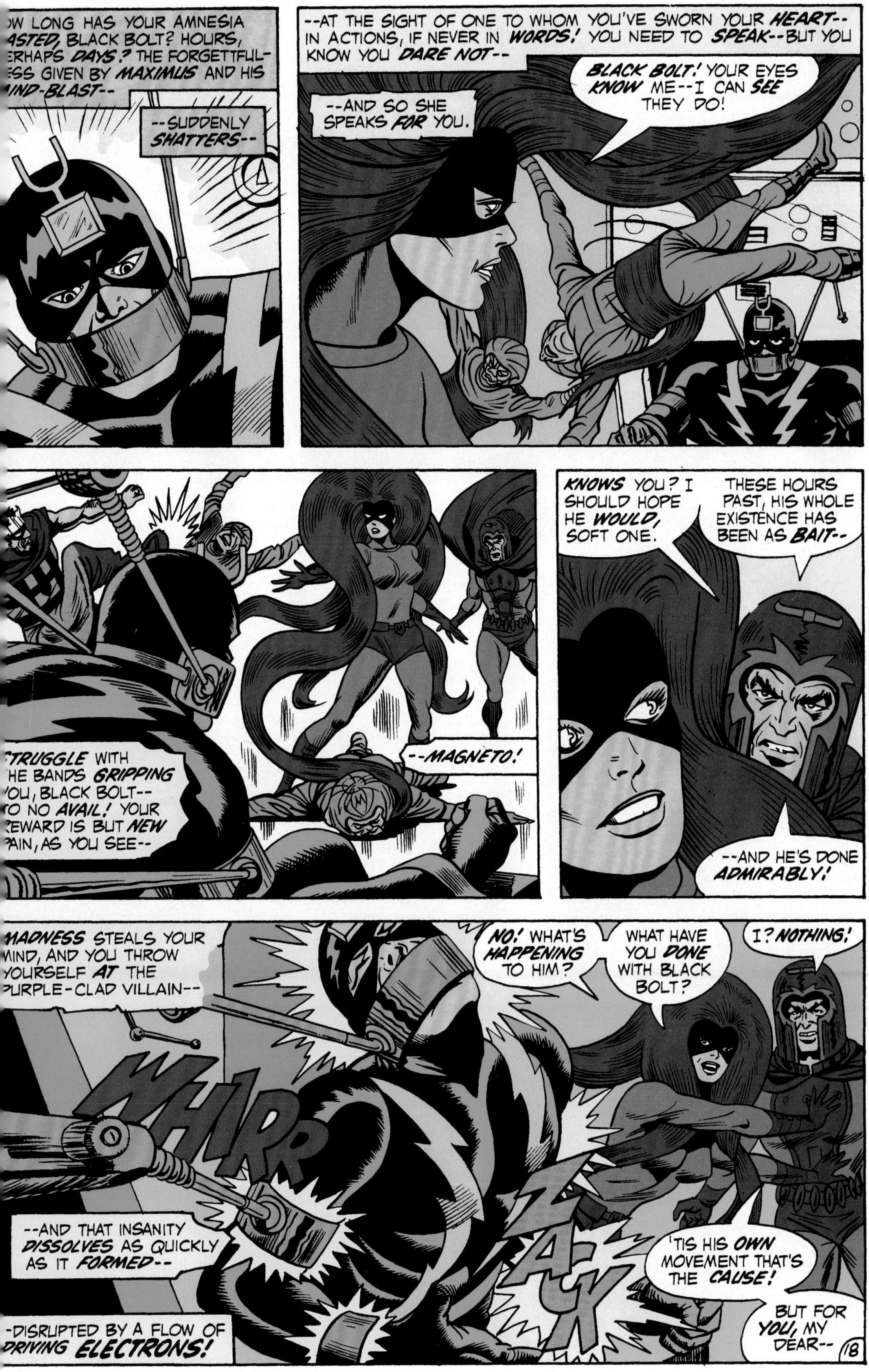

OW LONG HAS YOUR AMNESIA ASTED, BLACK BOLT? HOURS, ERHAPS DAYS? THE FORGETTFUL-ESS GIVEN BY MAXIMUS AND HIS IND-BLAST--
--SUDDENLY SHATTERS--
--AT THE SIGHT OF ONE TO WHOM YOU'VE SWORN YOUR HEART-- IN ACTIONS, IF NEVER IN WORDS! YOU NEED TO SPEAK--BUT YOU KNOW YOU DARE NOT--
--AND SO SHE SPEAKS FOR YOU.
BLACK BOLT! YOUR EYES KNOW ME--I CAN SEE THEY DO!
TRUGGLE WITH HE BANDS GRIPPING YOU, BLACK BOLT-- TO NO AVAIL! YOUR EWARD IS BUT NEW PAIN, AS YOU SEE--
--MAGNETO!
KNOWS YOU? I SHOULD HOPE HE WOULD, SOFT ONE.
THESE HOURS PAST, HIS WHOLE EXISTENCE HAS BEEN AS BAIT--
--AND HE'S DONE ADMIRABLY!
MADNESS STEALS YOUR MIND, AND YOU THROW YOURSELF AT THE PURPLE-CLAD VILLAIN--
NO! WHAT'S HAPPENING TO HIM?
WHAT HAVE YOU DONE WITH BLACK BOLT?
I? NOTHING!
WHIRR
--AND THAT INSANITY DISSOLVES AS QUICKLY AS IT FORMED--
'TIS HIS OWN MOVEMENT THAT'S THE CAUSE!
ZACK
-DISRUPTED BY A FLOW OF DRIVING ELECTRONS!
BUT FOR YOU, MY DEAR--
18

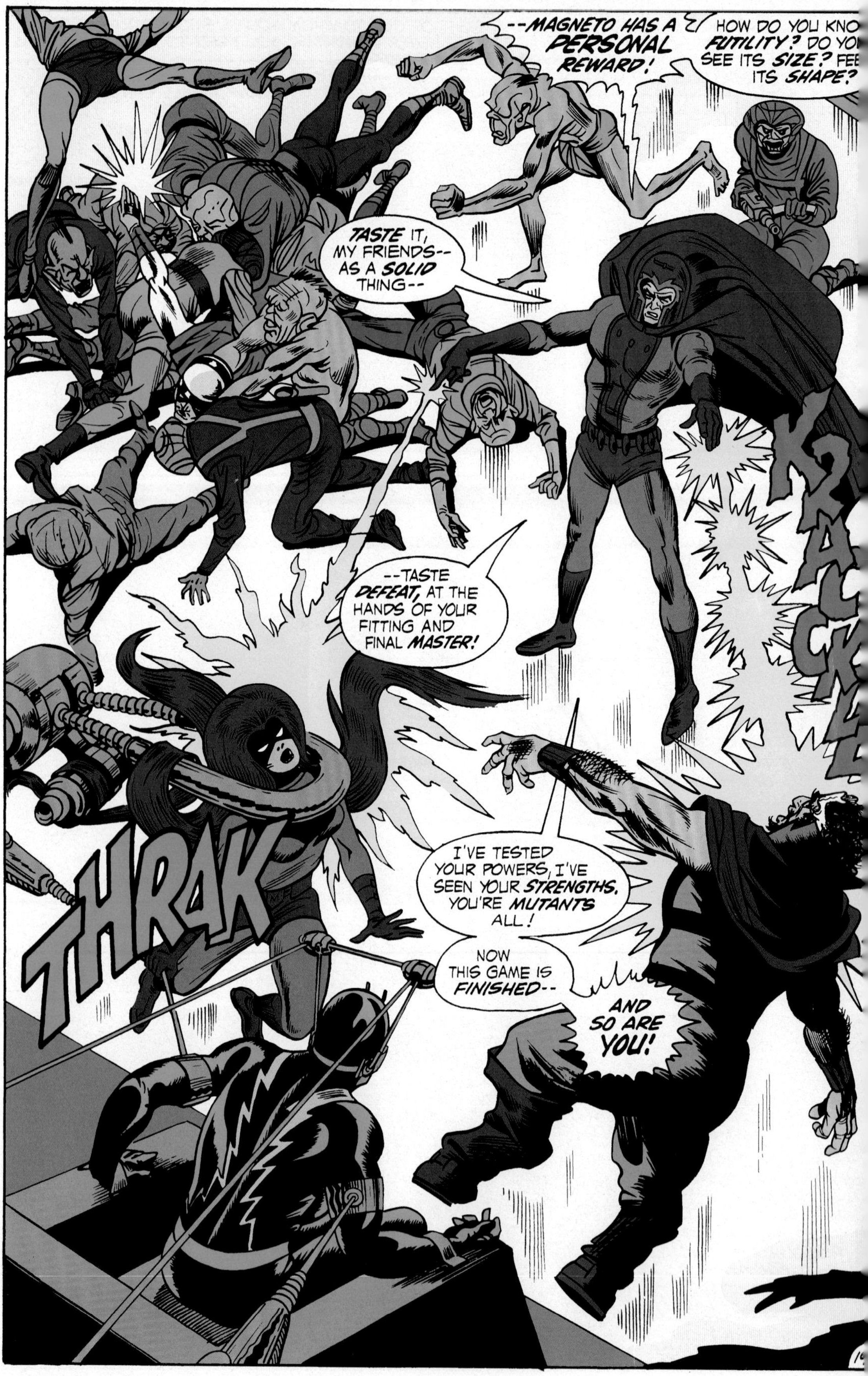
--MAGNETO HAS A PERSONAL REWARD!
HOW DO YOU KNO FUTILITY? DO YO SEE ITS SIZE? FEE ITS SHAPE?
TASTE IT, MY FRIENDS-- AS A SOLID THING--
--TASTE DEFEAT, AT THE HANDS OF YOUR FITTING AND FINAL MASTER!
THRAK
I'VE TESTED YOUR POWERS, I'VE SEEN YOUR STRENGTHS. YOU'RE MUTANTS ALL!
NOW THIS GAME IS FINISHED--
AND SO ARE YOU!

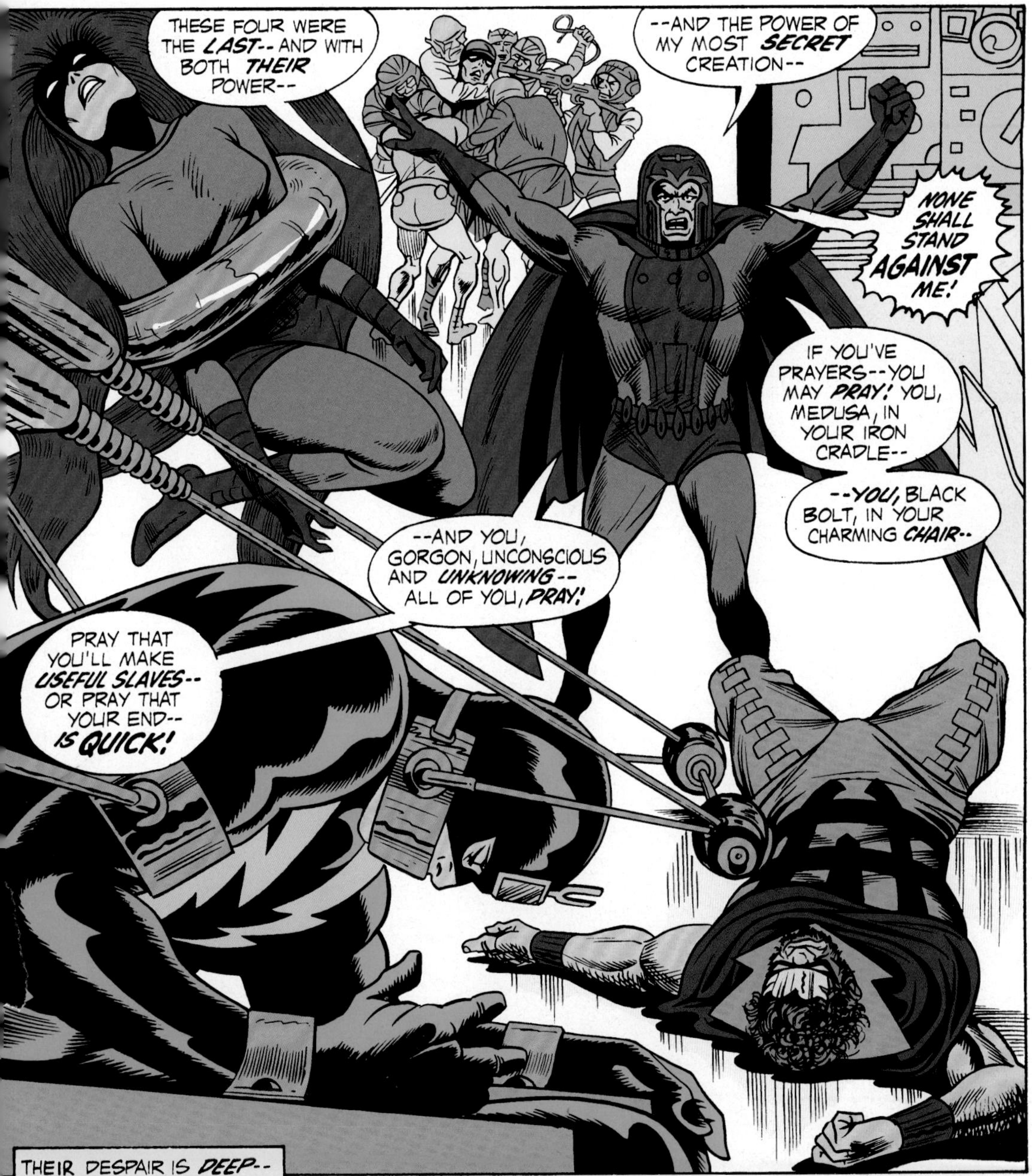
THESE FOUR WERE THE LAST-- AND WITH BOTH THEIR POWER--
--AND THE POWER OF MY MOST SECRET CREATION--
NONE SHALL STAND AGAINST ME!
IF YOU'VE PRAYERS--YOU MAY PRAY! YOU, MEDUSA, IN YOUR IRON CRADLE--
--YOU, BLACK BOLT, IN YOUR CHARMING CHAIR--
--AND YOU, GORGON, UNCONSCIOUS AND UNKNOWING-- ALL OF YOU, PRAY!
PRAY THAT YOU'LL MAKE USEFUL SLAVES-- OR PRAY THAT YOUR END-- IS QUICK!

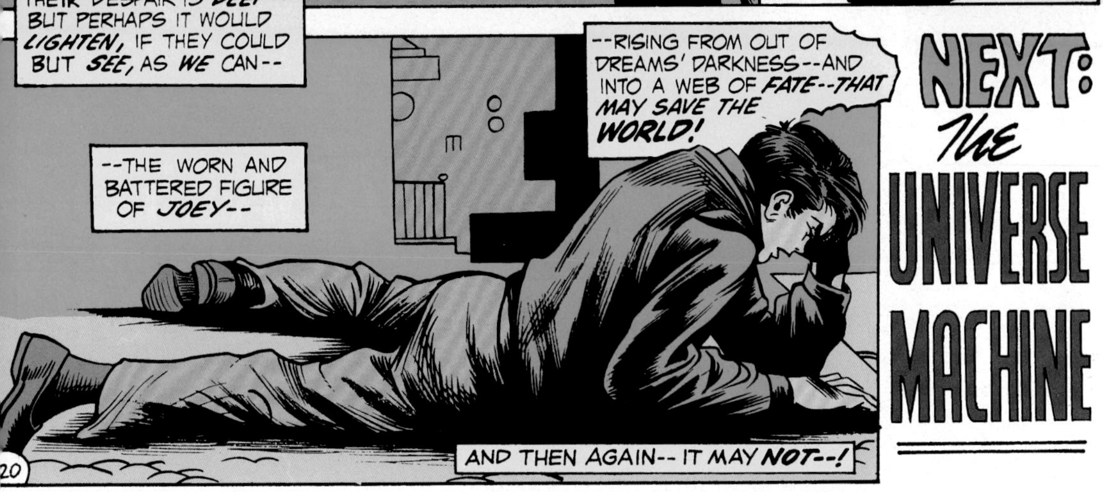
THEIR DESPAIR IS DEEP-- BUT PERHAPS IT WOULD LIGHTEN, IF THEY COULD BUT SEE, AS WE CAN--
--THE WORN AND BATTERED FIGURE OF JOEY--
--RISING FROM OUT OF DREAMS' DARKNESS--AND INTO A WEB OF FATE--THAT MAY SAVE THE WORLD!
AND THEN AGAIN-- IT MAY NOT--!
NEXT: THE UNIVERSE MACHINE
20

GET THE FULL STORY IN *MARVEL MASTERWORKS: THE INHUMANS VOL. 1* HARDCOVER!

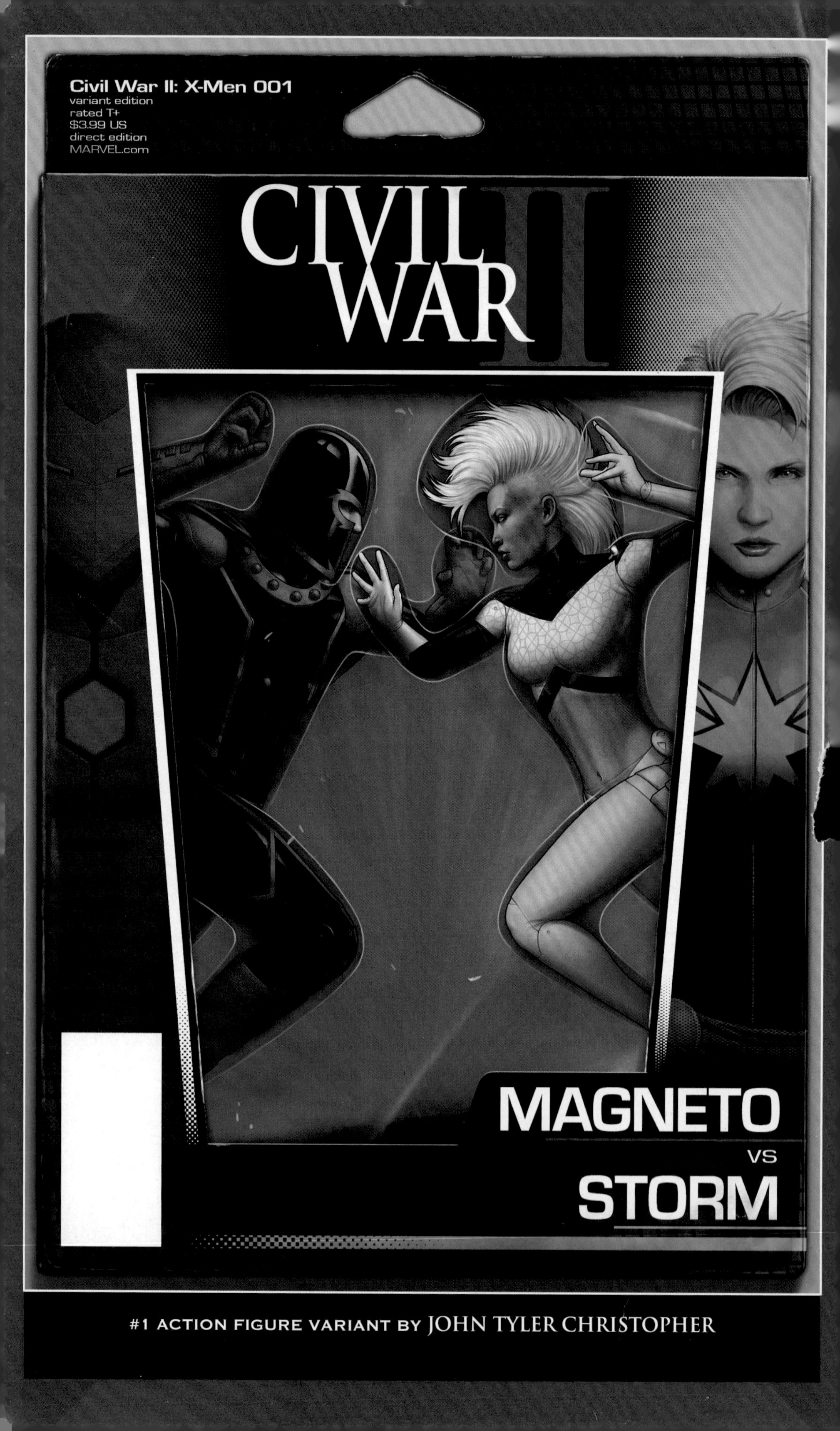
Civil War II: X-Men 001
variant edition
rated T+
$3.99 US
direct edition
MARVEL.com
CIVIL WAR II
MAGNETO
VS
STORM
#1 ACTION FIGURE VARIANT BY JOHN TYLER CHRISTOPHER

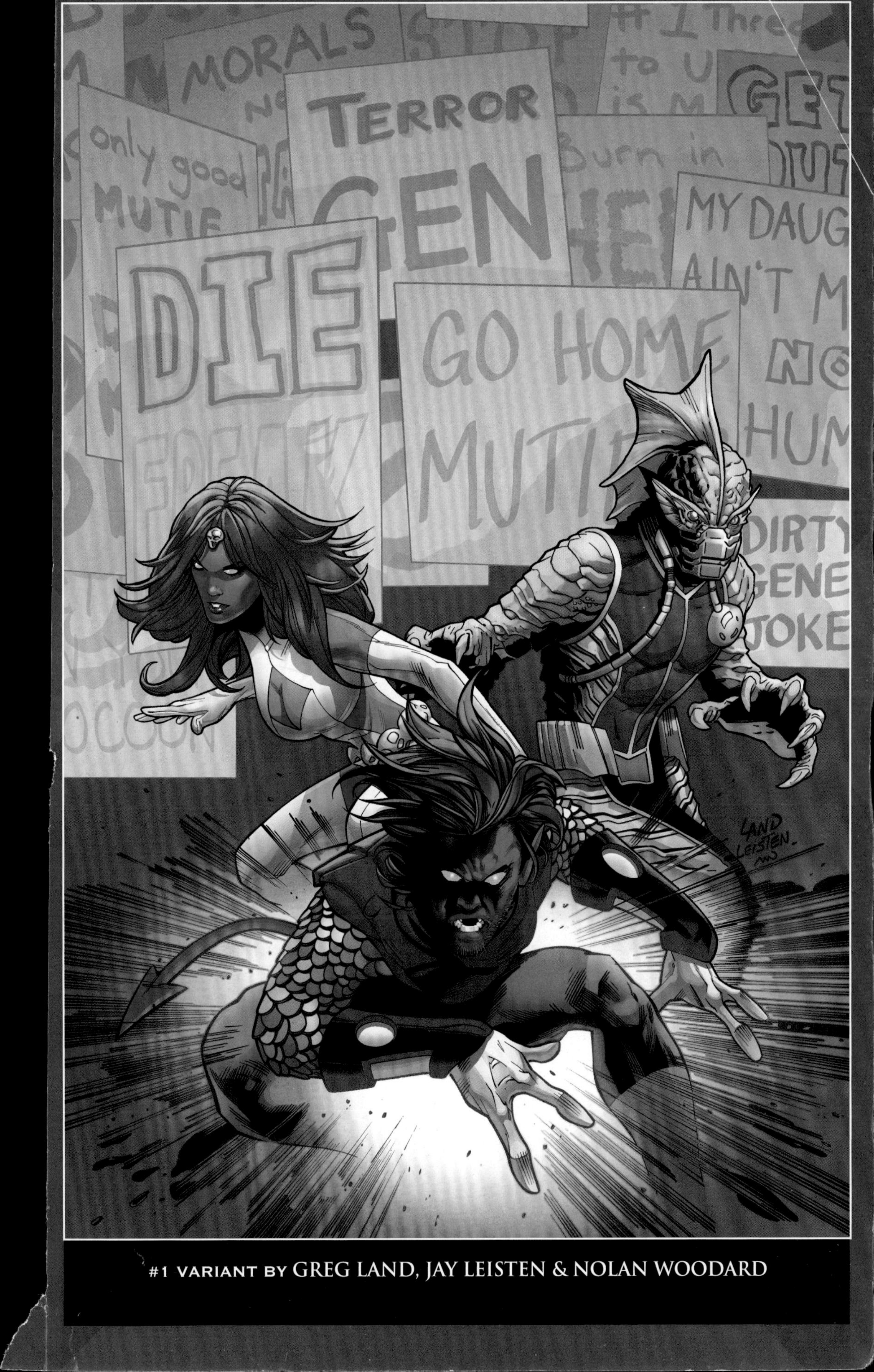
MORALS
#1 Threa
to U
TERROR
only good
MUTIE
GEN
Burn in
MY DAUG
AIN'T M
DIE
GO HOME
MUTI
DIRTY
GENE
JOKE
OCOON
LAND
LEISTEN

#1 VARIANT BY GREG LAND, JAY LEISTEN & NOLAN WOODARD

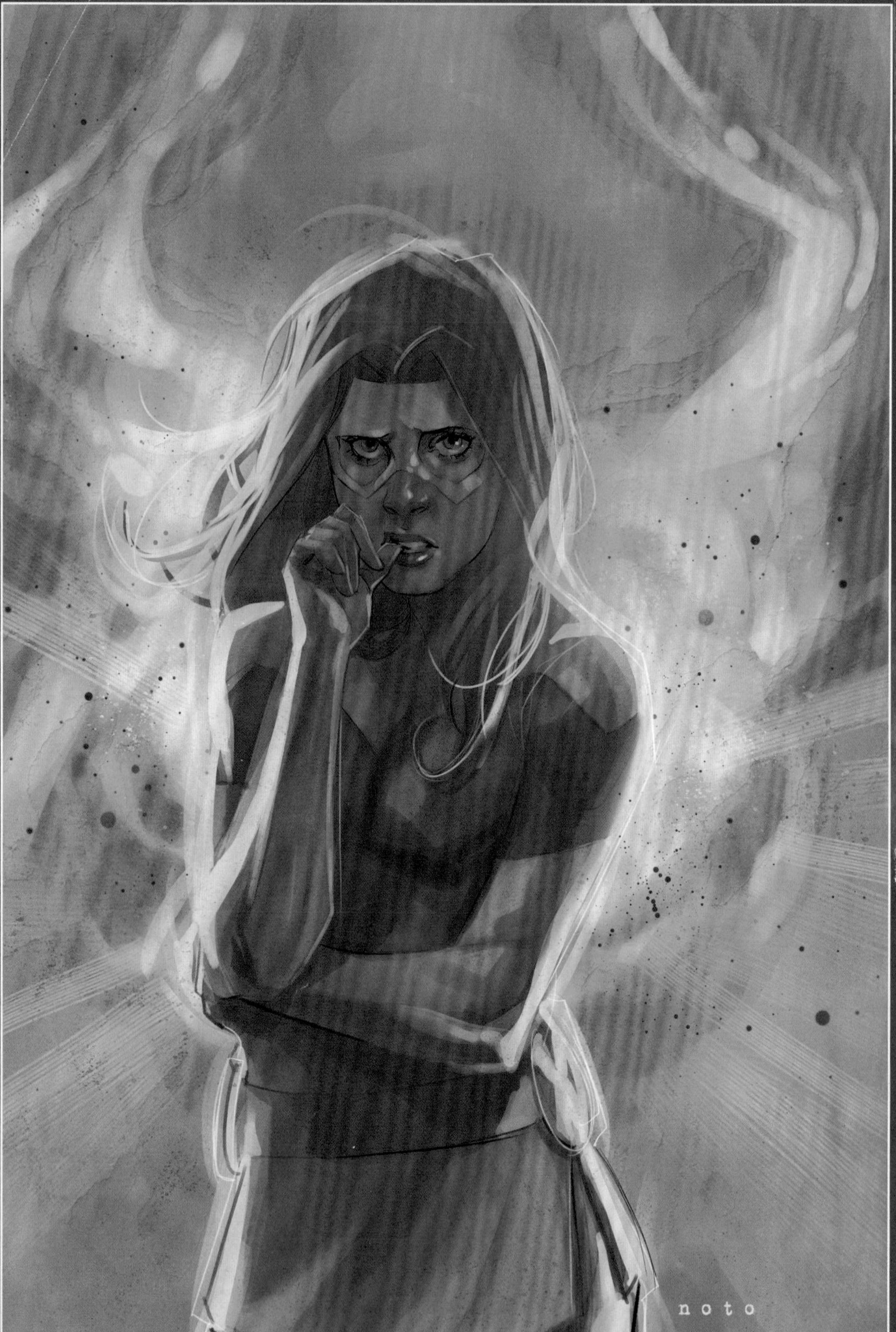
noto

#1 VARIANT BY PHIL NOTO

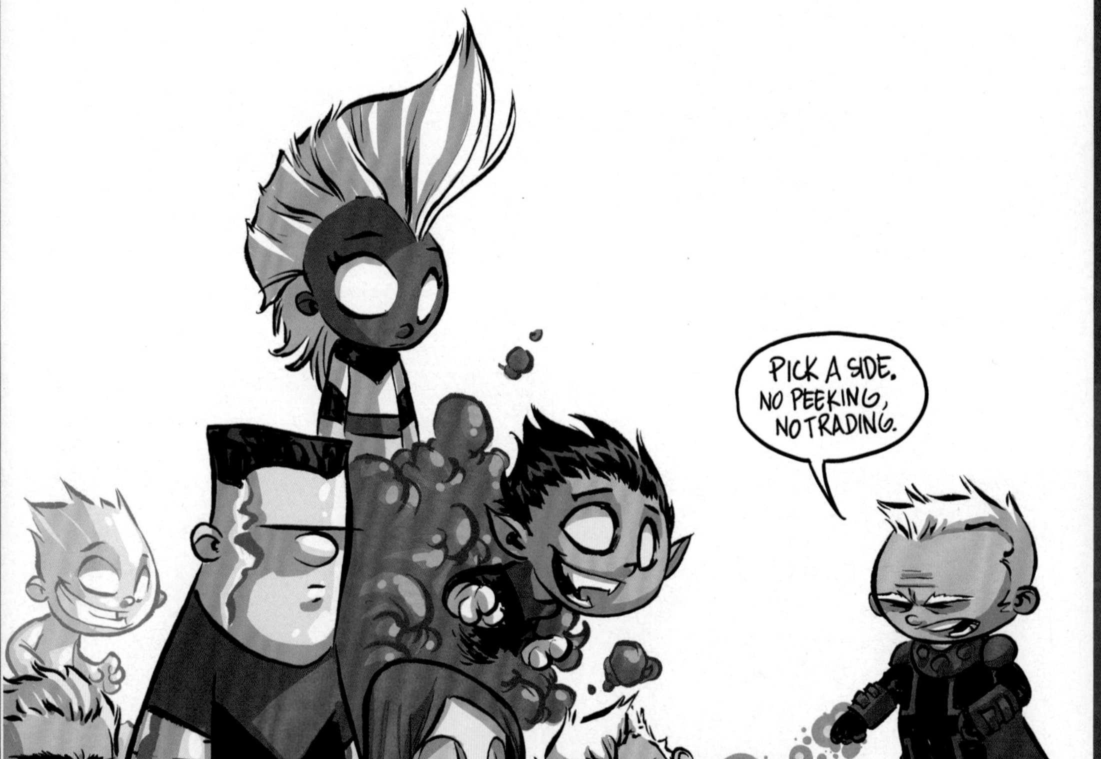
PICK A SIDE. NO PEEKING, NO TRADING.
SY 16

#1 VARIANT BY SKOTTIE YOUNG

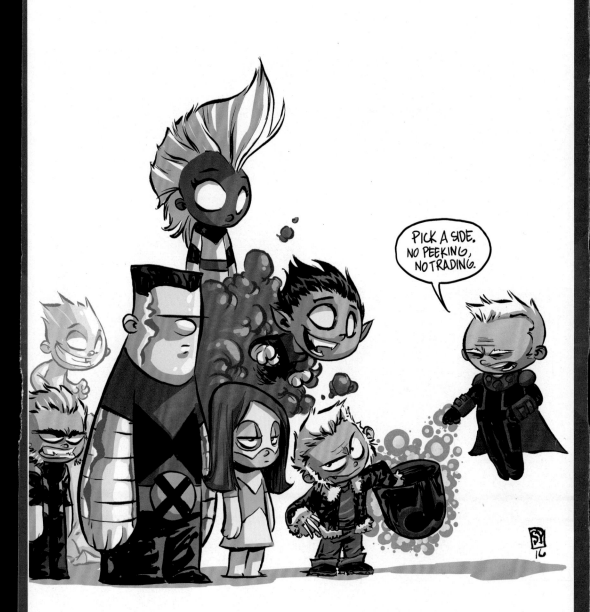

#2 VARIANT BY
VICTOR IBAÑEZ & JASON KEITH

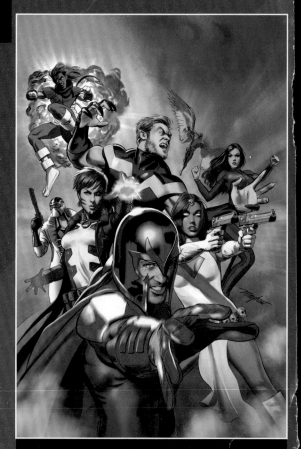

#3 VARIANT BY
MIKE MAYHEW